T&P BOOKS

CW01496529

CHECHEN
VOCABULARY

ENGLISH-CHECHEN

The most useful words
To expand your lexicon and sharpen
your language skills

9000 words

Chechen vocabulary for English speakers - 9000 words

By Andrey Taranov

T&P Books vocabularies are intended for helping you learn, memorize, and revise foreign words. The dictionary is divided into themes, covering all major spheres of everyday activities, business, science, culture, etc.

The process of learning words using T&P Books' theme-based dictionaries gives you the following advantages:

- Correctly grouped source information predetermines success at subsequent stages of word memorization
- Availability of words derived from the same root allowing memorization of word units (rather than separate words)
- Small units of words facilitate the process of establishing associative links needed for consolidation of vocabulary
- Level of language knowledge can be estimated by the number of learned words

T&P Books Publishing
www.tpbooks.com

ISBN: 978-1-78071-686-2

This book is also available in E-book formats.
Please visit www.tpbooks.com or the major online bookstores.

CHECHEN VOCABULARY
for English speakers

T&P Books vocabularies are intended to help you learn, memorize, and review foreign words. The vocabulary contains over 9000 commonly used words arranged thematically.

- Vocabulary contains the most commonly used words
- Recommended as an addition to any language course
- Meets the needs of beginners and advanced learners of foreign languages
- Convenient for daily use, revision sessions, and self-testing activities
- Allows you to assess your vocabulary

Special features of the vocabulary

- Words are organized according to their meaning, not alphabetically
- Words are presented in three columns to facilitate the reviewing and self-testing processes
- Words in groups are divided into small blocks to facilitate the learning process
- The vocabulary offers a convenient and simple transcription of each foreign word

The vocabulary has 256 topics including:

Basic Concepts, Numbers, Colors, Months, Seasons, Units of Measurement, Clothing & Accessories, Food & Nutrition, Restaurant, Family Members, Relatives, Character, Feelings, Emotions, Diseases, City, Town, Sightseeing, Shopping, Money, House, Home, Office, Working in the Office, Import & Export, Marketing, Job Search, Sports, Education, Computer, Internet, Tools, Nature, Countries, Nationalities and more ...

T&P BOOKS' THEME-BASED DICTIONARIES

The Correct System for Memorizing Foreign Words

Acquiring vocabulary is one of the most important elements of learning a foreign language, because words allow us to express our thoughts, ask questions, and provide answers. An inadequate vocabulary can impede communication with a foreigner and make it difficult to understand a book or movie well.

The pace of activity in all spheres of modern life, including the learning of modern languages, has increased. Today, we need to memorize large amounts of information (grammar rules, foreign words, etc.) within a short period. However, this does not need to be difficult. All you need to do is to choose the right training materials, learn a few special techniques, and develop your individual training system.

Having a system is critical to the process of language learning. Many people fail to succeed in this regard; they cannot master a foreign language because they fail to follow a system comprised of selecting materials, organizing lessons, arranging new words to be learned, and so on. The lack of a system causes confusion and eventually, lowers self-confidence.

T&P Books' theme-based dictionaries can be included in the list of elements needed for creating an effective system for learning foreign words. These dictionaries were specially developed for learning purposes and are meant to help students effectively memorize words and expand their vocabulary.

Generally speaking, the process of learning words consists of three main elements:

- Reception (creation or acquisition) of a training material, such as a word list
- Work aimed at memorizing new words
- Work aimed at reviewing the learned words, such as self-testing

All three elements are equally important since they determine the quality of work and the final result. All three processes require certain skills and a well-thought-out approach.

New words are often encountered quite randomly when learning a foreign language and it may be difficult to include them all in a unified list. As a result, these words remain written on scraps of paper, in book margins, textbooks, and so on. In order to systematize such words, we have to create and continually update a "book of new words." A paper notebook, a netbook, or a tablet PC can be used for these purposes.

This "book of new words" will be your personal, unique list of words. However, it will only contain the words that you came across during the learning process. For example, you might have written down the words "Sunday," "Tuesday," and "Friday." However, there are additional words for days of the week, for example, "Saturday," that are missing, and your list of words would be incomplete. Using a theme dictionary, in addition to the "book of new words," is a reasonable solution to this problem.

The theme-based dictionary may serve as the basis for expanding your vocabulary.

It will be your big "book of new words" containing the most frequently used words of a foreign language already included. There are quite a few theme-based dictionaries available, and you should ensure that you make the right choice in order to get the maximum benefit from your purchase.

Therefore, we suggest using theme-based dictionaries from T&P Books Publishing as an aid to learning foreign words. Our books are specially developed for effective use in the sphere of vocabulary systematization, expansion and review.

Theme-based dictionaries are not a magical solution to learning new words. However, they can serve as your main database to aid foreign-language acquisition. Apart from theme dictionaries, you can have copybooks for writing down new words, flash cards, glossaries for various texts, as well as other resources; however, a good theme dictionary will always remain your primary collection of words.

T&P Books' theme-based dictionaries are specialty books that contain the most frequently used words in a language.

The main characteristic of such dictionaries is the division of words into themes. For example, the *City* theme contains the words "street," "crossroads," "square," "fountain," and so on. The *Talking* theme might contain words like "to talk," "to ask," "question," and "answer".

All the words in a theme are divided into smaller units, each comprising 3–5 words. Such an arrangement improves the perception of words and makes the learning process less tiresome. Each unit contains a selection of words with similar meanings or identical roots. This allows you to learn words in small groups and establish other associative links that have a positive effect on memorization.

The words on each page are placed in three columns: a word in your native language, its translation, and its transcription. Such positioning allows for the use of techniques for effective memorization. After closing the translation column, you can flip through and review foreign words, and vice versa. "This is an easy and convenient method of review – one that we recommend you do often."

Our theme-based dictionaries contain transcriptions for all the foreign words. Unfortunately, none of the existing transcriptions are able to convey the exact nuances of foreign pronunciation. That is why we recommend using the transcriptions only as a supplementary learning aid. Correct pronunciation can only be acquired with the help of sound. Therefore our collection includes audio theme-based dictionaries.

The process of learning words using T&P Books' theme-based dictionaries gives you the following advantages:

- You have correctly grouped source information, which predetermines your success at subsequent stages of word memorization

- Availability of words derived from the same root (lazy, lazily, lazybones), allowing you to memorize word units instead of separate words

- Small units of words facilitate the process of establishing associative links needed for consolidation of vocabulary

- You can estimate the number of learned words and hence your level of language knowledge

- The dictionary allows for the creation of an effective and high-quality revision process

- You can revise certain themes several times, modifying the revision methods and techniques

- Audio versions of the dictionaries help you to work out the pronunciation of words and develop your skills of auditory word perception

The T&P Books' theme-based dictionaries are offered in several variants differing in the number of words: 1.500, 3.000, 5.000, 7.000, and 9.000 words. There are also dictionaries containing 15,000 words for some language combinations. Your choice of dictionary will depend on your knowledge level and goals.

We sincerely believe that our dictionaries will become your trusty assistant in learning foreign languages and will allow you to easily acquire the necessary vocabulary.

TABLE OF CONTENTS

T&P Books' Theme-Based Dictionaries   4
Pronunciation guide   15
Abbreviations   17

BASIC CONCEPTS   18
Basic concepts. Part 1   18

1. Pronouns   18
2. Greetings. Salutations. Farewells   18
3. How to address   19
4. Cardinal numbers. Part 1   19
5. Cardinal numbers. Part 2   20
6. Ordinal numbers   21
7. Numbers. Fractions   21
8. Numbers. Basic operations   21
9. Numbers. Miscellaneous   22
10. The most important verbs. Part 1   22
11. The most important verbs. Part 2   23
12. The most important verbs. Part 3   24
13. The most important verbs. Part 4   25
14. Colors   26
15. Questions   27
16. Prepositions   27
17. Function words. Adverbs. Part 1   28
18. Function words. Adverbs. Part 2   30

Basic concepts. Part 2   31

19. Weekdays   31
20. Hours. Day and night   31
21. Months. Seasons   32
22. Time. Miscellaneous   34
23. Opposites   35
24. Lines and shapes   37
25. Units of measurement   38
26. Containers   39
27. Materials   40
28. Metals   41

HUMAN BEING 42
Human being. The body 42

29.	Humans. Basic concepts	42
30.	Human anatomy	42
31.	Head	43
32.	Human body	44

Clothing & Accessories 45

33.	Outerwear. Coats	45
34.	Men's & women's clothing	45
35.	Clothing. Underwear	46
36.	Headwear	46
37.	Footwear	46
38.	Textile. Fabrics	47
39.	Personal accessories	47
40.	Clothing. Miscellaneous	48
41.	Personal care. Cosmetics	49
42.	Jewelry	50
43.	Watches. Clocks	50

Food. Nutricion 52

44.	Food	52
45.	Drinks	54
46.	Vegetables	55
47.	Fruits. Nuts	55
48.	Bread. Candy	56
49.	Cooked dishes	57
50.	Spices	58
51.	Meals	58
52.	Table setting	59
53.	Restaurant	59

Family, relatives and friends 61

54.	Personal information. Forms	61
55.	Family members. Relatives	61
56.	Friends. Coworkers	62
57.	Man. Woman	63
58.	Age	64
59.	Children	64
60.	Married couples. Family life	65

Character. Feelings. Emotions 67

61.	Feelings. Emotions	67

62.	Character. Personality	68
63.	Sleep. Dreams	69
64.	Humour. Laughter. Gladness	70
65.	Discussion, conversation. Part 1	71
66.	Discussion, conversation. Part 2	72
67.	Discussion, conversation. Part 3	73
68.	Agreement. Refusal	74
69.	Success. Good luck. Failure	75
70.	Quarrels. Negative emotions	75

Medicine 78

71.	Diseases	78
72.	Symptoms. Treatments. Part 1	79
73.	Symptoms. Treatments. Part 2	80
74.	Symptoms. Treatments. Part 3	81
75.	Doctors	82
76.	Medicine. Drugs. Accessories	82
77.	Smoking. Tobacco products	83

HUMAN HABITAT 84
City 84

78.	City. Life in the city	84
79.	Urban institutions	85
80.	Signs	87
81.	Urban transport	88
82.	Sightseeing	89
83.	Shopping	89
84.	Money	90
85.	Post. Postal service	91

Dwelling. House. Home 93

86.	House. Dwelling	93
87.	House. Entrance. Lift	94
88.	House. Electricity	94
89.	House. Doors. Locks	94
90.	Country house	95
91.	Villa. Mansion	96
92.	Castle. Palace	96
93.	Apartment	97
94.	Apartment. Cleaning	97
95.	Furniture. Interior	97
96.	Bedding	98
97.	Kitchen	98
98.	Bathroom	100
99.	Household appliances	101
100.	Repairs. Renovation	101

101.	Plumbing	102
102.	Fire. Conflagration	102

HUMAN ACTIVITIES | 104
Job. Business. Part 1 | 104

103.	Office. Working in the office	104
104.	Business processes. Part 1	105
105.	Business processes. Part 2	106
106.	Production. Works	107
107.	Contract. Agreement	109
108.	Import & Export	109
109.	Finances	110
110.	Marketing	110
111.	Advertising	111
112.	Banking	112
113.	Telephone. Phone conversation	112
114.	Mobile telephone	113
115.	Stationery	114
116.	Various kinds of documents	114
117.	Kinds of business	115

Job. Business. Part 2 | 118

118.	Show. Exhibition	118
119.	Mass Media	119
120.	Agriculture	120
121.	Building. Building process	121
122.	Science. Research. Scientists	122

Professions and occupations | 124

123.	Job search. Dismissal	124
124.	Business people	124
125.	Service professions	126
126.	Military professions and ranks	126
127.	Officials. Priests	127
128.	Agricultural professions	128
129.	Art professions	128
130.	Various professions	129
131.	Occupations. Social status	130

Sports | 132

132.	Kinds of sports. Sportspersons	132
133.	Kinds of sports. Miscellaneous	133
134.	Gym	134

135.	Hockey	134
136.	Football	134
137.	Alpine skiing	136
138.	Tennis. Golf	136
139.	Chess	137
140.	Boxing	137
141.	Sports. Miscellaneous	138

Education   140

142.	School	140
143.	College. University	141
144.	Sciences. Disciplines	142
145.	Writing system. Orthography	142
146.	Foreign languages	144
147.	Fairy tale characters	145
148.	Zodiac Signs	145

Arts   146

149.	Theater	146
150.	Cinema	147
151.	Painting	148
152.	Literature & Poetry	149
153.	Circus	150
154.	Music. Pop music	150

Rest. Entertainment. Travel   152

155.	Trip. Travel	152
156.	Hotel	153
157.	Books. Reading	153
158.	Hunting. Fishing	155
159.	Games. Billiards	156
160.	Games. Playing cards	156
161.	Casino. Roulette	157
162.	Rest. Games. Miscellaneous	157
163.	Photography	158
164.	Beach. Swimming	159

TECHNICAL EQUIPMENT. TRANSPORT   161
Technical equipment   161

165.	Computer	161
166.	Internet. E-mail	162
167.	Electricity	163
168.	Tools	164

Transport   167

169.	Airplane	167
170.	Train	168
171.	Ship	169
172.	Airport	170
173.	Bicycle. Motorcycle	171

Cars   173

174.	Types of cars	173
175.	Cars. Bodywork	173
176.	Cars. Passenger compartment	175
177.	Cars. Engine	175
178.	Cars. Crash. Repair	176
179.	Cars. Road	177
180.	Traffic signs	178

PEOPLE. LIFE EVENTS   180
Life events   180

181.	Holidays. Event	180
182.	Funerals. Burial	181
183.	War. Soldiers	182
184.	War. Military actions. Part 1	183
185.	War. Military actions. Part 2	184
186.	Weapons	186
187.	Ancient people	187
188.	Middle Ages	188
189.	Leader. Chief. Authorities	190
190.	Road. Way. Directions	190
191.	Breaking the law. Criminals. Part 1	192
192.	Breaking the law. Criminals. Part 2	193
193.	Police. Law. Part 1	194
194.	Police. Law. Part 2	195

NATURE   197
The Earth. Part 1   197

195.	Outer space	197
196.	The Earth	198
197.	Cardinal directions	199
198.	Sea. Ocean	199
199.	Seas' and Oceans' names	200
200.	Mountains	201
201.	Mountains names	202
202.	Rivers	203
203.	Rivers' names	203

| 204. | Forest | 204 |
| 205. | Natural resources | 205 |

The Earth. Part 2 207

206.	Weather	207
207.	Severe weather. Natural disasters	208
208.	Noises. Sounds	208
209.	Winter	209

Fauna 211

210.	Mammals. Predators	211
211.	Wild animals	211
212.	Domestic animals	213
213.	Dogs. Dog breeds	214
214.	Sounds made by animals	214
215.	Young animals	215
216.	Birds	215
217.	Birds. Singing and sounds	216
218.	Fish. Marine animals	217
219.	Amphibians. Reptiles	218
220.	Insects	218
221.	Animals. Body parts	219
222.	Actions of animals	220
223.	Animals. Habitats	220
224.	Animal care	221
225.	Animals. Miscellaneous	221
226.	Horses	222

Flora 224

227.	Trees	224
228.	Shrubs	225
229.	Mushrooms	225
230.	Fruits. Berries	225
231.	Flowers. Plants	226
232.	Cereals, grains	227
233.	Vegetables. Greens	228

REGIONAL GEOGRAPHY 230
Countries. Nationalities 230

234.	Western Europe	230
235.	Central and Eastern Europe	232
236.	Former USSR countries	233
237.	Asia	234

238.	North America	236
239.	Central and South America	237
240.	Africa	238
241.	Australia. Oceania	238
242.	Cities	239
243.	Politics. Government. Part 1	240
244.	Politics. Government. Part 2	242
245.	Countries. Miscellaneous	243
246.	Major religious groups. Confessions	244
247.	Religions. Priests	245
248.	Faith. Christianity. Islam	245

MISCELLANEOUS

248

249.	Various useful words	248
250.	Modifiers. Adjectives. Part 1	249
251.	Modifiers. Adjectives. Part 2	252

MAIN 500 VERBS

255

252.	Verbs A-C	255
253.	Verbs D-G	257
254.	Verbs H-M	260
255.	Verbs N-S	262
256.	Verbs T-W	265

PRONUNCIATION GUIDE

Letter	Chechen sample	T&P phonetics alphabet	English sample
А а	самадала	[ɑ:]	father, answer
Аь аь	аьртадала	[æ:], [æ]	camp, bank
Б б	биллиард	[b]	baby, book
В в	ловзо кехат	[v]	very, river
Г г	горгал	[g]	game, gold
ГӀ гӀ	жирӀа	[ɣ]	between [g] and [h]
Д д	дӀаала	[d]	day, doctor
Е е	кевнахо	[e], [ɛ]	absent, pet
Ё ё	боксёр	[jɔ:], [ɜ:]	yourself, girl
Ж ж	мужалтах	[ʒ]	forge, pleasure
З з	ловза	[z]	zebra, please
И и	сирла	[ı], [i]	tin, see
Й й	лийча	[j]	yes, New York
К к	секунд	[k]	clock, kiss
Кх кх	кхиорхо	[q]	king, club
Къ къ	юккъе	tense [q]	quay
КӀ кӀ	кӀайн	tense [k]	bookcase
Л л	лаьстиг	[l]	lace, people
М м	Марша Ӏайла	[m]	magic, milk
Н н	Хьанна?	[n]	name, normal
О о	модельхо	[o], [ɔ]	drop, baught
Оь оь	пхоьлгӀа	[ø]	eternal, church
П п	пхийтта	[p]	pencil, private
ПӀ пӀ	пӀераска	tense [p]	soup plate
Р р	борзанан	[r]	rice, radio
С с	сандалеш	[s]	city, boss
Т т	туьйдарг	[t]	tourist, trip
ТӀ тӀ	тӀормиг	tense [t]	first time
У у	тукар	[u:]	pool, room
Уь уь	уьш	[y]	fuel, tuna
Ф ф	футбол	[f]	face, food
Х х	хьехархо	[h]	huge, humor
Хь хь	дагахь	[h], [x]	as in Scots loch
ХӀ хӀ	хӀордахо	[h]	home, have
Ц ц	мацахлера	[ts]	cats, tsetse fly
ЦӀ цӀ	цӀубдар	tense [ts]	cats
Ч ч	лечкъо	[tʃ]	church, French
ЧӀ чӀ	чӀорӀа	tense [tʃ]	Dutch champion

15

Letter	Chechen sample	T&P phonetics alphabet	English sample
Ш ш	шахматаш	[ʃ]	machine, shark
Щ щ	цергийг щётка	[ɕ]	sheep, shop
ъ	къонза	[ʰ]	hard sign - no sound
ы	лыжаш хехка	[ɪ]	big, America
ь	доьзал	[ʲ]	soft sign - no sound
Э э	эшар	[e]	elm, medal
Ю ю	юхадала	[y]	fuel, tuna
Юь юь	юьхьенца	[juː], [ju]	cued, cute
Я я	цӀанъян	[jɑ]	young, yard
Яь яь	яьшка	[jæ]	cognac
Ӏ Ӏ	Ӏамо	[ə]	driver, teacher

ABBREVIATIONS
used in the vocabulary

ab.	-	about
adj	-	adjectif
adv	-	adverb
attr	-	attributive noun
e.g.	-	for example
etc.	-	et cetera
fem.	-	feminine
masc.	-	masculine
noun	-	noun
pl	-	plural
pron.	-	pronoun
sb	-	somebody
sing.	-	singular
sth	-	something
vi	-	intransitive verb
vi, vt	-	intransitive, transitive verb
vt	-	transitive verb

BASIC CONCEPTS

Basic concepts. Part 1

1. Pronouns

I, me	со	[sɔ]
you	хьо	[hɔ]
he, she, it	иза	[iza]
we	вай	[vaj]
you	шу	[ʃu]
they	уьш	[yʃ]

2. Greetings. Salutations. Farewells

Hello! (familiar)	Маршалла ду хьоьга!	[marʃal:a du høga]
Hello! (formal)	Маршалла ду шуьга	[marʃal:a du ʃyga]
Good morning!	Iуьйре дика хуьлда!	[əujre dika hylda]
Good afternoon!	Де дика хуьлда!	[de dika hylda]
Good evening!	Суьйре дика хуьлда!	[syjre dika hylda]
to say hello	салам дала	[salam dala]
Hi! (hello)	Маршалла ду хьоьга!	[marʃal:a du høga]
greeting (noun)	маршалла, маршалла хаттар	[marʃal:a, marʃal:a hat:ar]
to greet (vt)	маршалла хатта	[marʃal:a hat:a]
How are you?	Муха ду гӏуллакхш?	[muha du ɣul:aqʃ]
What's new?	Хӏун ду керла?	[hun du kerla]
Bye-Bye! Goodbye!	Марша Iайла	[marʃa əajla]
See you soon!	Iодика хуьлда!	[əɔdika huʎda]
Farewell! (to a friend)	Iодика йойла хьа!	[əɔdika jojla ha]
Farewell (formal)	Iодика йойла шунна!	[əɔdika jojla ʃuŋa]
to say goodbye	Iодика ян	[əɔdika jan]
So long!	Iодика йойла!	[əɔdika jojla]
Thank you!	Баркалла!	[barkal:a]
Thank you very much!	Доаккха баркалла!	[dɔak:a barkal:a]
You're welcome	Хӏума дац!	[huma dats]
Don't mention it!	Хӏума дац!	[huma dats]
It was nothing	Хӏума дац!	[huma dats]
Excuse me! (familiar)	Бехк ма билл!	[behk ma bil:]

| Excuse me! (formal) | Бехк ма биллалаш! | [behk ma bil:alaʃ] |
| to excuse (forgive) | бехк ца билла | [behk tsa bil:a] |

to apologize (vi)	бехк цабиллар деха	[behk tsabil:ar deha]
My apologies	Суна бехк ма биллалаш!	[suna behk ma bil:alaʃ]
I'm sorry!	Бехк ма биллаш!	[behk ma bil:aʃ]
to forgive (vt)	бехк цабиллар	[behk tsabil:ar]

Don't forget!	Диц ма ло!	[dits ma lɔ]
Certainly!	Дера!	[dera]
Of course not!	Дера дац!	[dera dats]
OK! (I agree)	Реза ву!	[reza vu]
That's enough!	Тоьур ду!	[tøur du]

3. How to address

Mister, Sir	Эла!	[ɛla]
Ma'am	Сту!	[stu]
Miss	Йол!	[joə]
Young man	Жима стаг!	[ʒima stag]
Young man (little boy)	КӀант!	[k:ant]
Miss (little girl)	Жима йол!	[ʒima joə]

4. Cardinal numbers. Part 1

0 zero	ноль	[nɔʎ]
1 one	цхьаъ	[tshaʔ]
2 two	шиъ	[ʃi]
3 three	кхоъ	[qɔ]
4 four	диъ	[di]

5 five	пхиъ	[phi]
6 six	ялх	[jalh]
7 seven	ворхӀ	[vɔrh]
8 eight	бархӀ	[barh]
9 nine	исс	[is:]

10 ten	итт	[it:]
11 eleven	цхьайтта	[tshajt:a]
12 twelve	шийтта	[ʃi:t:a]
13 thirteen	кхойтта	[qɔjt:a]
14 fourteen	дейтта	[dejt:a]

15 fifteen	пхийтта	[phi:t:a]
16 sixteen	ялхитта	[jalhit:a]
17 seventeen	ВуьрхӀитта	[vyrhit:a]
18 eighteen	берхӀитта	[berhit:a]
19 nineteen	ткъесна	[tqhesna]

20 twenty	ткъа	[tqha]
21 twenty-one	ткъе цхьаъ	[tqhe tsha]
22 twenty-two	ткъе шиъ	[tqhe ʃi]
23 twenty-three	ткъе кхоъ	[tqhe qɔ]

30 thirty	ткъе итт	[tqhe it:]
31 thirty-one	ткхе цхьайтта	[tqe tshajt:a]
32 thirty-two	ткъе шийтта	[tqhe ʃi:t:a]
33 thirty-three	ткъе кхойтта	[tqhe qɔjt:a]

40 forty	шовзткъа	[ʃɔvztqha]
41 forty-one	шовзткъе цхьаъ	[ʃɔvztqhe tsha]
42 forty-two	шовзткъе шиъ	[ʃɔvztqhe ʃi]
43 forty-three	шовзткъе кхоъ	[ʃɔvztqhe qɔ]

50 fifty	шовзткъе итт	[ʃɔvztqhe it:]
51 fifty-one	шовзткъе цхьайтта	[ʃɔvztqhe tshajt:a]
52 fifty-two	шовзткъе шийтта	[ʃɔvztqhe ʃi:t:a]
53 fifty-three	шовзткъе кхойтта	[ʃɔvztqhe qɔjt:a]

60 sixty	кхузткъа	[quztqha]
61 sixty-one	кхузткъе цхьаъ	[quztqhe tsha]
62 sixty-two	кхузткъе шиъ	[quztqhe ʃi]
63 sixty-three	кхузткъе кхоъ	[quztqhe qɔ]

70 seventy	кхузткъа итт	[quztqha it:]
71 seventy-one	кхузткъе цхьайтта	[quztqhe tshajt:a]
72 seventy-two	кхузткъе шийтта	[quztqhe ʃi:t:a]
73 seventy-three	кхузткъе кхойтта	[quztqhe qɔjt:a]

80 eighty	дезткъа	[deztqha]
81 eighty-one	дезткъе цхьаъ	[deztqhe tsha]
82 eighty-two	дезткъе шиъ	[deztqhe ʃi]
83 eighty-three	дезткъе кхоъ	[deztqhe qɔ]

90 ninety	дезткъа итт	[deztqha it:]
91 ninety-one	дезткъе цхьайтта	[deztqhe tshajt:a]
92 ninety-two	дезткъе шийтта	[deztqhe ʃi:t:a]
93 ninety-three	дезткъе кхойтта	[deztqhe qɔjt:a]

5. Cardinal numbers. Part 2

100 one hundred	бле	[bəe]
200 two hundred	ши бле	[ʃi bəe]
300 three hundred	кхо бле	[qɔ bəe]
400 four hundred	диъ бле	[di bəe]
500 five hundred	пхи бле	[phi bəe]

| 600 six hundred | ялх бле | [jalh bəe] |
| 700 seven hundred | ворхl бле | [vɔrh bəe] |

800 eight hundred	бархӀ бӀе	[barh bəe]
900 nine hundred	исс бӀе	[is: bəe]
1000 one thousand	эзар	[ɛzar]
2000 two thousand	ши эзар	[ʃi ɛzar]
3000 three thousand	кхо эзар	[qɔ ɛzar]
10000 ten thousand	итт эзар	[it: ɛzar]
one hundred thousand	бӀе эзар	[bəe ɛzar]
million	миллион	[mil:iɔn]
billion	миллиард	[mil:iard]

6. Ordinal numbers

first	хьалхара	[halhara]
second	шолгӀа	[ʃɔlɣa]
third	кхоалгӀа	[qɔalɣa]
fourth	доьалгӀа	[døalɣa]
fifth	пхоьлгӀа	[phølɣa]
sixth	йолхалгӀа	[jolhalɣa]
seventh	ворхӀалгӀа	[vɔrhalɣa]
eighth	бархӀалгӀа	[barhalɣa]
ninth	уьссалгӀа	[ys:alɣa]
tenth	итталгӀа	[it:alɣa]

7. Numbers. Fractions

fraction	дакъалла	[daqhal:a]
one half	шоалгӀачун цхьаъ	[ʃɔalɣaʧun tsha]
one third	кхоалгӀачун цхьаъ	[qɔalɣaʧun tsha]
one quarter	доьалгӀачун цхьаъ	[døalɣaʧun tsha]
one eighth	бархӀалгӀачун цхьаъ	[barhalɣʧun tsha]
one tenth	итталгӀачун цхьаъ	[it:alɣaʧun tsha]
two thirds	кхоалгӀачун шиъ	[qɔalɣaʧun ʃi]
three quarters	доьалгӀачун кхоъ	[døalɣaʧun qɔ]

8. Numbers. Basic operations

subtraction	тӀерадаккхар	[theradak:ar]
to subtract (vi, vt)	тӀерадаккха	[theradak:a]
division	декъар	[deqhar]
to divide (vt)	декъа	[deqha]
addition	вовшахтохар	[vɔvʃahtɔhar]
to add up (vt)	вовшахтоха	[vɔvʃahtɔha]

to add (vi)	тӀетоха	[thetɔha]
multiplication	эцар	[ɛtsar]
to multiply (vi, vt)	эца	[ɛtsa]

9. Numbers. Miscellaneous

digit, figure	цифра	[tsifra]
number	терахь	[terah]
numeral	терахьдош	[terahdɔʃ]
minus	минус	[minus]
plus	тӀетоха	[thetɔha]
formula	формула	[fɔrmula]

calculation	ларар	[larar]
to count (vi, vt)	лара	[lara]
to count up	лара	[lara]
to compare (vt)	дуста	[dusta]

How much?	Мел?	[mel]
How many?	Маса?	[masa]
sum, total	жамӀ	[ʒamə]
result	хилам	[hilam]
remainder	бухадиснарг	[buhadisnarg]

a few …	масех	[maseh]
the rest	бухадиснарг	[buhadisnarg]
one and a half	цхьаъ ах	[tsha ah]
dozen	цӀов	[tshɔv]

in half	шин декъе	[ʃin deqhe]
equally (evenly)	цхьабосса	[tshabɔs:a]
half	ах	[ah]
time (instance)	цкъа	[tsqha]

10. The most important verbs. Part 1

to advise (vt)	хьехам бан	[heham ban]
to agree (say yes)	реза хила	[reza hila]
to answer (vi, vt)	жоп дала	[ʒɔp dala]
to apologize (vi)	бехк цабиллар деха	[behk tsabil:ar deha]
to arrive (vi)	дан	[dan]

to ask (~ sb to do sth)	деха	[deha]
to ask (e.g., ~ oneself)	хатта	[hat:a]
to be afraid	кхера	[qera]

| to be hungry | хӀума яаа лаа | [huma ja:: la:] |
| to be interested in … | довза лаа | [dɔvza la:] |

to be necessary	оьшуш хила	[øʃuʃ hila]
to be surprised	цецдала	[tsetsdala]
to be thirsty	мала лаа	[mala la:]

to begin (vi, vt)	доло	[dɔlɔ]
to belong to ...	хила	[hila]
to boast (vi)	куралла ян	[kural:a jan]
to break (split into pieces)	кегдан	[kegdan]

to call (for help)	кхайкха	[qajqa]
can (modal verb)	мага	[maga]
to catch (vt)	леца	[letsa]
to change (vt)	хийца	[hi:tsa]
to choose (select)	харжар	[harʒar]

to come down	охьадан	[ɔhadan]
to come in (enter)	чудахар	[ʧudahar]
to compare (vt)	дуста	[dusta]
to complain (vi, vt)	латкъа	[latqha]
to continue (vi, vt)	дахдан	[dahdan]

to control (vt)	тӀехьажа	[thehaʒa]
to cook (dinner)	кечдан	[ketʃdan]
to cost (vt)	деха	[deha]
to count (add up)	лара	[lara]
to count on ...	дагахь хила	[dagah hila]
to create (vt)	кхолла	[qɔl:a]
to cry (weep)	делха	[delha]

11. The most important verbs. Part 2

to deceive (vi, vt)	Ӏехо	[aehɔ]
to decorate (tree, street)	хаздан	[hazdan]
to defend (a country etc.)	лардан	[lardan]
to demand (request firmly)	тӀедожо	[thedɔʒɔ]

to dig (vi, vt)	ахка	[ahka]
to direct (supervise)	куьйгаллз дан	[kyjgal:z dan]
to discuss (talk about)	дийцаре дилла	[di:tsare dil:a]
to do (vt)	дан	[dan]
to doubt (have doubts)	шекьхила	[ʃəkʲhila]
to drop (let fall)	охьаэго	[ɔhaəgɔ]

to exist (vi)	хила	[hila]
to expect (foresee)	хиндерг хаа	[hinderg ha:]
to explain (vi, vt)	кхето	[qetɔ]

to fall (vi)	охьаэга	[ɔhaəga]
to find (vt)	каро	[karɔ]
to finish (vt)	чекхдаккха	[ʧeqdak:a]

to fly (vi)	лела	[lela]
to follow … (come after)	тІаьхьадаха	[thæhadaha]
to forget (vi, vt)	дицдала	[ditsdala]
to forgive (vt)	геч дан	[getʃ dan]

to give (vt)	дала	[dala]
to go (to walk)	даха	[daha]
to go for a swim	лийча	[li:tʃa]
to go out	арадалар	[aradalar]
to guess right	хаа	[ha:]

to have (vt)	хила	[hila]
to have breakfast	марта даа	[marta da:]
to have dinner	пхьор дан	[phɔr dan]
to have lunch	делкъана хІума яа	[delqhana huma ja:]

to hear (vi, vt)	хаза	[haza]
to help (assist, aid)	гІо дан	[ɣɔ dan]
to hide (vt)	дІадилла	[dəadil:a]
to hint (vi)	къедо	[qhedɔ]
to hope (vi, vt)	догдаха	[dɔgdaha]
to hunt (vi, vt)	талла эха	[tal:a ɛha]
to hurry (vi)	сихдала	[sihdala]

12. The most important verbs. Part 3

to inform (vi, vt)	информаци ян, хаам бан	[informatsi jan, ha:m ban]
to insist (vi, vt)	тІера ца вала	[thera tsa vala]
to insult (vt)	сий дайа	[si: daja]
to invite (vt)	схьакхайкха	[shaqajqa]
to joke (vi)	забарш ян	[zabarʃ jan]

to keep (vt)	лардан	[lardan]
to keep silence	къамел ца дан	[qhamel tsa dan]
to kill (vt)	ден	[den]
to know (sb)	довза	[dɔvza]
to know (sth)	хаа	[ha:]

to laugh (vi)	дела	[dela]
to liberate (vt)	мукъадаккха	[muqhadak:a]
to like (I like …)	хазахета	[hazaheta]
to look for … (search)	леха	[leha]
to love sb	деза	[deza]

to make a mistake	гІалатдала	[ɣalatdala]
to mean (signify)	маьІна хила	[mæəna hila]
to mention (talk about)	хьахо	[haho]
to miss (school etc.)	юкъахдита	[juqhahdita]
to mix up (confuse)	тило	[tilɔ]

to notice (see)	ган	[gan]
to object (vi, vt)	дуьхьал хила	[dyhal hila]
to observe (see)	тергам бан	[tergam ban]
to open (vt)	схьаделла	[shadel:a]
to order (meal etc.)	заказ ян	[zakaz jan]
to order (military)	омра дан	[ɔmra dan]
to own (possess)	хила	[hila]
to participate (vi)	дакъа лаца	[daqha latsa]
to pay (vi, vt)	ахча дала	[ahtʃa dala]
to permit (allow)	магийта	[magi:ta]
to plan (vi, vt)	план хӀотто	[plan hot:ɔ]
to play (vi, vt)	ловза	[lɔvza]
to pray (vi, vt)	ламаз дан	[lamaz dan]
to prefer (vt)	гӀоли хета	[ɣɔli heta]
to promise (vt)	вайда дан	[vaəda dan]
to pronounce (say)	ала	[ala]
to propose (vt)	хьахо	[haho]
to punish (vt)	тӀазар дан	[taəzar dan]
to read (vi, vt)	еша	[eʃa]
to recommend (vt)	мага дан	[maga dan]
to refuse (vi, vt)	дуьхьал хила	[dyhal hila]
to regret (be sorry)	дагахьбаллам хила	[dagahbal:am hila]
to rent (of a tenant)	лаца	[latsa]
to repeat (say again)	юхаала	[juha:la]
to reserve, to book	резервировать ян	[rezerwirovatʲ jan]
to run (vi)	дада	[dada]

13. The most important verbs. Part 4

to save (rescue)	кӀелхьардаккха	[k:elhardak:a]
to say (e.g., ~ thank you)	ала	[ala]
to scold (vt)	дов дан	[dɔv dan]
to see (vi, vt)	ган	[gan]
to sell (goods)	дохка	[dɔhka]
to send (vt)	дӀадахьийта	[dəadahi:ta]
to shoot (vi)	кхийса	[qi:sa]
to shout (vi)	мохь бетта	[mɔh bet:a]
to show (vi, vt)	гайта	[gajta]
to sign (document)	куьг тӀало	[kyg taəɔ]
to sit down (vi)	охьахаа	[ɔhaha:]
to smile (vi)	дела къежа	[dela qheʒa]
to speak (vi, vt)	мотт бийца	[mɔt: bi:tsa]
to steal (money, etc.)	лечкъо	[letʃqhɔ]
to stop (cease)	дӀасацо	[dəasatsɔ]

to stop (vi)	саца	[satsa]
to study (vt)	Iамо	[əamɔ]
to swim (vi)	нека дан	[neka dan]
to take (vt)	схьаэца	[shaətsa]
to think (vi, vt)	ойла ян	[ɔjla jan]
to threaten (vt)	кхерам тийса	[qeram ti:sa]
to touch (by hands)	куьг тоха	[kyg tɔha]
to translate (word, text)	талмажалла дан	[talmaʒal:a dan]
to trust (vt)	теша	[teʃa]
to try (attempt)	хьажа	[haʒa]
to turn (change direction)	дIадерза	[dəaderza]
to underestimate (vt)	ма-дарра ца лара	[ma dar:a tsa lara]
to understand (vi, vt)	кхета	[qeta]
to unite (join)	цхьанатоха	[tshænatɔha]
to wait (vi, vt)	хьежа	[heʒa]
to want (wish, desire)	лаа	[la:]
to warn (of the danger)	дIахьедан	[dəahedan]
to work (vi)	болх бан	[bɔlh ban]
to write (vi, vt)	яздан	[jazdan]
to write down	дIаяздан	[dəajazdan]

14. Colors

color	бос	[bɔs]
shade (nuance)	амат	[amat]
tone	бос	[bɔs]
rainbow	стелалад	[stelaəad]
white	кIайн	[k:ajn]
black	IаьРжа	[əærʒa]
gray	сира	[sira]
green	баьццара	[bætsara]
yellow	можа	[mɔʒa]
red	цIен	[tshen]
blue	сийна	[si:na]
light blue	сийна	[si:na]
pink	сирла-цIен	[sirla tshen]
orange	цIехо-можа	[tsheho mɔʒa]
violet	цIехо-сийна	[tsheho si:na]
brown	боьмаша	[bømaʃa]
golden	дашо	[daʃo]
silvery	детиха	[detiha]
beige	бежеви	[beʒewi]

cream	беда-можа	[beda moʒa]
turquoise	бирюзан бос	[biryzan bɔs]
cherry	баьллийн бос	[bæl:i:n bɔs]
lilac	сирла-сийна	[sirla si:na]
raspberry	камарийн бос	[kamari:n bɔs]
light	сирла	[sirla]
dark	Iаьржа	[əærʒa]
bright	къегина	[qhegina]
colored (pencils)	бесара	[besara]
color (e.g., ~ film)	бос болу	[bɔs bɔlu]
black-and-white	кIайн-Iаьржа	[k:ajn əærʒa]
plain (one color)	цхьана бесара	[tshana besara]
multicolored	бес-бесара	[bes besara]

15. Questions

Who?	Мила?	[mila]
What?	ХIун?	[hun]
Where? (at, in)	Мичахь?	[mitʃah]
Where (to)?	Мича?	[mitʃa]
Where ... from?	Мичара?	[mitʃara]
When?	Маца?	[matsa]
Why? (aim)	Стенна?	[stena]
Why? (reason)	ХIунда?	[hunda]
What for?	Стенан?	[stenan]
How? (in what way)	Муха?	[muha]
What? (which?)	Муьлха?	[mylha]
Which?	МасалгIа?	[masalɣa]
To whom?	Хьанна?	[hana]
About whom?	Хьанах лаьцна?	[hanah lætsna]
About what?	Стенах лаьцна?	[stenah lætsna]
With whom?	Хьаьнца?	[hæntsa]
How many? How much?	Маса?	[masa]
Whose?	Хьенан?	[henan]

16. Prepositions

with (accompanied by)	цхьан	[tshan]
without	доцуш	[dɔtsuʃ]
to (indicating direction)	чу	[tʃu]
before (in time)	хьалха	[halha]
in front of ...	хьалха	[halha]
under (beneath, below)	кIел	[k:el]

above (in a higher position)	тӀехула	[thehula]
on (e.g., ~ the table)	тӀехь	[theh]
in (e.g., ~ ten minutes)	даьлча	[dælʧa]
over (across the top of)	хула	[hula]

17. Function words. Adverbs. Part 1

Where? (at, in)	Мичахь?	[miʧah]
here	хьоккхузахь	[hɔk:uzah]
there (in a particular place)	цигахь	[ʦigah]
somewhere	цхьанхьа-м	[ʦhanha m]
nowhere (not anywhere)	цхьаннахьа а	[ʦhaŋaha a]
by (near, beside)	уллехь	[ul:eh]
by the window	кора уллехь	[kɔra ul:eh]
Where (to)?	Мича?	[miʧa]
here (e.g., come ~!)	кхузахь	[quzah]
there (e.g., to go ~)	цига	[ʦiga]
from here	хӀоккхузара	[hɔk:uzara]
from there	цигара	[ʦigara]
near (in space)	герга	[gerga]
far (distant in space)	гена	[gena]
near (e.g., ~ Paris)	улло	[ul:ɔ]
nearby	юххе	[juhe]
not far	гена доцу	[gena dɔʦu]
left	аьрру	[ær:u]
on the left	аьрру аӀорхьара	[ær:u aɣɔrhara]
to the left	аьрру аӀор	[ær:u aɣɔr]
right	аьтту	[æt:u]
on the right	аьтту аӀорхьара	[æt:u aɣɔrhara]
to the right	аьтту аӀор	[æt:u aɣɔr]
in front	хьалха	[halha]
front (attr)	хьалхара	[halhara]
ahead (in space)	хьалха	[halha]
behind	тӀехьа	[theha]
from behind	тӀаьхьа	[thæha]
back (towards the rear)	юхо	[juho]
middle	юкъ	[juqh]
in the middle	юккъе	[jukqhe]
at the side	аӀор	[aɣɔr]

everywhere	массанхьа	[mas:anha]
around (in all directions)	гонаха	[gonaha]
from inside	чухула	[tʃuhula]
somewhere (to go)	цхьанхьа	[tshanha]
straight (directly)	нийсса дла	[ni:s:a dəa]
back (e.g., come ~)	юха	[juha]
from anywhere	миччара а	[mitʃara a]
from somewhere	цхьанхьара	[tshanhara]
firstly	цкъа-делахь	[tsqha delah]
secondly	шолгla-делахь	[ʃolɣa delah]
thirdly	кхоалгla-делахь	[qoalɣa delah]
suddenly	цlexxьана	[tshehana]
at first	юьхьенца	[juhentsa]
for the first time	дуьххьара	[dyhara]
long before …	хьалхе	[halhe]
anew (over again)	юха	[juha]
for good	гуттаренна	[gut:areŋa]
never	цкъа а	[tsqha a]
again	кхин цкъа а	[qin tsqha a]
now	хlинца	[hintsa]
often	кест-кеста	[kest kesta]
then	хlетахь	[hetah]
urgently (quickly)	чехка	[tʃehka]
usually	нехан санна	[nehan saŋa]
by the way, …	шен метта	[ʃen met:a]
possible (e.g., that is ~)	тарлун ду	[tarlun du]
probably	хила мегаш хила	[hila megaʃ hila]
maybe	хила мега	[hila mega]
besides …	цул совнаха, …	[tsul sovnaha]
that's why …	цундела	[tsundela]
in spite of …	делахь а …	[delah a]
thanks to …	бахьана долуш …	[bahana doluʃ]
what (pron.)	хlун	[hun]
that	а	[a]
something	цхьаъ-м	[tsha m]
anything (something)	цхьа хlума	[tsha huma]
nothing	хlумма а дац	[hum:a a dats]
who (pron.)	мила	[mila]
someone	цхьаъ	[tsha]
somebody	цхьаъ	[tsha]
nobody	цхьа а	[tsha a]
nowhere (not to any place)	цхьанхха а	[tshanha a]
nobody's	цхьаьннан а	[tshæŋan a]

somebody's	цхьаьннан	[tshæŋɑn]
so (e.g., I'm ~ glad)	иштта	[iʃt:ɑ]
also (as well)	санна	[sɑŋɑ]
too (as well)	а	[ɑ]

18. Function words. Adverbs. Part 2

Why?	ХІунда?	[hundɑ]
for some reason	цхьанна-м	[tshɑŋɑ m]
because ...	цундела	[tsundelɑ]
for some purpose	цхьана хІуманна	[tshɑnɑ humɑŋɑ]

and	а-а	[ɑ ɑ]
or	я	[jɑ]
but	амма	[ɑm:ɑ]

too (excessively)	дукха	[duqɑ]
only (exclusively)	бен	[ben]
exactly	нийсса	[ni:s:ɑ]
about (more or less)	герга	[gergɑ]

approximately	герггарчу хьесапехь	[gerg:ɑrtʃu hesɑpeh]
approximate	герггарчу хьесапера	[gerg:ɑrtʃu hesɑperɑ]
almost	гергга	[gerg:ɑ]
the rest	бухадиснарг	[buhɑdisnɑrg]

other, another	кхин	[qin]
each	хІоп	[hɔr]
any (no matter which)	муьлхха а	[mylhɑ ɑ]
many, much (a lot of)	дукха	[duqɑ]
many people	дуккха а	[duk:ɑ ɑ]
all (everyone)	дерриг	[der:ig]

in exchange for ...	цхьана ... хийцина	[tshɑnɑ hi:tsinɑ]
in exchange	метта	[met:ɑ]
by hand (made)	куьйга	[kyjgɑ]
hardly (negative opinion)	те	[te]

probably	схьахетарехь	[shɑhetɑreh]
on purpose	хуъушехь	[hyuʃeh]
by accident	ларамаза	[lɑrɑmɑzɑ]

very	чІоарла	[tʃhɔɑɣɑ]
for example	масала	[mɑsɑlɑ]
between	юккъехь	[jukqheh]
among	юккъехь	[jukqheh]
especially	къасттина	[qhɑst:inɑ]

Basic concepts. Part 2

19. Weekdays

Monday	оршот	[ɔrʃɔt]
Tuesday	шинара	[ʃinara]
Wednesday	кхаара	[qɑːra]
Thursday	еара	[eɑra]
Friday	пıераска	[pheraska]
Saturday	шот	[ʃɔt]
Sunday	кıиранде	[kːirande]

today	тахана	[tahana]
tomorrow	кхана	[qana]
the day after tomorrow	лама	[lama]
yesterday	селхана	[selhana]
the day before yesterday	стомара	[stɔmara]

day	де	[de]
workday	белхан де	[belhan de]
holiday	деза де	[deza de]
day off	мукъа де	[muqha de]
weekend	мукъаденош	[muqha denɔʃ]

all day long	деррига де	[derːiga de]
next day	шолгıачу дийнахь	[ʃɔlɣatʃu diːnah]
two days ago	ши де хьалха	[ʃi de halha]
the day before	де хьалха	[de halha]
daily	хıор денна хуьлу	[hɔr deŋa hylu]
every day	хıор денна хуьлу	[hɔr deŋa hylu]

week	кıира	[kːira]
last week	дıадаханчу кıирнахь	[dəadahantʃu kːirnah]
next week	тıедогıучу кıирнахь	[thedoɣutʃu kːirnah]
weekly (adj)	хıор кıиранан	[hɔr kːiranan]
every week	хıор кıирна	[hɔr kːirna]
twice a week	кıирнахь шозза	[kːirnah ʃɔzːa]
every Tuesday	хıор шинара	[hɔr ʃinara]

20. Hours. Day and night

morning	ıуьйре	[əyjre]
in the morning	ıуьйранна	[əyjraŋa]
noon, midday	делкъе	[delqhe]

in the afternoon	делкъан тlаьхьа	[delqhan thæha]
evening	суьйре	[syjre]
in the evening	сарахь	[sarah]
night	буьса	[bysa]
at night	буса	[busa]
midnight	буьйсанан юкъ	[byjsanan juqh]
second	секунд	[sekund]
minute	минот	[minɔt]
hour	сахьт	[saht]
half an hour	ахсахьт	[ahsaht]
quarter of an hour	сахьтах пхийтта	[sahtah phi:t:a]
fifteen minutes	l5 минот	[phi:t:a minɔt]
24 hours	де-буьйса	[de byjsa]
sunrise	малх схьакхетар	[malh shaqetar]
dawn	сатасар	[satasar]
early morning	lуьйранна хьалххехь	[əyjraŋa halheh]
sunset	чубузар	[ʧubuzar]
early in the morning	lуьйранна хьалххе	[əyjraŋa halhe]
this morning	тахан lуьйранна	[tahan əyjraŋa]
tomorrow morning	кхана lуьйранна	[qana əyjraŋa]
this afternoon	тахана дийнахь	[tahana di:nah]
in the afternoon	делкъан тlаьхьа	[delqhan thæha]
tomorrow afternoon	кхана делкъан тlаьхьа	[qana delqhan thæha]
tonight (this evening)	тахана суьйранна	[tahana syjraŋa]
tomorrow evening	кхана суьйранна	[qana syjraŋa]
at 3 o'clock sharp	нийсса кхоъ сахьт даьлча	[ni:s:a qø saht dælʧa]
about 4 o'clock	диъ сахьт гергга	[di saht gerg:a]
by 12 o'clock	шийтта сахьт долаж	[ʃi:t:a saht dɔlaʒ]
in 20 minutes	ткъа минот яьлча	[tqha minɔt jalʧa]
in an hour	цхьа сахьт даьлча	[tsha saht dælʧa]
on time	шен хеннахь	[ʃən heŋah]
term (end of period)	хан	[han]
a quarter of ...	сахьтах пхийтта яьлча	[sahtah phi:t:a jalʧa]
within an hour	сахьт даллалц	[saht dal:alts]
every 15 minutes	хlор пхийтта минот	[hɔr phi:t:a minɔt]
round the clock	дуьззина де-буьйса	[dyz:ina de byjsa]

21. Months. Seasons

January	январь	[janvarʲ]
February	февраль	[fevraʎ]

March	март	[mɑrt]
April	апрель	[ɑpreʎ]
May	май	[mɑj]
June	июнь	[ijuɲ]

July	июль	[ijuʎ]
August	август	[ɑvgust]
September	сентябрь	[sentʲabrʲ]
October	октябрь	[ɔktʲabrʲ]
November	ноябрь	[nɔjabrʲ]
December	декабрь	[dekabrʲ]

spring	бlаьсте	[bææste]
in spring	бlаьста	[bææstɑ]
spring (attr)	бlаьстенан	[bææstenɑn]

summer	аьхке	[æhke]
in summer	аьхка	[æhkɑ]
summer (attr)	аьхкенан	[æhkenɑn]

fall	гуьйре	[gyjre]
in the fall	гурахь	[gurɑh]
fall (attr)	гуьйренан	[gyjrenɑn]

winter	lа	[əɑ]
in winter	lай	[əɑj]
winter (attr)	lаьнан	[əænɑn]

month	бутт	[but:]
this month	кху баттахь	[qu bɑt:ɑh]
next month	тlеболгу баттахь	[thebɔɣu bɑt:ɑh]
last month	байна баттахь	[bɑjnɑ bɑt:ɑh]

a month ago	цхьа бутт хьалха	[tshɑ but: hɑlhɑ]
in a month	цхьа бутт баьлча	[tshɑ but: bæltʃɑ]
in two months	ши бутт баьлча	[ʃi but: bæltʃɑ]
a whole month	беррига бутт	[ber:igɑ but:]
all month long	дийнна бутт	[di:ŋɑ but:]

monthly (~ magazine)	хlоп беттан	[hɔr bet:ɑn]
monthly (adv)	хlоп баттахь	[hɔr bɑt:ɑh]
every month	хlоп бутт	[hɔr but:]
twice a month	баттахь 2	[bɑt:ɑh ʃɔz:ɑ]

year	шо	[ʃɔ]
this year	кхушара	[quʃɑrɑ]
next year	тlедолгучу шарахь	[thedɔɣutʃu ʃɑrɑh]
last year	стохка	[stɔhkɑ]

a year ago	шо хьалха	[ʃɔ hɑlhɑ]
in a year	шо даьлча	[ʃɔ dæltʃɑ]
in two years	ши шо даьлча	[ʃi ʃɔ dæltʃɑ]

a whole year	деррига шо	[derːiga ʃo]
all year long	дийнна шо	[diːŋa ʃo]
every year	хlоп шо	[hor ʃo]
annual (adj)	хlоп шеран	[hor ʃeran]
annually	хlоп шарахь	[hor ʃarah]
4 times a year	шарахь 4	[ʃarah døazːa]
date (e.g., today's ~)	де	[de]
date (e.g., ~ of birth)	терахь	[terah]
calendar (of dates)	календарь	[kalendarʲ]
half a year	ахшо	[ahʃo]
six months	ахшо	[ahʃo]
season (summer etc.)	зам	[zam]
century	оьмар	[ømar]

22. Time. Miscellaneous

time	хан	[han]
instant (noun)	бlарган негlап туху юкъ	[beargan neɣar tuhu juqh]
moment	бlарган негlап туху юкъ	[beargan neɣar tuhu juqh]
instant (adj)	цlеххьана	[tʃʃehana]
period (length of time)	хенан юкъ	[henan juqh]
life	дахар	[dahar]
eternity	абаде	[abade]
epoch	мур	[mur]
era	зама	[zama]
cycle	цикл	[tʃsikl]
period	мур	[mur]
term (period)	хан	[han]
the future	тlедорly	[thedoɣu]
future (attr)	тlедорly	[thedoɣu]
next time	тlаьхьахула	[thæhahula]
the past	дlадахнарг	[deadahnarg]
past (recent)	дlадахнар	[deadahnar]
last time	тохар	[tohar]
later	тlаккха	[thakːa]
after	тlаьхьа	[thæha]
nowadays	хlинца	[hintsa]
now	хlинцца	[hintsa]
immediately	хьем ца беш	[hem tsa beʃ]
soon	кеста	[kesta]
in advance (beforehand)	хьалххе	[halhe]
a long time ago	тоххара	[tohara]
recently	дукха хан йоццуш	[duqa han jotsuʃ]
destiny	кхел	[qel]

| memories (recollection) | диццадалар | [diʦadalar] |
| archives | архив | [arhiv] |

during ...	хеннахь ...	[heŋah]
long, a long time	дукха	[duqa]
not long	дукха дац	[duqa daʦ]
early (in the morning)	хьалха	[halha]
late (not early)	тІаьхьа	[thæha]

forever (for good)	даиманна	[daimaŋa]
to start (begin)	доло	[dɔlɔ]
to postpone (vt)	тІаьхьадаккха	[thæhadak:a]

at the same time	цхьана хеннахь	[ʦhana heŋah]
permanently	даимлера	[daimlera]
constant (noise, pain)	хаддаза	[had:aza]
temporary	ханна	[haŋa]

sometimes	наггахь	[nag:ah]
rarely	кеста ца хуьлу	[kesta ʦa hylu]
often	кест-кеста	[kest kesta]

23. Opposites

| rich | хьал долу | [hal dɔlu] |
| poor | къен | [qhen] |

| ill, sick | цомгуш | [ʦɔmguʃ] |
| healthy | могуш | [mɔguʃ] |

| big | доккха | [dɔk:a] |
| small | жима | [ʒima] |

| quickly | сиха | [siha] |
| slowly | меллаша | [mel:aʃa] |

| fast | маса | [masa] |
| slow | меллаша | [mel:aʃa] |

| cheerful | самукъане | [samuqhane] |
| sad | гІайгІане | [ɣajɣane] |

| together | цхьана | [ʦhana] |
| separately | къастина | [qhastina] |

| aloud (read) | хезаш | [hezaʃ] |
| silently | ша-шена | [ʃa ʃena] |

| tall | лекха | [leqa] |
| low | лоха | [lɔha] |

deep	кӏоарга	[kːɔarga]
shallow	гомха	[gɔmha]
yes	хьаъ	[ha]
no	хӏан-хӏа	[han ha]
distant	генара	[genara]
nearby (adj)	герггара	[gergːara]
far	гена	[gena]
nearby (adv)	юххехь	[juheh]
long	деха	[deha]
short	доца	[dɔʦa]
kind	дика	[dika]
evil	вон	[vɔn]
married	зуда ялийна	[zuda jaliːna]
single	зуд ялоза	[zud jalɔza]
to forbid (vt)	дехка	[dehka]
to permit (vi, vt)	магийта	[magiːta]
end	чаккхе	[ʧakːe]
beginning	юьхь	[juh]
left	аьрру	[ærːu]
right	аьтту	[ætːu]
first	хьалхара	[halhara]
last	тӏаьххьара	[thæhara]
crime	зулам	[zulam]
punishment	тӏазар	[taezar]
to order (vi, vt)	буьйр дан	[byjr dan]
to obey (vi, vt)	муьтӏахь хила	[mythah hila]
straight	нийса	[niːsa]
curved	гона	[gɔna]
Paradise	ялсамани	[jalsamani]
Hell	жоьжахати	[ʒøʒahati]
to be born	хила	[hila]
to die (vi, vt)	дала	[dala]
strong	нуьцкъала	[nyʦqhala]
weak	гӏийла	[ɣiːla]

old	къена	[qhena]
young	къона	[qhɔna]
old	тиша	[tiʃa]
new	цlина	[tshina]
hard	чloarla	[tʃhɔaɣa]
soft	кleда	[k:eda]
warm	мела	[mela]
cold	шийла	[ʃi:la]
fat	стомма	[stɔm:a]
slim	оза	[ɔza]
narrow	готта	[gɔt:a]
wide	шуьйра	[ʃyjra]
good	дика	[dika]
bad	вон	[vɔn]
brave	майра	[majra]
cowardly	осала	[ɔsala]

24. Lines and shapes

square	квадрат	[kvadrat]
square (attr)	квадратан	[kvadratan]
circle	го	[gɔ]
round	горга	[gɔrga]
triangle	кхосаберг	[qɔsaberg]
triangular	кхо са болу	[qɔ sa bɔlu]
oval	овал	[ɔval]
oval (attr)	овалан	[ɔvalan]
rectangle	нийса саберг	[ni:sa saberg]
rectangular	нийса сенаш долу	[ni:sa senaʃ dɔlu]
pyramid	пирамида	[piramida]
rhombus	ромб	[rɔmb]
trapezoid	трапеци	[trapetsi]
cube	куб	[kub]
prism	призма	[prizma]
circumference	хlоз	[hɔz]
sphere	тlехула	[thehula]
sphere (ball)	горгал	[gɔrgal]
diameter	диаметр	[diametr]

radius	радиус	[radius]
perimeter	периметр	[perimetr]
center	центр	[ʦentr]
horizontal	ана	[ana]
vertical	ирх	[irh]
parallel (noun)	параллель	[paral:eʎ]
parallel (adj)	параллельни	[paral:eʎni]
line	сиз	[siz]
stroke	сиз	[siz]
straight line	нийсаниг	[ni:sanig]
curve	гома сиз	[gɔma siz]
thin (layer)	дуткъа	[dutqha]
contour (outline)	гӀаларт	[ɣalart]
intersection	хадор	[hadɔr]
right angle (angle of 90°)	нийса саберг	[ni:sa saberg]
segment	сегмент	[segment]
sector	сектор	[sektɔr]
side (of triangle)	арло	[aɣɔ]
angle	са	[sa]

25. Units of measurement

weight	дозалла	[dɔzal:a]
length	йохалла	[johal:a]
width	шоралла	[ʃoral:a]
height	лакхалла	[laqal:a]
depth	кӀоргалла	[k:ɔrgal:a]
volume	дукхалла	[duqal:a]
area	майда	[majda]
gram	грамм	[gram:]
milligram	миллиграмм	[mil:igram:]
kilogram	килограмм	[kilɔgram:]
ton	тонна	[tɔŋa]
pound (unit of weight)	герка	[gerka]
ounce	унци	[unʦi]
meter	метр	[metr]
millimeter	миллиметр	[mil:imetr]
centimeter	сантиметр	[santimetr]
kilometer	километр	[kilɔmetr]
mile	миля	[miʎa]
inch	дюйм	[dyjm]
foot	фут	[fut]
yard	ярд	[jard]
square meter	квадратни метр	[kvadratni metr]
hectare	гектар	[gektar]

liter	литр	[litr]
degree	градус	[gradus]
volt	вольт	[voʌt]
ampere	ампер	[amper]
horsepower	говран ницкъ	[gɔvran nitsqh]
quantity	дукхалла	[duqal:a]
a little bit of …	кӏезиг	[k:ezig]
half	ах	[ah]
dozen	цӏов	[tshɔv]
piece (item)	цхьаъ	[tsha]
size	барам	[baram]
scale (of model, drawing)	масштаб	[masʃtab]
minimum	уггар кӏезиг	[ug:ar k:ezig]
the smallest	уггара кӏезигаха долу	[ug:ara k:ezigaha dɔlu]
medium	юккъера	[jukqhera]
maximum	уггар дукха	[ug:ar duqa]
the largest	уггара дукхаха долу	[ug:ara duqaha dɔlu]

26. Containers

jar (glass)	банка	[baŋka]
can	банка	[baŋka]
bucket	ведар	[wedar]
barrel	боьшка	[bøʃka]
basin (for washing)	тас	[tas]
tank (for liquid, gas)	бак	[bak]
flask (for water, wine)	фляжк	[fʌaʒk]
jerrycan	канистр	[kanistr]
cistern (tank)	цистерна	[tsisterna]
mug	кружка	[kruʒka]
cup (of coffee etc.)	кад	[kad]
saucer	боьшхап	[bɔʃhap]
glass (~ of water)	стака	[staka]
glass (~ of vine)	кад	[kad]
stew pot	яй	[jaj]
bottle (e.g., ~ of wine)	шиша	[ʃiʃa]
neck (of the bottle)	бертиг	[bertig]
carafe	сурийла	[suri:la]
pitcher (earthenware)	кӏудал	[k:udal]
vessel (container)	пхьерӏа	[pheʁa]
pot (crock)	кхаба	[qaba]
vase	ваза	[vaza]
bottle (e.g., ~ of perfume)	флакон	[flakɔn]

vial, small bottle	шиша	[ʃiʃa]
tube (of toothpaste)	тюбик	[tybik]
sack (bag)	гали	[gali]
bag (paper, plastic)	пакет	[paket]
package (small parcel)	пакет	[paket]
pack (of cigarettes etc.)	ботт	[bɔt:]
pack	дӏахьарчорг	[dəahartʃɔrg]
box (e.g., shoebox)	гӏутакх	[ɣutaq]
box (for transportation)	яьшка	[jaʃka]
basket (for carrying)	тускар	[tuskar]

27. Materials

material	коьчал	[køtʃal]
wood	дитт	[dit:]
wooden	дечиган	[detʃigan]
glass (noun)	ангали	[aŋali]
glass (attr)	ангалин	[aŋalin]
stone (noun)	тӏулг	[thulg]
stone (attr)	тӏулган	[thulgan]
plastic (noun)	пластик	[plastik]
plastic (attr)	пластмассови	[plastmas:ɔwi]
rubber (noun)	резина	[rezina]
rubber (attr)	резинин	[rezinin]
material, fabric (noun)	кӏади	[k:adi]
fabric (attr)	кӏадах	[k:adah]
paper (noun)	кехат	[kehat]
paper (attr)	кехатан	[kehatan]
cardboard (noun)	мужалт	[muʒalt]
cardboard (attr)	мужалтан	[muʒaltan]
polythene	полиэтилен	[pɔliɛtilen]
cellophane	целлофан	[tsel:ɔfan]
plywood	фанера	[fanera]
porcelain (noun)	кӏайн кхийра	[k:ajn qi:ra]
porcelain (attr)	кӏайчу кхийран	[k:ajtʃu qi:ran]
clay (noun)	поппар	[pɔp:ar]
clay (attr)	кхийра	[qi:ra]
ceramics (noun)	кхийра	[qi:ra]
ceramic (attr)	кхийран	[qi:ran]

28. Metals

metal (noun)	металл	[metal:]
metal (attr)	металлан	[metal:an]
alloy (noun)	лалам	[lalam]
gold (noun)	деши	[deʃi]
gold, golden	дашо	[daʃo]
silver (noun)	дети	[deti]
silver (attr)	дато	[datɔ]
iron (noun)	эчиг	[ɛtʃig]
iron, made of iron	аьчка	[ætʃka]
steel (noun)	болат	[bolat]
steel (attr)	болатан	[bɔlatan]
copper (noun)	цIаста	[tshasta]
copper (attr)	цIастан	[tshastan]
aluminum (noun)	наштар	[naʃtar]
aluminum (attr)	наштаран	[naʃtaran]
bronze (noun)	борза	[bɔrza]
bronze (attr)	борзанан	[bɔrzanan]
brass	латунь	[latuɲ]
nickel	никель	[nikeʎ]
platinum	кIайн деши	[k:ajn deʃi]
mercury	гинсу	[ginsu]
tin	гIели	[ɣeli]
lead	даш	[daʃ]
zinc	цинк	[tsiŋk]

HUMAN BEING

Human being. The body

29. Humans. Basic concepts

human, human being	стаг	[stag]
man (adult male)	боьрша стаг	[børʃa stag]
woman	зуда	[zuda]
child	бер	[ber]
girl	жима йол	[ʒima joə]
boy	кӏант	[k:ant]
teenager	кхиазхо	[qiazho]
old man	воккха стаг	[vok:a stag]
old woman	йоккха стаг	[jok:a stag]

30. Human anatomy

organism	организм	[organizm]
heart	дог	[dog]
blood	цӏий	[tshi:]
artery	дегапха	[degapha]
vein	пха	[pha]
brain	хье	[he]
nerve	нерв	[nerv]
nerves	нерваш	[nervaʃ]
vertebra	букъдаьлахк	[buqhdæəahk]
spine	букъсурт	[buqhsurt]
stomach (organ)	хьер	[her]
intestines	чуьйраш	[ʧyjraʃ]
intestine	йоьхь	[jøh]
liver	долах	[doəah]
kidney	чениг	[ʧhenig]
bone	даьлахк	[dæəahk]
skeleton	скелет	[skelet]
rib	пӏенда	[phenda]
skull	туьта	[tyta]
muscle	дилха	[dilha]
biceps	пхьаьрсан пхьид	[phærsan phid]

triceps	трицепс	[tritseps]
tendon	хьорзам	[hɔrzam]
joint	хоттар	[hot:ar]
lungs	пехаш	[pehaʃ]
genitals	стен-боьршаллин органаш	[sten børʃal:in ɔrganaʃ]
skin	цIока	[tshɔka]

31. Head

head	корта	[kɔrta]
face	юьхь	[juh]
nose	мара	[mara]
mouth	бага	[baga]

eye	бIаьрга	[bæærga]
eyes	бIаьргаш	[bæærgaʃ]
pupil	йолбIаьрг	[jɔəbæærg]
eyebrow	цIоцкъам	[tshɔtsqham]
eyelash	бIарган неIарийн чоьш	[bəargan neɣari:n tʃøʃ]
eyelid	бIаьрганеIар	[bæərganeɣar]

tongue	мотт	[mɔt:]
tooth	церг	[tserg]
lips	балдаш	[baldaʃ]
cheekbones	бIаьрадаьIахкаш	[bææradææahkaʃ]
gum	доьлаш	[dølaʃ]
palate	стигал	[stigal]

nostrils	меран IуьргаШ	[meran əyrgaʃ]
chin	чIениг	[tʃhenig]
jaw	мочхал	[mɔtʃhal]
cheek	бесни	[besni]

forehead	хьаж	[haʒ]
temple	лергаюх	[lergajuh]
ear	лерг	[lerg]
back of the head	кIесаркIаг	[k:esark:ag]
neck	ворта	[vɔrta]
throat	къамкъарг	[qhamqharg]

hair	месаш	[mesaʃ]
hairstyle	тойина месаш	[tɔjina mesaʃ]
haircut	месаш дIахедор	[mesaʃ dəahedɔr]
wig	парик	[parik]

mustache	мекхаш	[meqaʃ]
beard	маж	[maʒ]
to have (a beard etc.)	лело	[lelɔ]
braid	кIажар	[k:aʒar]

sideburns	бакенбардаш	[bakenbardaʃ]
red-haired	хьаьрса	[hærsa]
gray (hair)	къоьжа	[qhøʒa]
bald	кӏунзал	[k:unzal]
bald patch	кӏунзал	[k:unzal]
ponytail	цӏога	[tshɔga]
bangs	кӏужал	[k:uʒal]

32. Human body

hand	тӏара	[thara]
arm	куьйг	[kyjg]
finger, toe	пӏелг	[phelg]
thumb	нана пӏелг	[nana phelg]
little finger	цӏаза-пӏелг	[tshaza phelg]
nail	мӏара	[meara]
fist	буй	[buj]
palm	кераюкъ	[kerajuqh]
wrist	куьйган хьакхолг	[kyjgan haqolg]
forearm	пхьарс	[phars]
elbow	гола	[gɔla]
shoulder	белш	[belʃ]
leg	ког	[kɔg]
foot	коган кӏело	[kɔgan k:elɔ]
knee	гола	[gɔla]
calf (part of leg)	пхьид	[phid]
hip	варе	[vare]
heel	кӏажа	[k:aʒa]
body	дегӏ	[deɣ]
stomach (abdomen)	гай	[gaj]
chest	накха	[naqa]
breast	накха	[naqa]
side (of the body)	арло	[aɣɔ]
back	букъ	[buqh]
lower back	хоттарш	[hot:arʃ]
waist	гӏодаюкъ	[ɣɔdajuqh]
navel	цӏонга	[tshɔŋa]
buttocks	хенан маьлиг	[henan mæəig]
behind	тӏехье	[thehe]
beauty mark	кӏеда	[k:eda]
birthmark	минга	[miŋa]
tattoo	дагар	[dagar]
scar	мо	[mɔ]

Clothing & Accessories

33. Outerwear. Coats

clothes	бедар	[bedɑr]
outer clothing	тӀехула юху бедар	[thehulɑ juhu bedɑr]
winter clothing	Ӏаьнан барзакъ	[əænɑn bɑrzɑqh]
overcoat	пальто	[pɑʎtɔ]
fur coat	кетар	[ketɑr]
fur jacket	йоца кетар	[jotsɑ ketɑr]
down coat	месийн гоь	[mesiːn gø]
jacket (e.g., leather ~)	куртка	[kurtkɑ]
raincoat	плащ	[plɑɕ]
waterproof	хи чекх ца долу	[hi ʈʃeq tsɑ dɔlu]

34. Men's & women's clothing

shirt	коч	[kɔʈʃ]
pants	хеча	[heʈʃɑ]
jeans	джинсаш	[dʒinsɑʃ]
jacket (of man's suit)	пиджак	[pidʒɑk]
suit	костюм	[kɔstym]
dress (frock)	бедар	[bedɑr]
skirt (garment)	юпка	[jupkɑ]
blouse	блузка	[bluzkɑ]
knitted jacket	кофта	[kɔftɑ]
jacket (of woman's suit)	жакет	[ʒɑket]
shawl	йовлакх	[jovlɑq]
T-shirt	футболк	[futbɔlk]
shorts (short trousers)	шорташ	[ʃɔrtɑʃ]
tracksuit	спортан костюм	[spɔrtɑn kɔstym]
bathrobe	оба	[ɔbɑ]
pajamas	пижама	[piʒɑmɑ]
sweater	свитер	[switer]
pullover	пуловер	[pulɔwer]
vest	жилет	[ʒilet]
tailcoat	фрак	[frɑk]
tuxedo	смокинг	[smɔkiŋ]

uniform	форма	[fɔrma]
workwear	белхан бедар	[belhan bedar]
overalls	комбинезон	[kɔmbinezɔn]
coat (e.g., doctor's ~)	оба	[ɔba]

35. Clothing. Underwear

underwear	чухулаюху хIуманаш	[tʃuhulajuhu humanaʃ]
undershirt (underwear)	майка	[majka]
socks	пазаташ	[pazataʃ]

nightgown	вуьжуш юху коч	[vyʒuʃ juhu kɔtʃ]
bra	бюстгалтер	[bystgalter]
knee highs	пазаташ	[pazataʃ]
pantyhose	колготкаш	[kɔlgɔtkaʃ]
stockings	пазаташ	[pazataʃ]
bathing suit	луьйчушъюхург	[lyjtʃuʃʲjuhurg]

36. Headwear

hat	куй	[kuj]
fedora	шляпа	[ʃʎapa]
baseball cap	бейсболк	[bejsbɔlk]
flatcap	кепка	[kepka]

beret	берет	[beret]
hood	бошлакх	[bɔʃlaq]
panama	панамка	[panamka]
knitted hat	юьйцина куй	[jujtsina kuj]

headscarf	йовлакх	[jovlaq]
women's hat	шляпин цуьрг	[ʃʎapin tsyrg]
scarf (headscarf)	касенка	[kaseŋka]

hard hat	каска	[kaska]
garrison cap	пилотка	[pilɔtka]
helmet	гIем	[ɣem]

derby	яй	[jaj]
top hat	цилиндр	[tsilindr]

37. Footwear

footwear	мача	[matʃa]
ankle boots	батенкаш	[bateŋkaʃ]
shoes (wingtip shoes)	туфлеш	[tufleʃ]

| boots (e.g., cowboy ~) | эткаш | [ɛtkaʃ] |
| slippers | кӀархаш | [k:arhaʃ] |

tennis shoes	красовкаш	[krasɔvkaʃ]
sneakers	кеди	[kedi]
sandals	сандалеш	[sandaleʃ]

cobbler	эткийн пхьар	[ɛtki:n phar]
heel (of shoe)	кӀажа	[k:aʒa]
pair (of shoes)	шиъ	[ʃi]

shoestring	чимчарӏа	[ʧimʧarɣa]
to lace (vt)	чимчарӏа дӏадехка	[ʧimʧarɣa dəadehka]
shoehorn	Ӏайг	[əajg]
shoe polish	мачийн крем	[maʧi:n krem]

38. Textile. Fabrics

cotton (noun)	бамба	[bamba]
cotton (attr)	бамбан	[bamban]
flax (noun)	вета	[weta]
flax (attr)	ветан	[wetan]

silk (noun)	чилла	[ʧil:a]
silk (attr)	чилланан	[ʧil:anan]
wool (noun)	тӏапрӏа	[tharɣa]
woolen	тӏепрӏан	[therɣan]

velvet	бархат	[barhat]
suede	замша	[zamʃa]
corduroy	хут	[hut]

nylon (noun)	нейлон	[nejlɔn]
nylon (attr)	нейлонан	[nejlɔnan]
polyester (noun)	полиэстер	[poliɛster]
polyester (attr)	полиэстеран	[poliɛsteran]

leather (noun)	тӏаьрсиг	[thærsig]
leather (attr)	тӏаьрсиган	[thærsigan]
fur (noun)	чо	[ʧɔ]
fur (e.g., ~ coat)	чо болу	[ʧɔ bɔlu]

39. Personal accessories

gloves	карнаш	[karnaʃ]
mittens	каранаш	[karanaʃ]
scarf (long)	шарф	[ʃarf]
glasses	куьзганаш	[kyzganaʃ]

frame (for spectacles)	куьзганийн гура	[kyzgani:n gura]
umbrella	зонтик	[zɔntik]
walking stick	Iасалг	[əasalg]
hairbrush	щётка	[ɕɔtka]
fan (accessory)	мохтухург	[mɔhtuhurg]

necktie	галстук	[galstuk]
bow tie	галстук-бабочка	[galstuk babɔʧka]
suspenders	доьхкарш	[døhkarʃ]
handkerchief	мерах хьокху йовлакх	[merah hɔqu jovlaq]

comb (for hair)	ехк	[ehk]
barrette	маха	[maha]
hairpin	мIара	[məara]
buckle	кIега	[k:ega]

belt	доьхка	[døhka]
shoulder strap	бухка	[buhka]

bag (handbag)	тIормиг	[thɔrmig]
purse	тIормиг	[thɔrmig]
backpack	рюкзак	[rykzak]

40. Clothing. Miscellaneous

fashion	мода	[mɔda]
in vogue	модехь долу	[mɔdeh dɔlu]
fashion designer	модельхо	[mɔdeʎhɔ]

collar	кач	[kaʧ]
pocket	киса	[kisa]
pocket (e.g., ~ camera)	кисанан	[kisanan]
sleeve	пхьош	[phɔʃ]
hanging tab (loop)	лалам	[lalam]
fly (on trousers)	ширинка	[ʃiriŋka]

zipper (fastener)	догIа	[dɔɣa]
fastener	туьйдарг	[tyjdarg]
button	нуьйда	[nyjda]
buttonhole	туьйдарг	[tyjdarg]
to come off (ab. button)	дIадала	[deadala]

to sew (vi, vt)	тега	[tega]
to embroider (vi, vt)	дага	[daga]
embroidery	дагар	[dagar]
sewing needle	маха	[maha]
thread	тай	[taj]
seam	эвна	[ɛvna]
to get dirty (vi)	бехдала	[behdala]
stain (mark, spot)	таммагIа	[tam:aɣa]

to crease, crumple (vi)	хьерча	[hertʃa]
to tear (vt)	датӀо	[dathɔ]
clothes moth	неца	[netsa]

41. Personal care. Cosmetics

toothpaste	цергийн паста	[tsergi:n pasta]
toothbrush	цергийг щётка	[tsergi:g ɕɔtka]
to brush one's teeth	цергаш цӀанъян	[tsergaʃ tshanʰjan]

razor	урс	[urs]
shaving cream	маж йошуш хьокху крем	[maʒ joʃuʃ hɔqu krem]
to shave (vi)	даша	[daʃa]

| soap | саба | [saba] |
| shampoo | шампунь | [ʃampuɲ] |

scissors	тукар	[tukar]
nail file	ков	[kɔv]
nail clippers	мӀараш йоху морзах	[maəraʃ johu mɔrzah]
tweezers	пинцет	[pintset]

cosmetics	косметика	[kɔsmetika]
face mask	маска	[maska]
manicure	маникюр	[manikyr]
to have a manicure	маникюр ян	[manikyr jan]
pedicure	педикюр	[pedikyr]

make-up bag	косметичка	[kɔsmetitʃka]
powder (for face)	пудра	[pudra]
powder compact	пудрадухкург	[pudraduhkurg]
blusher	цӀен басарш	[tshen basarʃ]

perfume (bottled)	духӀи	[duhi]
toilet water	туалетан хи	[tualetan hi]
lotion	лосьон	[lɔsʲɔn]
cologne	латӀап	[eathar]

eyeshadow	тенеш	[teneʃ]
eyeliner	бӀаргах хьокху къолам	[beargah hɔqu qhɔlam]
mascara	тушь	[tuʃ]

lipstick	балдех хьокху хьакхар	[baldeh hɔqu haqar]
nail polish, enamel	мӀарат хьокху лак	[maərat hɔqu lak]
hair spray	месашт хьокху лак	[mesaʃt hɔqu lak]
deodorant	дезодарант	[dezɔdarant]

| cream | крем | [krem] |
| face cream | юьхьах хьокху крем | [juhah hɔqu krem] |

hand cream	куьйгах хьокху крем	[kyjgah hɔqu krem]
anti-wrinkle cream	хершнаш дуьхьал крем	[herʃnaʃ dyhal krem]
day (attr)	дийнан	[di:nan]
night (attr)	буьйсанан	[byjsanan]

tampon	тампон	[tampɔn]
toilet paper	хьаштаг1ан кехат	[haʃtaɣan kehat]
hair dryer	месашъякъорг	[mesaʃˀjaqhɔrg]

42. Jewelry

jewelry	мехела х1ума	[mehela huma]
precious (e.g., ~ stone)	мехала	[mehala]
hallmark	ц1еналла	[tʃhenal:a]

ring	ч1уг	[tʃhug]
wedding ring	т1орд	[thɔrd]
bracelet	х1оз	[hɔz]

earrings	ч1агарш	[tʃhagarʃ]
necklace (~ of pearls)	туьтеш	[tyteʃ]
crown	таж	[taʒ]
beads (necklace)	туьтеш	[tyteʃ]

diamond	бриллиант	[bril:iant]
emerald	изумруд	[izumrud]
ruby	ц1ен алмаз	[tʃhen almaz]
sapphire	сапфир	[sapfir]
pearl	жовх1ар	[ʒɔvhar]
amber	янтар	[jantar]

43. Watches. Clocks

watch (wristwatch)	пхьаьрсах доьхку сахьт	[phærsah døhku saht]
dial	циферблат	[tsiferblat]
hand (of clock, watch)	сахьтан цамза	[sahtan tsamza]
bracelet	сахьтан х1оз	[sahtan hɔz]
watch strap	ремешок	[remeʃɔk]

battery	батарейка	[batarejka]
to be dead (battery)	охьахаа	[ɔhaha:]
to change a battery	хийца	[hi:tsa]
to run fast	сихадала	[sihadala]
to run slow	т1ехь лела	[theh lela]

| wall clock | пенах уллу сахьт | [penah ul:u saht] |
| hourglass | г1амаран сахьт | [ɣamaran saht] |

sundial	маьлхан сахьт	[mælhan saht]
alarm clock	сомавоккху сахьт	[somavɔk:u saht]
watchmaker	сахьтийн пхьар	[sahti:n phar]
to repair (vt)	тадан	[tadan]

Food. Nutricion

44. Food

meat	жижиг	[ʒiʒig]
chicken	котам	[kɔtam]
young chicken	кӀорни	[k:ɔrni]
duck	бад	[bad]
goose	гӀаз	[ɣaz]
game	экха	[ɛqa]
turkey	москал-котам	[mɔskal kɔtam]
pork	хьакхин жижиг	[haqin ʒiʒig]
veal	эсан жижиг	[ɛsan ʒiʒig]
lamb	уьстагӀан жижиг	[ystaɣan ʒiʒig]
beef	бежанан жижиг	[beʒanan ʒiʒig]
rabbit	пхьагал	[phagal]
sausage (salami etc.)	марш	[marʃ]
hot dog (frankfurter)	йоьхь	[jøh]
bacon	бекон	[bekɔn]
ham	дакъийна хьакхин жижиг	[daqhi:na haqin ʒiʒig]
gammon (ham)	хьакхин гӀорӀ	[haqin ɣɔɣ]
pâté	паштет	[paʃtet]
liver	дoӀax	[dɔəah]
lard	хьакхин дума	[haqin duma]
ground beef	аьхьана жижиг	[æhana ʒiʒig]
tongue	мотт	[mɔt:]
egg	xloa	[hɔa]
eggs	xloaш	[hɔaʃ]
egg white	кӀайн xloa	[k:ajn hɔa]
egg yolk	буьйра	[byjra]
fish	чlapa	[ʧhara]
seafood	xloрдан сурсаташ	[hɔrdan sursataʃ]
caviar	зирх	[zirh]
crab	краб	[krab]
shrimp	креветка	[krewetka]
oyster	устрица	[ustritsa]
spiny lobster	лангуст	[laŋust]
octopus	бархӀкогберг	[barhkɔgberg]
squid	кальмар	[kaʎmar]

sturgeon	ирлу	[irɣu]
salmon	лосось	[lɔsɔsʲ]
halibut	палтус	[paltus]
cod	треска	[treska]
mackerel	скумбри	[skumbri]
tuna	тунец	[tunets]
eel	жӏаьлин чӏара	[ʒæælin tʃħara]
trout	бакъ чӏара	[baqh tʃħara]
sardine	сардина	[sardina]
pike	гӏазкхийн чӏара	[ɣazqiːn tʃħara]
herring	сельдь	[seʌdʲ]
bread	бепиг	[bepig]
cheese	нехча	[nehtʃa]
sugar	шекар	[ʃəkar]
salt	туьха	[tyha]
rice	дуга	[duga]
pasta	макаронаш	[makarɔnaʃ]
noodles	гарзанаш	[garzanaʃ]
butter	налха	[nalha]
vegetable oil	ораматийн даьтта	[ɔramatiːn dæt:a]
sunflower oil	хӏун даьтта	[hun dæt:a]
margarine	маргарин	[margarin]
olives	оливкаш	[ɔlivkaʃ]
olive oil	оливкан даьтта	[ɔlivkan dæt:a]
milk	шура	[ʃura]
condensed milk	юкъйина шура	[juqhjɪna ʃura]
yogurt	йогурт	[jogurt]
sour cream	тӏо	[thɔ]
cream (of milk)	гӏаймакх	[ɣajmaq]
mayonnaise	майнез	[majnez]
cream (filling for biscuits)	крем	[krem]
cereal grains	ӏов	[ɔv]
flour	дама	[dama]
canned food	консерваш	[kɔnservaʃ]
cornflakes	хьаьжкӏийн чуьппалгаш	[hæʒkːiːn tʃypːalgaʃ]
honey	моз	[mɔz]
jelly (e.g., strawberry ~)	джем	[dʒem]
chewing gum	셰eгӏаз	[seɣaz]

45. Drinks

water	хи	[hi]
drinking water	молу хи	[mɔlu hi]
mineral water	дарбане хи	[darbane hi]

still	газ йоцуш	[gaz jotsuʃ]
carbonated	газ тоьхна	[gaz tøhna]
sparkling	газ йолуш	[gaz joluʃ]
ice	ша	[ʃa]
with ice	ша болуш	[ʃa bɔluʃ]

non-alcoholic	алкоголь йоцу	[alkɔgɔʎ jotsu]
soft drink	алкоголь йоцу маларш	[alkɔgɔʎ jotsu malarʃ]
cool soft drink	хьогаллин малар	[hɔgal:in malar]
lemonade	лимонад	[limɔnad]

liquor	алкоголь йолу маларш	[alkɔgɔʎ jolu malarʃ]
wine	чагӀар	[ʧaɣar]
white wine	кӀай чагӀар	[k:aj ʧaɣar]
red wine	цӀен чагӀар	[tshen ʧaɣar]

liqueur	ликёр	[likзr]
champagne	шампански	[ʃampanski]
vermouth	вермут	[wermut]

whisky	виски	[wiski]
vodka	къаьракъа	[qhæraqha]
gin	джин	[dʒin]
cognac	коньяк	[kɔɲjak]
rum	ром	[rɔm]

coffee	къахьо	[qhahɔ]
black coffee	Ӏаьржа къахьо	[əærʒa qhahɔ]
coffee with milk	шура тоьхна къахьо	[ʃura tøhna qhahɔ]
cappuccino	гӀаймакх тоьхна къахьо	[ɣajmaq tøhna qhahɔ]
instant coffee	дешаш долу къахьо	[deʃaʃ dɔlu qhahɔ]

milk	шура	[ʃura]
cocktail	коктейль	[kɔktejʎ]
milk shake	шурин коктейль	[ʃurin kɔktejʎ]

juice	мутта	[mut:a]
tomato juice	помидорийн мутта	[pɔmidɔri:n mut:a]
orange juice	апельсинан мутта	[apeʎsinan mut:a]
freshly squeezed juice	керла йаккха мутта	[kerla jak:a mut:a]

beer	йий	[ji:]
light beer	сирла йий	[sirla ji:]
dark beer	Ӏаьржа йий	[əærʒa ji:]
tea	чай	[ʧaj]

| black tea | Iаьржа чай | [əærʒa ʧaj] |
| green tea | баьццара чай | [bætsara ʧaj] |

46. Vegetables

| vegetables | хасстоьмаш | [has:tømaʃ] |
| greens | гIабуц | [ɣabuts] |

tomato	помидор	[pɔmidɔr]
cucumber	наьрс	[nærs]
carrot	жIонка	[ʒəɔŋka]
potato	картол	[kartɔl]
onion	хох	[hoh]
garlic	саьрмасекх	[særmaseq]

cabbage	копаста	[kɔpasta]
cauliflower	къорза копаста	[qhɔrza kɔpasta]
Brussels sprouts	брюссельски копаста	[brys:eʎski kɔpasta]
broccoli	брокколи копаст	[brɔk:ɔli kɔpast]

beet	бурак	[burak]
eggplant	баклажан	[baklaʒan]
zucchini	кабачок	[kabaʧɔk]
pumpkin	гIабакх	[ɣabaq]
turnip	хорсам	[horsam]

parsley	чам-буц	[ʧam buts]
dill	оччам	[ɔʧam]
lettuce	салат	[salat]
celery	сельдерей	[seʎderej]
asparagus	спаржа	[sparʒa]
spinach	шпинат	[ʃpinat]

pea	кхоьш	[qøʃ]
beans	кхоьш	[qøʃ]
corn (maize)	хьаьжкIа	[hæʒk:a]
kidney bean	кхоь	[qø]

bell pepper	бурч	[burʧ]
radish	цIен хорсам	[tshen horsam]
artichoke	артишок	[artiʃok]

47. Fruits. Nuts

fruit	стом	[stom]
apple	Iаж	[əaʒ]
pear	кхор	[qor]
lemon	лимон	[limɔn]

orange	апельсин	[apeʌsin]
strawberry	цӏазам	[ʦhazam]
mandarin	мандарин	[mandarin]
plum	хьач	[haʧ]
peach	гӏаммагӏа	[ɣam:aɣa]
apricot	туьрк	[tyrk]
raspberry	комар	[kɔmar]
pineapple	ананас	[ananas]
banana	банан	[banan]
watermelon	хорбаз	[horbaz]
grapes	кемсаш	[kemsaʃ]
cherry	балл	[bal:]
cherry (sweet cherry)	балл	[bal:]
melon	гӏабакх	[ɣabaq]
grapefruit	грейпфрут	[grejpfrut]
avocado	авокадо	[avɔkadɔ]
papaya	папайя	[papaja]
mango	манго	[maŋɔ]
pomegranate	гранат	[granat]
redcurrant	цӏен кхезарш	[ʦhen qezarʃ]
blackcurrant	ӏаьржа кхезарш	[əærʒa qezarʃ]
gooseberry	кӏудалгаш	[k:udalgaʃ]
bilberry	ӏаьржа балл	[əærʒa bal:]
blackberry	мангалкомар	[maŋalkɔmar]
raisin	кишмаш	[kiʃmaʃ]
fig	инжир	[inʒir]
date	хурма	[hurma]
peanut	орахис	[ɔrahis]
almond	миндаль	[mindaʎ]
walnut	бочабӏар	[bɔʧabəar]
hazelnut	хӏунан бӏар	[hunan bəar]
coconut	кокосови бӏар	[kɔkɔsɔwi bəar]
pistachios	фисташкаш	[fistaʃkaʃ]

48. Bread. Candy

confectionery (pastry)	кхачанан хӏуманаш	[qaʧanan humanaʃ]
bread	бепиг	[bepig]
cookies	пичени	[piʧeni]
chocolate (noun)	шоколад	[ʃɔkɔlad]
chocolate (attr)	шоколадан	[ʃɔkɔladan]
candy	кемпет	[kempet]
cake (e.g., cupcake)	пирожни	[pirɔʒni]

cake (e.g., birthday ~)	торт	[tɔrt]
pie (e.g., apple ~)	чуда	[tʃuda]
filling (for cake, pie)	чуйоьллинарг	[tʃujøl:inarg]

jam	варени	[vareni]
marmalade	мармелад	[marmelad]
wafer	вафлеш	[vafleʃ]
ice-cream	морожени	[mɔrɔʒeni]

49. Cooked dishes

course, dish	даар	[dɑːr]
cuisine	даарш	[dɑːrʃ]
recipe	рецепт	[retsept]
portion	порци	[pɔrtsi]

| salad | салат | [salat] |
| soup | чорпа | [tʃɔrpa] |

clear soup (broth)	чорпа	[tʃɔrpa]
sandwich (bread)	бутерброд	[buterbrɔd]
fried eggs	хӏоаш	[hɔaʃ]

cutlet	котлет	[kɔtlet]
hamburger (beefburger)	гамбургер	[gamburger]
beefsteak	бифштекс	[bifʃteks]
roast meat	гӏурма	[ɣurma]

side dish	гарнир	[garnir]
spaghetti	спагетти	[spaget:i]
mashed potatoes	картолийн худар	[kartɔli:n hudar]
pizza	пицца	[pitsa]
porridge (oatmeal, etc)	худар	[hudar]
omelet	омлет	[ɔmlet]

boiled (e.g., ~ beef)	кхехкийна	[qehki:na]
smoked	кхаьгна	[qæʁna]
fried	кхерзина	[qerzina]
dried	дакъийна	[daqhi:na]
frozen	гӏорийна	[ɣɔri:na]
pickled	берамала доьллина	[beramala døl:ina]

sweet (in taste)	мерза	[merza]
salty	дуьра	[dyra]
cold	шийла	[ʃi:la]
hot	довха	[dɔvha]
bitter	къаьхьа	[qhæha]
tasty	чоме	[tʃɔme]
to cook (vt)	кхехко	[qehkɔ]
to cook (vi)	кечдан	[ketʃdan]

| to fry (vt) | кхарза | [qarza] |
| to heat up (food) | дохдан | [dɔhdan] |

to salt (vt)	туьха таса	[tyha tasa]
to pepper (vt)	бурч таса	[burtʃ tasa]
to grate (vt)	сатоха	[satɔha]
peel (noun)	чкъуьйриг	[tʃqhyjrig]
to peel (vt)	цӏанъян	[tshanʰjan]

50. Spices

salt	туьха	[tyha]
salty	дуьра	[dyra]
to salt (vt)	туьха таса	[tyha tasa]

black pepper	Iаьржа бурч	[əærʒa burtʃ]
red pepper	цӏен бурч	[tshen burtʃ]
mustard	кӏолла	[k:ɔl:a]
horseradish	кӏон орам	[k:ɔn ɔram]

seasoning (condiment)	чамбийриг	[tʃambi:rig]
spice	мерза юург	[merza ju:rg]
sauce	берам	[beram]
vinegar	къонза	[qhɔnza]

anise	анис	[anis]
basil	базилик	[bazilik]
cloves	гвоздика	[gvɔzdika]
ginger	Iамбар	[əambar]
coriander	кориандр	[kɔriandr]
cinnamon	корица	[kɔritsa]

sesame	кунжут	[kunʒut]
bay leaf	лавран гӏа	[lavran ɣa]
paprika	паприка	[paprika]
caraway	циц	[tsits]
saffron	шафран	[ʃafran]

51. Meals

| food (noun) | даар | [da:r] |
| to eat (vi, vt) | яаа | [ja::] |

breakfast	марта	[marta]
to have breakfast	марта даа	[marta da:]
lunch	делкъан кхача	[delqhan qatʃa]
to have lunch	делкъана хӏума яа	[delqhana huma ja:]
dinner (evening meal)	пхьор	[phɔr]

to have dinner	пхьор дан	[phɔr dan]
appetite	аппетит	[ap:etit]
Enjoy your meal!	Гоза доийла!	[ɣɔza dɔi:la]
to open (e.g., ~ a bottle)	схьаела	[shaela]
to spill (liquid)	lано	[əanɔ]
to spill out (vi)	lана	[əana]
to boil (vi)	кхехка	[qehka]
to boil (vt)	кхехко	[qehkɔ]
boiled	кхехкийна	[qehki:na]
to cool (vt)	шелдан	[ʃeldan]
to cool down (vi)	шелдала	[ʃeldala]
taste, flavor	чам	[tʃam]
aftertaste	кхин чам	[qin tʃam]
to be on a diet	аздала	[azdala]
diet	диета	[dieta]
vitamin	втамин	[vtamin]
calorie	калорий	[kalɔri:]
vegetarian (noun)	дилхазахо	[dilhazaho]
vegetarian (adj)	дилхаза	[dilhaza]
fats (nutrient)	дилхдаьтта	[dilhdæt:a]
proteins	кlайн хloa	[k:ajn hɔa]
carbohydrates	углеводаш	[uglevɔdaʃ]
slice (of lemon, ham)	цастар	[tsastar]
piece (of cake, pie)	юьхк	[juhk]
crumb (of bread)	цуьрг	[tsyrg]

52. Table setting

spoon	lайг	[əajg]
knife	урс	[urs]
fork	мlара	[məara]
cup (of coffee)	кад	[kad]
dinner plate	бошхап	[bɔʃhap]
saucer	бошхап	[bɔʃhap]
napkin (on table)	салфетка	[salfetka]
toothpick	цергахъуттург	[tsergahʰəut:urg]

53. Restaurant

restaurant	ресторан	[restɔran]
café	кафе	[kafe]

coffee house	кофейни	[kɔfejni]
pub, bar	бар	[bar]
tearoom	чайнан салон	[tʃajnan salɔn]

waiter	официант	[ɔfitsiant]
waitress	официантка	[ɔfitsiantka]
bartender	бармен	[barmen]

menu	меню	[meny]
wine list	чагаран карта	[tʃaɣaran karta]
to book a table	стол цхьанна тӀехь чӀагӀдан	[stɔl tshana theh tʃhaɣdan]

course, dish	даар	[da:r]
to order (meal)	заказ ян	[zakaz jan]
to make an order	заказ ян	[zakaz jan]
aperitif	аперетив	[aperetiv]
appetizer	тӀекхоллург	[theqɔl:urg]
dessert	десерт	[desert]

check	счёт	[stʃɔt]
to pay the check	счётан мах бала	[stʃɔtan mah bala]
to give change	юхадогӀург дала	[juhadɔɣurg dala]
tip	чайнна хӀума	[tʃajna huma]

Family, relatives and friends

54. Personal information. Forms

name, first name	цle	[ʦhe]
family name	фамили	[famili]
date of birth	вина терахь	[wina terah]
place of birth	вина меттиг	[wina met:ig]
nationality	къам	[qham]
place of residence	веха меттиг	[weha met:ig]
country	мохк	[mɔhk]
profession (occupation)	говзалла	[gɔvzal:a]
gender, sex	стен-боьршалла	[sten børʃal:a]
height	локхалла	[lɔqal:a]
weight	дозалла	[dɔzal:a]

55. Family members. Relatives

mother	нана	[nana]
father	да	[da]
son	воl	[vɔə]
daughter	йоl	[jɔə]
younger daughter	жимаха йоl	[ʒimaha jɔə]
younger son	жимаха воl	[ʒimaha vɔə]
elder daughter	йоккхаха йоl	[jok:aha jɔə]
elder son	воккхаха воl	[vɔk:aha vɔə]
brother	ваша	[vaʃa]
sister	йиша	[jıʃa]
cousin (masc.)	шича	[ʃitʃa]
cousin (fem.)	шича	[ʃitʃa]
mom	нана	[nana]
dad, daddy	дада	[dada]
parents	да-нана	[da nana]
child (boy or girl)	бер	[ber]
children	бераш	[beraʃ]
grandmother	баба	[baba]
grandfather	дада	[dada]

grandson	кlентан, йоlан кlант	[k:entan], [joəan k:ant]
granddaughter	кlентан, йоlан йоl	[k:entan], [joəan joə]
grandchildren	кlентан, йоlан бераш	[k:entan], [joəan beraʃ]

uncle	ден ваша, ненан ваша	[den vaʃa], [nenan vaʃa]
aunt	деца, неца	[detsa], [netsa]
nephew	вешин кlант,	[weʃin k:ant,
	йишин кlант	jiʃin k:ant]

niece	вешин йоl, йишин йоl	[weʃin joə], [jiʃin joə]
mother-in-law	стуннана	[stuŋana]
father-in-law	марда	[marda]
son-in-law	нуц	[nuts]
stepmother	десте	[deste]
stepfather	ненан майра	[nenan majra]

baby (infant)	декхаш долу бер	[deqaʃ dɔlu ber]
infant	бер	[ber]
little boy, kid	жиманиг	[ʒimanig]

wife	зуда	[zuda]
husband	майра	[majra]
spouse (husband)	майра	[majra]
spouse (wife)	сесаг	[sesag]

married (man)	зуда ялийна	[zuda jali:na]
married (woman)	марехь	[mareh]
single (unmarried)	зуда ялоза	[zuda jalɔza]
bachelor	зуда йоцург	[zuda jotsurg]
divorced (man)	йитина	[jitina]
widow	жеро	[ʒerɔ]
widower	жера-стаг	[ʒera stag]

relative	гергара стаг	[gergara stag]
close relative	юххера гергара стаг	[juhera gergara stag]
distant relative	генара гергара стаг	[genara gergara stag]
relatives	гергара нах	[gergara nah]

orphan (boy or girl)	бо	[bɔ]
guardian (of minor)	верас	[weras]
to adopt (a boy)	кlантан хlотта	[k:antan hɔt:a]
to adopt (a girl)	йоьlан да хlотта	[jøəan da hɔt:a]

56. Friends. Coworkers

friend (man)	доттаrl	[dɔt:aɣ]
friend (girlfriend)	доттаrl	[dɔt:aɣ]
friendship	доттаrlалла	[dɔt:aɣal:a]
to be friends	доттаrlалла лело	[dɔt:aɣal:a lelɔ]
buddy (man)	доттаrl	[dɔt:aɣ]

buddy (woman)	доттагl	[dɔt:aɣ]
comrade (politics)	белхан накъост	[belhan naqhɔst]
partner	декъашхо	[deqhaʃho]
business partner	гlуллакхе партнёр	[ɣul:aqe partnɜr]
chief (boss)	куьйгалхо	[kyjgalho]
boss, superior	хьаькам	[hæːkam]
subordinate	муьтlахь верг	[mythah werg]
colleague	коллега	[kɔl:ega]
acquaintance (person)	вевза стаг	[wevza stag]
fellow traveler	некъаннакъост	[neqhaŋaqhɔst]
classmate	классхо	[klas:ho]
neighbor (man)	лулахо	[lulaho]
neighbor (woman)	лулахо	[lulaho]
neighbors	лулахой	[lulahoj]

57. Man. Woman

woman	зуда	[zuda]
girl (young woman)	йоl	[joə]
bride	нускал	[nuskal]
beautiful	хаза	[haza]
tall	лекха зуда	[leqa zuda]
slender	куц долу зуда	[kuts dɔlu zuda]
short	лохачу дегlахь стаг	[lɔhatʃu deɣah stag]
blonde (noun)	блондинка	[blɔndiŋka]
brunette (noun)	брюнетка	[brynetka]
ladies'	зударийн	[zudariːn]
virgin (girl)	йоlстаг	[joəstag]
pregnant	берахниг	[berahnig]
man (adult male)	боьрша стаг	[bɵrʃa stag]
blond (noun)	блондин	[blɔndin]
brunet (noun)	брюнет	[brynet]
tall	лекха	[leqa]
short	лохачу дегlахь стаг	[lɔhatʃu deɣah stag]
rude (rough)	кlоршаме	[k:ɔrʃame]
stocky	воьртала	[vɵrtala]
robust	чlорla	[tʃhɔɣa]
strong	нуьцкъала	[nytsqhala]
strength (physical power)	ницкъ	[nitsqh]
stout, fat	дерстина	[derstina]
swarthy	lаьржачу аматехь	[əærʒatʃu amateh]

| well-built | куц долу стаг | [kuts dɔlu stag] |
| elegant | оьзда | [øzda] |

58. Age

age	хан	[han]
youth (young age)	къоналла	[qhɔnal:a]
young	къона	[qhɔna]

| younger | жимаха | [ʒimaha] |
| older | воккхаха | [vɔk:aha] |

young man	къонаниг	[qhɔnanig]
teenager	кхиазхо	[qiazho]
guy, fellow	жима стаг	[ʒima stag]

| old man | воккха стаг | [vɔk:a stag] |
| old woman | йоккха стаг | [jok:a stag] |

adult	кхиъна	[qina]
middle-aged	юккъерчу шеран	[juk:ʰertʃu ʃeran]
elderly	хан тӀехтилла	[han thehtil:a]
old	къена	[qhena]

retirement	пенси	[pensi]
to retire (from job)	пенси ваха	[pensi vaha]
retiree	пенсионер	[pensiɔner]

59. Children

child (boy or girl)	бер	[ber]
children	бераш	[beraʃ]
twins	шала дина бераш	[ʃala dina beraʃ]

cradle (for baby)	ага	[aga]
rattle (for baby)	экарг	[ɛkarg]
diaper	подгузник	[pɔdguznik]

pacifier	тӀармала	[tharmaəa]
baby carriage	гӀудалкх	[ɣudalq]
kindergarten	берийн беш	[beri:n beʃ]
babysitter	баба	[baba]

childhood	бералла	[beral:a]
doll	тайниг	[tajnig]
toy	ловзо хӀума	[lɔvzɔ huma]
construction set	конструктор	[kɔnstruktɔr]
well-bred	бакъхьара	[baqhara]

ill-bred	оьздангалла йоцу	[øzdaŋal:a joʦu]
spoiled	боча Іамийна	[boʧa əami:na]
to be naughty	харцхьара лела	[harʦhara lela]
naughty	вон лела	[vɔn lela]
naughtiness	харцхьаралла	[harʦharal:a]
naughty boy	харцхьарниг	[harʦharnig]
obedient	ладугІу	[laduɣu]
disobedient	ладугІуш доцу	[laduɣuʃ dɔʦu]
docile	кхетаме	[qetame]
clever (smart)	хьекъале	[heqhale]
child prodigy	вундеркинд	[vunderkind]

60. Married couples. Family life

to kiss (vt)	барташ даха	[bartaʃ daha]
to kiss (vi)	обанаш баха	[ɔbanaʃ baha]
family (noun)	доьзал	[døzal]
family (attr)	доьзалан	[døzalan]
couple	шиъ	[ʃi]
marriage (state)	брак	[brak]
hearth (home)	цІийнан кхерч	[ʦhi:nan qerʧ]
dynasty	династи	[dinasti]
date	вовшехкхетар	[vɔvʃəhqetar]
kiss	уба	[uba]
love (for sb)	безам	[bezam]
to love (sb)	деза	[deza]
beloved	везарг	[wezarg]
tenderness	кІеда-мерзалла	[k:eda merzal:a]
tender (affectionate)	кІеда-мерза	[k:eda merza]
faithfulness	тешаме хилар	[teʃame hilar]
faithful	тешаме	[teʃame]
care (attention)	гІайгІа	[ɣajɣa]
caring (thoughtful)	гІайгІа йолу	[ɣajɣa jolu]
newlyweds	къона мар-нускал	[qhona mar nuskal]
honeymoon	нускалан хан	[nuskalan han]
to get married (woman)	маре яха	[mare jaha]
to get married (man)	зуда яло	[zuda jalɔ]
wedding	ловзар	[lɔvzar]
golden wedding	дашо ловзар	[daʃo lɔvzar]
anniversary	шо кхачар	[ʃɔ qaʧar]
lover (man)	везарг	[wezarg]
mistress	езарг	[ezarg]

adultery	ямартло	[jamartlɔ]
to commit adultery	ямартло яр	[jamartlɔ jar]
jealous (fearful of rivals)	эмгаралле	[ɛmgaral:e]
to be jealous	эмгаралла дан	[ɛmgaral:a dan]
divorce	дӀасакъастар	[dəasaqhastar]
to divorce (vi)	дӀасакъаста	[dəasaqhasta]
to quarrel (vi)	эгӀар	[ɛɣar]
to become reconciled	тан	[tan]
together	цхьана	[ʦhana]
sex (sexual activity)	секс	[seks]
happiness	ирс	[irs]
happy	ирсе	[irse]
misfortune (accident)	ирс цахилар	[irs ʦahilar]
unhappy	ирс доцу	[irs dɔʦu]

Character. Feelings. Emotions

61. Feelings. Emotions

feeling (emotion)	синхаам	[sinha:m]
feelings	синхаамаш	[sinha:maʃ]
to feel (vt)	хаадала	[ha:dala]
hunger	мацалла	[matsal:a]
to be hungry	хlума яаа лаа	[huma ja:: la:]
thirst	хьогалла	[hɔgal:a]
to be thirsty	мала лаа	[mala la:]
sleepiness	наб яр	[nab jar]
to feel sleepy	наб ян лаа	[nab jan la:]
tiredness	гlелдалар	[ɣeldalar]
tired	гlелделла	[ɣeldel:a]
to get tired	гlелдала	[ɣeldala]
mood (humor)	дог-ойла	[dɔg ɔjla]
boredom	сахьийзар	[sahi:zar]
to be bored	сагатдала	[sagatdala]
seclusion	ша къастар	[ʃa qhastar]
to seclude oneself	ша къаста	[ʃa qhasta]
to worry (make anxious)	сагатдан	[sagatdan]
to be worried	сагатдан	[sagatdan]
anxiety	сагатдар	[sagatdar]
worrying (noun)	сагатдар	[sagatdar]
preoccupied	гlайгlане	[ɣajɣane]
to be nervous	дог этла	[dɔg ɛtha]
to panic (vi)	доха	[dɔha]
hope	сатуьйсийла	[satyjsi:la]
to hope (vi, vt)	догдаха	[dɔgdaha]
certainty	тешна хилар	[teʃna hilar]
certain, sure	тешна	[teʃna]
uncertainty	тешна цахилар	[teʃna tsahilar]
uncertain	тешна доцу	[teʃna dɔtsu]
drunk	вехна	[wehna]
sober	дахазниг	[dahaznig]
weak	гlийла	[ɣi:la]
lucky	ирсе	[irse]
to scare (vt)	кхеро	[qerɔ]

| fury (madness) | хьерадалар | [heradalar] |
| rage (fury) | луьралла | [lyral:a] |

depression	депресси	[depres:i]
discomfort (unease)	дискомфорт	[diskomfort]
comfort	комфорт	[komfort]
to regret (be sorry)	дагахьбаллам хила	[dagahbal:am hila]
regret	дагахьбаллам	[dagahbal:am]
bad luck	аьтто боцуш хилар	[æt:o botsuʃ hilar]
sadness	халахетар	[halahetar]

shame (feeling)	эхь	[ɛh]
merriment	синкъерам	[sinqheram]
enthusiasm	энтузиазм	[ɛntuziazm]
enthusiast	энтузиаст	[ɛntuziast]
to show enthusiasm	энтузиазм гучаяккха	[ɛntuziazm gutʃajak:a]

62. Character. Personality

character	амал	[amal]
character flaw	эшар	[ɛʃar]
mind	хьекъал	[heqhal]

conscience	эхь-бехк	[ɛh behk]
habit (custom)	марзделларг	[marzdel:arg]
ability	хьунар хилар	[hunar hilar]
can (e.g., ~ swim)	хаа	[ha:]

patient	собаре	[sobare]
impatient	собар доцу	[sobar dotsu]
curious (inquisitive)	хаа гӀерта	[ha: ɣerta]
curiosity	хаа гӀертар	[ha: ɣertar]

modesty	эсалалла	[ɛsalal:a]
modest	эсала	[ɛsala]
immodest	оьзда доцу	[øzda dotsu]

laziness	мало	[malo]
lazy	мела	[mela]
lazy person (masc.)	малонча	[malontʃa]

cunning (noun)	хӀилла	[hil:a]
cunning (attr)	хӀиллане	[hil:ane]
distrust	цатешам	[tsateʃam]
distrustful	тешамза	[teʃamza]

generosity	комаьршалла	[komærʃal:a]
generous	комаьрша	[komærʃa]
talented	похӀме	[pohme]
talent	похӀма	[pohma]

courageous	майра	[majra]
courage	майралла	[majral:a]
honest	дог цена	[dog tshena]
honesty	дог ценалла	[dog tshenal:a]

careful (cautious)	ларлуш долу	[larluʃ dolu]
brave	майра	[majra]
serious	ладаме	[ladame]
strict (severe, stern)	къовламе	[qhɔvlame]

determined (resolute)	хадам боллуш	[hadam bɔl:uʃ]
indecisive	ирке	[irke]
shy, timid	стешха	[steʃha]
shyness, timidity	стешхалла	[steʃhal:a]

trust (confidence)	тешам	[teʃam]
to trust (vt)	теша	[teʃa]
trusting (naïve)	тешаш долу	[teʃaʃ dolu]

sincerely	даггара	[dag:ara]
sincere	даггара	[dag:ara]
sincerity	догценалла	[dogtshenal:a]
open (person)	дуьххьал дІа	[dyhal dea]

calm	тийна	[ti:na]
frank, sincere	дог цена	[dog tshena]
naive	дог диллина стаг	[dog dil:ina stag]
absent-minded	тидаме доцу	[tidame dɔtsu]
funny (amusing)	беламе	[belame]

greed	сутаралла	[sutaral:a]
greedy	сутара	[sutara]
stingy	бІаьрмециган	[beærmetsigan]
evil	вон	[vɔn]
stubborn	духахьара	[duhahara]
unpleasant (person)	там боцу	[tam bɔtsu]

selfish person (masc.)	эгоист	[ɛgɔist]
selfish	эгоизме	[ɛgɔizme]
coward	стешха стаг	[steʃha stag]
cowardly	осала	[ɔsala]

63. Sleep. Dreams

to sleep (vi)	наб ян	[nab jan]
sleep, sleeping	наб	[nab]
dream	гІан	[ɣan]
to dream (in sleep)	гІенаш ган	[ɣenaʃ gan]
sleepy (person)	набаран	[nabaran]
bed	маьнга	[mæŋa]

mattress	гоь	[gø]
blanket (e.g., comforter)	юргӀа	[jurɣa]
pillow	гӀайба	[ɣajba]
sheet (for bed)	шаршу	[ʃarʃu]

insomnia	наб цакхетар	[nab tsaqetar]
sleepless	наб йоцу	[nab jotsu]
sleeping pill	наб йойту молханаш	[nab jojtu mɔlhanaʃ]
to take a sleeping pill	наб йойту молханаш мала	[nab jojtu mɔlhanaʃ mala]

to feel sleepy	наб ян лаа	[nab jan la:]
to yawn (vi)	бага гӀетто	[baga ɣet:ɔ]
to go to bed	наб я ваха	[nab ja vaha]
to make up the bed	мотт билла	[mɔt: bil:a]
to fall asleep	наб кхета	[nab qeta]

nightmare	Ӏаламат	[əalamat]
snoring	хар	[har]
to snore (vi)	хур-тӀур дан	[hur thur dan]

alarm clock	сомавоккху сахьт	[sɔmavɔk:u saht]
to wake (vt)	самадаккха	[samadak:a]
to wake up (vi)	самадала	[samadala]
to get up (vi)	хьалагӀатта	[halaɣat:a]
to wash up (vi)	дӀадиладала	[dəadiladala]

64. Humour. Laughter. Gladness

humor (wit, fun)	белам	[belam]
sense (of humor)	синхаам	[sinha:m]
to have fun	сакъера	[saqhera]
merry, cheerful	самукъане	[samuqhane]
merriment	сакъерар	[saqherar]

smile	делакъажар	[delaqhaʒar]
to smile (vi)	дела къежа	[dela qheʒa]
to start laughing	деладала	[deladala]
to laugh (vi)	дела	[dela]
laugh, laughter	белам	[belam]

anecdote	анекдот	[anekdɔt]
funny (amusing)	беламе	[belame]
funny (odd)	беламе	[belame]

to joke (vi)	забарш ян	[zabarʃ jan]
joke (verbal)	забар	[zabar]
joy (such a ~)	хазахетар	[hazahetar]
to be glad	хазахета	[hazaheta]
glad, cheerful	хазахоьтуьйту	[hazahøtyjtu]

65. Discussion, conversation. Part 1

communication	тӀекере	[thekere]
to communicate	тӀекере хила	[thekere hila]
conversation	къамел	[qhamel]
dialog	диалог	[dialɔg]
discussion (debate)	дискусси	[diskus:i]
debate	къовсам	[qhɔvsam]
to debate (vi)	къийса	[qhi:sa]
interlocutor	къамелхо	[qhamelho]
topic (theme)	тема	[tema]
point of view	хетарг	[hetarg]
opinion (viewpoint)	хетарг	[hetarg]
speech (talk)	мотт	[mɔt:]
discussion (of report etc.)	дийцаре диллар	[di:tsare dil:ar]
to discuss (proposal etc.)	дийцаре дилла	[di:tsare dil:a]
talk (conversation)	къамел	[qhamel]
to talk (vi)	къамел дан	[qhamel dan]
meeting	дуьхьалдахар	[dyhaldahar]
to meet (vi, vt)	вовшахкхета	[vɔvʃahqeta]
proverb	кица	[kitsa]
saying	кица	[kitsa]
riddle (poser)	хӀетал-метал	[hetal metal]
to ask a riddle	хӀетал-метал ала	[hetal metal ala]
password	пароль	[parɔʎ]
secret	хьулам	[hulam]
oath (vow)	дуй	[duj]
to swear (an oath)	дуй баа	[duj ba:]
promise	валда	[vaəda]
to promise (vt)	валда дан	[vaəda dan]
advice (counsel)	хьехам	[heham]
to advise (vt)	хьехам бан	[heham ban]
to listen (vi)	ладогӀа	[ladɔɣa]
news	керланиг	[kerlanig]
sensation (news)	сенсаци	[sensatsi]
information (facts)	хабар	[habar]
conclusion (decision)	жамӀ	[ʒamə]
voice	аз	[az]
compliment	тамехь дош	[tameh dɔʃ]
kind (nice)	безаме	[bezame]
word	дош	[dɔʃ]
phrase	фраза	[fraza]
answer	жоп	[ʒɔp]

response	дуьхьал	[dyhal]
truth (true facts)	бакъдерг	[baqhderg]
lie (untruth)	аьшпаш	[æʃpaʃ]
thought	ойла	[ɔjla]
idea (plan, inspiration)	ойла	[ɔjla]
fantasy	дагадар	[dagadar]

66. Discussion, conversation. Part 2

respected	лоруш долу	[lɔruʃ dɔlu]
to respect (vt)	лара	[lara]
respect	ларам	[laram]
Dear ...	хьомсара	[hɔmsara]
to introduce (present)	довзо	[dɔvzɔ]
intention	дагахь хилар	[dagah hilar]
to intend (have in mind)	ойла хилар	[ɔjla hilar]
wish	алар	[alar]
to wish (~ good luck)	ала	[ala]
surprise (astonishment)	цецдалар	[tsetsdalar]
to surprise (amaze)	цецдаккха	[tsetsdak:a]
to be surprised	цецдала	[tsetsdala]
to give (vt)	дала	[dala]
to take (get hold of)	схьаэца	[shaetsa]
to give back (vt)	юхадерзо	[juhaderzɔ]
to return (give back)	юхадала	[juhadala]
to apologize (vi)	бехк цабиллар деха	[behk tsabil:ar deha]
apology	бехк цабиллар	[behk tsabil:ar]
to forgive (vt)	геч дан	[getʃ dan]
to talk (speak)	къамел дан	[qhamel dan]
to listen (vi)	ладоґlа	[ladɔɣa]
to hear sb out	ладоґlа	[ladɔɣa]
to understand (vt)	кхета	[qeta]
to show (display)	гайта	[gajta]
to look at ...	хьежа	[heʒa]
to call (with one's voice)	кхайкха	[qajqa]
to disturb (vt)	новкъарло ян	[nɔvqharlɔ jan]
to pass (to hand sth)	дlадала	[dədala]
request (demand)	дехар	[dehar]
to request (ask)	деха	[deha]
demand (firm request)	тlедожор	[thedɔʒɔr]
to demand (request firmly)	тlедожо	[thedɔʒɔ]
to tease sb	хичаш ян	[hitʃaʃ jan]

to mock (deride)	дела	[dela]
mockery, derision	кхардам	[qardam]
nickname	харц цӀе	[harts tshe]

hint (indirect suggestion)	къадор	[qhadɔr]
to hint (vi)	къедо	[qhedɔ]
to mean (what do you ~ ?)	дагахь хила	[dagah hila]

description	сурт хӀоттор	[surt hɔt:ɔr]
to describe (vt)	сурт хӀотто	[surt hɔt:ɔ]
praise (compliments)	хастам	[hastam]
to praise (vt)	хесто	[hestɔ]

disappointment	безам балар	[bezam balar]
to disappoint (vt)	безам байа	[bezam baja]
to be disappointed	безам бан	[bezam ban]

supposition	моттар	[mɔt:ar]
to suppose (assume)	мотта	[mɔt:a]
warning (caution)	лардар	[lardar]
to warn	лардан	[lardan]

67. Discussion, conversation. Part 3

| to talk into (persuade) | бертадало | [bertadalɔ] |
| to calm down (vt) | дог тедан | [dɔg tedan] |

silence (~ is golden)	вистцахилар	[wisttsahilar]
to keep silent	къамел ца дан	[qhamel tsa dan]
to whisper (vt)	шабар-шибар дан	[ʃabar ʃibar dan]
whisper	шабар-шибар	[ʃabar ʃibar]

| frankly, sincerely | дог цӀена | [dɔg tshena] |
| in my opinion … | суна хетарехь | [suna hetareh] |

detail (of the story)	ма-дарра хилар	[ma dar:a hilar]
detailed	ма-дарра	[ma dar:a]
in detail	ма-дарра	[ma dar:a]

| hint, clue | дӀаалар | [dea:lar] |
| to give a hint | дӀаала | [dea:la] |

look (glance)	бӀаьрахьажар	[bæærahaʒar]
to have a look	хьажа	[haʒa]
fixed (look)	хийцалуш йоцу	[hi:tsaluʃ jotsu]
to blink (vi)	бӀаьргаш детта	[bæærgaʃ det:a]
to wink (vi)	бӀаьрг тало	[bæærg taeɔ]
to nod (in assent)	корта тало	[kɔrta taeɔ]
sigh	садаккхар	[sadak:ar]
to sigh (vi)	са даккха	[sa dak:a]

to shudder (vi)	тохадала	[tɔhadala]
gesture	ишар ян	[iʃar jan]
to touch (one's arm etc.)	дӀахьакхадала	[dəahaqadala]
to seize (by the arm)	леца	[letsa]
to tap (on the shoulder)	детта	[det:a]

Look out!	Ларло!	[larlɔ]
Really?	Баккъалла?	[bakqhal:a]
Are you sure?	Тешна вуй хьо?	[teʃna vuj hɔ]
Good luck!	Аьтто хуьлда!	[æt:ɔ hylda]
I see!	Кхета!	[qeta]
It's a pity!	Халахета!	[halaheta]

68. Agreement. Refusal

agreement	резахилар	[rezahilar]
to agree (say yes)	реза хила	[reza hila]
approval	магор	[magɔr]
to approve (vt)	маго	[magɔ]
refusal	цадалар	[tsadalar]
to refuse (vi, vt)	дуьхьал хила	[dyhal hila]

Great!	Чlорla дика ду!	[tʃhɔɣa dika du]
All right!	Дика ду!	[dika du]

OK! (I agree)	Мегар ду!	[megar du]
That's wrong!	Хlара нийса дац!	[hara ni:sa dats]

forbidden	цамагийна	[tsamagi:na]
it's forbidden	ца мега	[tsa mega]

it's impossible	хила йиш яц	[hila jiʃ jats]
incorrect (adj)	нийса доцу	[ni:sa dɔtsu]

to reject (~ a demand)	юхатоха	[juhatɔha]
to support (cause, idea)	тlетан	[thetan]
to accept (~ an apology)	тlеэца	[thætsa]

to confirm (vt)	чlарlдан	[tʃhaɣdan]
confirmation	чlарlдар	[tʃhaɣdar]
permission	пурба	[purba]
to permit (allow)	магийта	[magi:ta]

decision	сацам бар	[satsam bar]
to say nothing	дист ца хила	[dist tsa hila]

condition (term)	диллар	[dil:ar]
excuse (pretext)	бахьана	[bahana]
praise (compliments)	хастам	[hastam]
to praise (vt)	хестадан	[hestadan]

69. Success. Good luck. Failure

success	кхиам	[qiɑm]
successfully	кхиаме	[qiɑme]
successful	кхиам болу	[qiɑm bɔlu]
good luck	аьтто	[æt:ɔ]
Good luck!	Аьтто хуьлда!	[æt:ɔ hyldɑ]
lucky (e.g., ~ day)	аьтто болу	[æt:ɔ bɔlu]
lucky (fortunate)	аьтто болу	[æt:ɔ bɔlu]
failure (lack of success)	бохам	[bɔham]
bad luck (failure)	аьтто ца хилар	[æt:ɔ ʦa hilɑr]
misfortune (bad luck)	аьтто боцуш хилар	[æt:ɔ bɔʦuʃ hilɑr]
unsuccessful (attempt)	ца даьлла	[ʦa dæl:ɑ]
catastrophe	ирча бохам	[irʧa bɔham]
pride	дозалла	[dɔzɑl:ɑ]
proud	кура	[kurɑ]
to be proud	дозалла дан	[dɔzɑl:ɑ dɑn]
winner (of competition)	толамхо	[tɔlɑmhɔ]
to win (vi)	тола	[tɔlɑ]
to lose (not win)	эша	[ɛʃɑ]
try	гӏортар	[ɣɔrtɑr]
to try (vi)	гӏорта	[ɣɔrtɑ]
chance (opportunity)	хьал	[hɑl]

70. Quarrels. Negative emotions

shout (scream)	мохь	[mɔh]
to shout (vi)	мохь бетта	[mɔh bet:ɑ]
to cry out (yell)	мохь тоха	[mɔh tɔha]
quarrel	дов	[dɔv]
to quarrel (vi)	эрӏар	[ɛɣɑr]
fight (argument)	дов	[dɔv]
to have a fight	девнаш даха	[devnaʃ dɑha]
conflict	конфликт	[kɔnflikt]
misunderstanding	цакхетар	[ʦaqetɑr]
insult	сийсаздаккхар	[si:sazdɑk:ɑr]
to insult (vt)	сий дайа	[si: dɑjɑ]
insulted	юьхьаьрж хӏоттина	[juheærʒ hɔt:inɑ]
offense (e.g., to take ~)	халахетар	[halɑhetɑr]
to offend (sb)	халахетар дан	[halɑhetɑr dɑn]
to take offense	халахета	[halɑhetɑ]
indignation	эргӏаддахар	[ɛrɣad:ɑhar]
to be indignant	эргӏаддала	[ɛrɣad:ɑlɑ]

complaint	латкъам	[latqham]
to complain (vi, vt)	латкъа	[latqha]
apology	бехк цабиллар	[behk tsabil:ar]
to apologize (vi)	бехк цабиллар деха	[behk tsabil:ar deha]
to beg pardon	бехк цабиллар деха	[behk tsabil:ar deha]
criticism	критика	[kritika]
to criticize (vt)	критиковать дан	[kritikovatʲ dan]
accusation	бехкедар	[behkedar]
to accuse (vt)	бехкедан	[behkedan]
revenge	чӀир	[tʃhir]
to avenge (vt)	чӀир леха	[tʃhir leha]
to pay back	дӀадекъа	[dəadeqha]
disdain	цадашар	[tsadaʃar]
to despise (vt)	ца даша	[tsa daʃa]
hatred, hate	цабезам	[tsabezam]
to hate (vt)	ца деза	[tsa deza]
nervous	нервийн	[nervi:n]
to be nervous	дог этӀа	[dɔg ɛtha]
angry (mad)	оьгӀазе	[øɣaze]
to make angry	оьгӀаздахийта	[øɣazdahi:ta]
humiliation	кӀезиг хетар	[k:ezig hetar]
to humiliate (vt)	кӀезиг хета	[k:ezig heta]
to humiliate oneself	кӀезиг хила	[k:ezig hila]
shock	шовкъ	[ʃovqh]
to shock (vt)	юьхьӀаьржахӀотто	[juhəærʒahɔt:ɔ]
trouble (e.g., to be in ~)	цатам	[tsatam]
unpleasant	там боцу	[tam bɔtsu]
fear (dread)	кхерам	[qeram]
terrible (storm, heat)	Ӏаламат чӀорӀа	[əalamat tʃhɔɣa]
scary (e.g., ~ story)	инзаре	[inzare]
horror	Ӏадор	[əadɔr]
awful (crime, news)	къемате	[qhemate]
to cry (weep)	делха	[delha]
to start crying	делха	[delha]
tear	бӀаьрхи	[bəærhi]
fault	бехк	[behk]
guilt (feeling)	бехк	[behk]
disgrace (dishonor)	эхь	[ɛh]
protest	дуьхьалхилар	[dyhalhilar]
stress (nervous tension)	стресс	[stres:]
to disturb (vt)	новкъарло ян	[nɔvqharlɔ jan]

to be angry (with …)	оьгӀазъэха	[øɣazʰɛha]
mad, angry	вон	[vɔn]
to end (e.g., relationship)	дӀасацо	[dəasatsɔ]
to scold sb	дов дан	[dɔv dan]
to be scared	тила	[tila]
to hit (strike with hand)	тоха	[tɔha]
to fight (vi)	лета	[leta]
to settle (a conflict)	дӀадерзо	[dəaderzɔ]
discontented	реза доцу	[reza dɔtsu]
furious (look)	буьрса	[byrsa]
It's not good!	ХӀара дика дац!	[hara dika dats]
It's bad!	ХӀара вон ду!	[hara vɔn du]

Medicine

71. Diseases

sickness	лазар	[lazar]
to be sick	цомгуш хила	[ʦɔmguʃ hila]
health	могушалла	[mɔguʃal:a]
runny nose	шелвалар	[ʃəlvalar]
tonsillitis	ангина	[aɲina]
cold	шелдалар	[ʃəldalar]
to catch a cold	шелдала	[ʃəldala]
bronchitis	бронхит	[brɔnhit]
pneumonia	пехашна хьу кхетар	[pehaʃna hu qetar]
flu, influenza	грипп	[grip:]
near-sighted	б1орзагал	[bəɔrzagal]
far-sighted	генара гун	[genara gun]
strabismus	б1аг1апа хилар	[bəaɣara hilar]
cross-eyed	б1аг1апа	[bəaɣara]
cataract	б1аьрган марха	[bəærgan marha]
glaucoma	глаукома	[glaukɔma]
stroke	инсульт	[insuʌt]
heart attack	дог дат1ар	[dɔg dathar]
myocardial infarction	миокардан инфаркт	[miokardan infarkt]
paralysis	энаш лацар	[ɛnaʃ laʦar]
to paralyze (vt)	энаша лаца	[ɛnaʃa laʦa]
allergy	аллергий	[al:ergi:]
asthma	астма	[astma]
diabetes	диабет	[diabet]
toothache	цергийн лазар	[ʦergi:n lazar]
caries	кариес	[karies]
diarrhea	диарея	[diareja]
constipation	чо юкъялар	[ʧʃɔ juqhjalar]
stomach upset	чохьлазар	[ʧʃohlazar]
food poisoning	отравлени	[ɔtravleni]
to have a food poisoning	кхачанан отравлени	[qaʧʃanan ɔtravleni]
arthritis	артрит	[artrit]
rickets	рахит-цамгар	[rahit ʦamgar]
rheumatism	энаш	[ɛnaʃʃ]

atherosclerosis	атеросклероз	[aterɔsklerɔz]
gastritis	гастрит	[gastrit]
appendicitis	сов йоьхь дестар	[sɔv jøh destar]
cholecystitis	холецистит	[hɔleʦistit]
ulcer	дал	[daə]

measles	кхартанаш	[qartanaʃ]
German measles	хьара	[hara]
jaundice	маждар	[maʒdar]
hepatitis	гепатит	[gepatit]

schizophrenia	шизофрени	[ʃizɔfreni]
hydrophobia, rabies	хьарадалар	[haradalar]
neurosis	невроз	[nevrɔz]
concussion	хье лазор	[he lazɔr]

cancer	дал	[daə]
sclerosis	склероз	[sklerɔz]
multiple sclerosis	тидаме доцу	[tidame dɔʦu]

alcoholism	алкоголан цамгар	[alkɔgɔlan ʦamgar]
alcoholic (noun)	алкоголхо	[alkɔgɔlho]
syphilis	чlурамцамгар	[ʧhuramʦamgar]
AIDS	СПИД	[spid]

tumor	дестар	[destar]
malignant	кхераме	[qerame]
benign	зуламе доцу	[zulame dɔʦu]

fever	хорша	[hɔrʃa]
malaria	хорша	[hɔrʃa]
gangrene	гангрена	[gaŋrena]
seasickness	хlорд хьахар	[hɔrd hahar]
epilepsy	эпилепси	[ɛpilepsi]

epidemic	ун	[un]
typhus	тиф	[tif]
tuberculosis	йовхарийн цамгар	[jovhari:n ʦamgar]
cholera	чоьнан ун	[ʧønan un]
plague (bubonic ~)	lаьржа ун	[əærʒa un]

72. Symptoms. Treatments. Part 1

symptom	билгало	[bilgalɔ]
temperature	температура	[temperatura]
high temperature	лекха температур	[leqa temperatur]
pulse	синпха	[sinpha]

| giddiness | корта хьовзар | [kɔrta hovzar] |
| hot | довха | [dɔvha] |

shivering	шелона дегадар	[ʃelɔna degadar]
pale (e.g., ~ face)	беда	[beda]
cough	йовхарш	[jovharʃ]
to cough (vi)	йовхарш етта	[jovharʃ et:a]
to sneeze (vi)	хьоршамаш детта	[hɔrʃamaʃ det:a]
faint	дог вон хилар	[dɔg vɔn hilar]
to faint (vi)	дог кӀадделла охьавожа	[dɔg k:ad:el:a ɔhavɔʒa]
bruise	Iарждарг	[əarʒdarg]
bump (lump)	бӀара	[bəara]
to bruise oneself	дӀакхета	[dəaqeta]
bruise	дӀатохар	[dəatɔhar]
to get bruised	дӀакхета	[dəaqeta]
to limp (vi)	астагӀлелха	[astaɣlelha]
dislocation	чуьрдаккхар	[tʃyrdak:ar]
to dislocate (vt)	чуьрдаккхар	[tʃyrdak:ar]
fracture	кагдалар	[kagdalar]
to get a fracture	кагдар	[kagdar]
cut (e.g., on the finger)	хадор	[hadɔr]
to cut oneself	хада	[hada]
bleeding	цӀий эхар	[tshi: ɛhar]
burn (injury)	дагор	[dagɔr]
to burn oneself	даго	[dagɔ]
to prick (vt)	Iотта	[əɔt:a]
to prick oneself	Iоттадала	[əɔt:adala]
to injure (vt)	лазо	[lazɔ]
injury	лазор	[lazɔr]
wound	чов	[tʃɔv]
trauma	лазор	[lazɔr]
to be delirious	харц лен	[harts len]
to stutter (vi)	толкха лен	[tɔlqa len]
sunstroke	малх хьахар	[malh hahar]

73. Symptoms. Treatments. Part 2

pain (physical)	лазар	[lazar]
splinter (in foot, finger)	сирхат	[sirhat]
sweat (perspiration)	хьацар	[hatsar]
to sweat (perspire)	хьацар дала	[hatsar dala]
vomiting	Iеттор	[əet:ɔr]
convulsions	пхенаш озор	[phenaʃ ɔzɔr]
pregnant	берахниг	[berahnig]

to be born	**хила**	[hila]
delivery, labor	**бер хилар**	[ber hilar]
to be in labor	**бер дар**	[ber dar]
abortion	**аборт**	[abɔrt]
respiration	**са дахар**	[sa dahar]
inhalation	**са чуозар**	[sa ʧuɔzar]
exhalation	**са арахецар**	[sa arahetsar]
to breathe out	**са арахеца**	[sa arahetsa]
to breathe in	**са чуоза**	[sa ʧuɔza]
disabled person	**заьlапхо**	[zæəapho]
cripple	**заьlапхо**	[zæəapho]
drug addict	**наркоман**	[narkɔman]
deaf	**къора**	[qhɔra]
dumb	**мотт ца хуург**	[mɔt: tsa hu:rg]
deaf-and-dumb	**мотт ца хуург**	[mɔt: tsa hu:rg]
mad, insane	**хьерадьалла**	[heradʲal:a]
madman	**хьераваьлларг**	[heravæl:arg]
madwoman	**хьерайалларг**	[herajal:arg]
to go insane	**хьервалар**	[hervalar]
gene	**ген**	[gen]
immunity	**иммунитет**	[im:unitet]
congenital	**вешшехь хилла**	[weʃəh hil:a]
virus	**вирус**	[wirus]
microbe	**микроб**	[mikrɔb]
bacterium	**бактери**	[bakteri]
infection	**инфекци**	[infektsi]

74. Symptoms. Treatments. Part 3

hospital	**больница**	[bɔʌnitsa]
patient	**пациент**	[patsient]
diagnosis	**диагноз**	[diagnɔz]
cure, treatment	**дарбанаш лелор**	[darbanaʃ lelɔr]
treatment	**дарба лелор**	[darba lelɔr]
to get treatment	**дарбанаш лелор**	[darbanaʃ lelɔr]
to treat (vt)	**дарба лело**	[darba lelɔ]
to nurse (look after)	**лело**	[lelɔ]
care (treatment)	**лелор**	[lelɔr]
operation, surgery	**эtlор**	[ɛthɔr]
to bandage (head, limb)	**дlадехка**	[dəadehka]
bandaging	**йоьхкург**	[jøhkurg]
vaccination	**маха тохар**	[maha tɔhar]

to vaccinate (vt)	маха тоха	[maha tɔha]
injection, shot	маха тохар	[maha tɔhar]
to give an injection	маха тоха	[maha tɔha]
amputation	ампутаци	[amputatsi]
to amputate (vt)	дӀадаккха	[dəadak:a]
coma	кома	[kɔma]
to be in a coma	коме хила	[kɔme hila]
intensive care	реанимаци	[reanimatsi]
to recover (~ from flu)	тодала	[tɔdala]
state (patient's ~)	хьал	[hal]
consciousness	кхетам	[qetam]
memory (faculty)	эс	[ɛs]
to extract (tooth)	дӀадаккха	[dəadak:a]
filling (in tooth)	йома	[joma]
to fill (a tooth)	йома йилла	[joma jil:a]
hypnosis	гипноз	[gipnɔz]
to hypnotize (vt)	гипноз ян	[gipnɔz jan]

75. Doctors

doctor	лор	[lɔr]
nurse (in hospital)	лорйиша	[lɔrjiʃa]
private physician	шен лор	[ʃen lɔr]
children's doctor	берийн лор	[beri:n lɔr]
dentist	дантист	[dantist]
ophthalmologist	окулист	[ɔkulist]
internist	терапевт	[terapevt]
surgeon	хирург	[hirurg]
psychiatrist	психиатр	[psihiatr]
pediatrician	педиатр	[pediatr]
psychologist	психолог	[psihɔlɔg]
gynecologist	гинеколог	[ginekɔlɔg]
cardiologist	кардиолог	[kardiɔlɔg]

76. Medicine. Drugs. Accessories

medicine, drug	молха	[mɔlha]
remedy	дарба	[darba]
to prescribe (vt)	дайх диена	[dajh diena]
prescription	рецепт	[retsept]
tablet, pill	буьртиг	[byrtig]
ointment	хьакхар	[haqar]

ampule	ампула	[ɑmpulɑ]
mixture	микстура	[miksturɑ]
syrup	сироп	[sirɔp]
pill	буьртиг	[byrtig]
powder	хIур	[hur]

bandage	бинт	[bint]
cotton wool	бамба	[bɑmbɑ]
iodine	йод	[jod]

Band-Aid	белхьам	[belhɑm]
eyedropper	пипетка	[pipetkɑ]
thermometer	градусъюстург	[grɑdusʰjusturg]
syringe	маха	[mɑhɑ]

| wheelchair | гIудалкх | [ɣudɑlq] |
| crutches | Iасанаш | [əɑsɑnɑʃ] |

painkiller	лаза ца войту молханаш	[lɑzɑ tsɑ vɔjtu mɔlhɑnɑʃ]
laxative	чуьйнадохуьйтург	[tʃyjnɑdɔhyjturg]
spirit	спирт	[spirt]
medicinal herbs	дарбанан буц	[dɑrbɑnɑn buts]
herbal	бецан	[betsɑn]

77. Smoking. Tobacco products

tobacco	тонка	[tɔŋkɑ]
cigarette	сигарет	[sigɑret]
cigar	сигара	[sigɑrɑ]
pipe	луьлла	[lyl:ɑ]
pack (of cigarettes)	цигаьркийн ботт	[tsigærki:n bɔt:]

matches	сирникаш	[sirnikɑʃ]
matchbox	сирникийн ботт	[sirniki:n bɔt:]
lighter	цIетухург	[tshetuhurg]
ashtray	чимтосург	[tʃimtɔsurg]
cigarette case	портсигар	[pɔrtsigɑr]

| cigarette holder | муштакх | [muʃtɑq] |
| filter | луьттург | [lyt:urg] |

to smoke (vi, vt)	оза	[ɔzɑ]
to light a cigarette	ийза дола	[i:zɑ dɔlɑ]
smoking	цигаьрка озар	[tsigærkɑ ɔzɑr]
smoker	цигаьркаузург	[tsigærkɑuzurg]

stub, butt (of cigarette)	цигаьркан юьхьиг	[tsigærkɑn juhig]
smoke	кIур	[k:ur]
ash	чим	[tʃim]

HUMAN HABITAT

City

78. City. Life in the city

city, town	гӀала	[ɣala]
capital	нана-гӀала	[nana gəala]
village (e.g., fishing ~)	юрт	[jurt]
small town	эвла	[ɛvla]
city map	гӀалин план	[ɣalin plan]
downtown	гӀалин юкъ	[ɣalin juqh]
suburb	гӀалин йист	[ɣalin jıst]
suburban	гӀалин йистера	[ɣalin jıstera]
outskirts	гӀалин йист	[ɣalin jıst]
environs (suburbs)	гӀалин гонахе	[ɣalin gonahe]
district (of city)	район	[rajon]
block	квартал	[kvartal]
residential block	нах беха квартал	[nah beha kvartal]
traffic	лелар	[lelar]
traffic lights	светофор	[swetofor]
public transportation	гӀалара транспорт	[ɣalara transport]
intersection	галморзе	[galmorze]
crosswalk	галморзе	[galmorze]
pedestrian underpass	лаьттан бухара дехьаволийла	[læt:an buhara dehavoli:la]
to cross (vt)	дехьа вала	[deha vala]
pedestrian	гӀашло	[ɣaʃlo]
sidewalk	тротуар	[trotuar]
bridge	тӀай	[thaj]
bank, quay	хийист	[hi:ist]
fountain	фонтан	[fontan]
alley (in park, garden)	аллей	[al:ej]
park	беш	[beʃ]
boulevard	бульвар	[buʎvar]
square	майда	[majda]
avenue (wide street)	проспект	[prospekt]
street	урам	[uram]
lane	урамалг	[uramalg]

dead end	кӀажбухе	[k:aჳbuhe]
house	цӀа	[tsha]
building	гӀишло	[ɣiʃlo]
skyscraper	стигал-бохь	[stigal bɔh]
facade	хьалхе	[halhe]
roof	тхов	[thov]
window	кор	[kɔr]
arch	нартол	[nartɔl]
column	колонна	[kɔlɔŋa]
corner	маьйиг	[mæəig]
store window	витрина	[witrina]
sign (on shop, bar etc.)	гойтург	[gɔjturg]
poster	афиша	[afiʃa]
advertising poster	рекламан плакат	[reklaman plakat]
billboard	рекламан у	[reklaman u]
garbage, trash	нехаш	[nehaʃ]
garbage can	урна	[urna]
to litter (vi)	нехаш яржо	[nehaʃ jarჳɔ]
garbage dump	нехаш дӀакхийсуьйла	[nehaʃ dəaqi:syjla]
phone booth	телефонан будка	[telefɔnan budka]
lightpost	фонаран зӀенар	[fɔnaran zəenar]
bench (park ~)	гӀант	[ɣant]
policeman	полици	[pɔlitsi]
police	полици	[pɔlitsi]
beggar	саӀадоьхург	[saɣadøhurg]
homeless, bum	цӀа доцу	[tsha dɔtsu]

79. Urban institutions

store	туька	[tyka]
drugstore, pharmacy	аптека	[apteka]
optical store	оптика	[ɔptika]
shopping mall	механ центр	[mehan tsentr]
supermarket	супермаркет	[supermarket]
bakery	сурсатийн туька	[sursati:n tyka]
baker	пурнхо	[purnho]
confectionery	кондитерски	[kɔnditerski]
grocery store	баккхал	[bak:al]
butcher shop	жижиг духку туька	[ჳiჳig duhku tyka]
produce store	хасстоьмийн туька	[has:tømi:n tyka]
market	базар	[bazar]
coffee house	кафе	[kafe]
restaurant	ресторан	[restɔran]

pub	**йийн туька**	[ji:n tyka]
pizzeria	**пиццерий**	[pitseri:]
hair salon	**парикмахерски**	[parikmaherski]
post office	**пошт**	[pɔʃt]
dry cleaners	**химцӀандар**	[himtshandar]
photo studio	**фотоателье**	[fɔtɔateʎje]
shoe store	**мачийн туька**	[matʃi:n tyka]
bookstore	**книшкийн туька**	[kniʃki:n tyka]
sporting goods store	**спортан туька**	[spɔrtan tyka]
clothes repair	**бедар таяр**	[bedar tajar]
formal wear rental	**бедарийн прокат**	[bedari:n prɔkat]
movie rental store	**фильман прокат**	[fiʎman prɔkat]
circus	**цирк**	[tsirk]
zoo	**дийнатийн парк**	[di:nati:n park]
movie theater	**кинотеатр**	[kinɔteatr]
museum	**музей**	[muzej]
library	**библиотека**	[bibliɔteka]
theater	**театр**	[teatr]
opera house	**опера**	[ɔpera]
nightclub	**буьйсанан клуб**	[byjsanan klub]
casino	**казино**	[kazinɔ]
mosque	**маьждиг**	[mæʒdig]
synagogue	**синагога**	[sinagɔga]
cathedral	**килс**	[kils]
temple	**зиярат**	[zijarat]
church	**килс**	[kils]
institute	**институт**	[institut]
university	**университет**	[uniwersitet]
school	**школа**	[ʃkɔla]
prefecture	**префектур**	[prefektur]
city hall	**мэри**	[mɛri]
hotel	**хьешийн цӀа**	[heʃi:n tsha]
bank	**банк**	[baŋk]
embassy	**векаллат**	[wekal:at]
travel agency	**турагенство**	[turagenstvɔ]
information office	**хаттараллин бюро**	[hat:aral:in byrɔ]
money exchange	**хуьицийла**	[hyitsi:la]
subway	**метро**	[metrɔ]
hospital	**больница**	[bɔʎnitsa]
gas station	**бензин дутту колонка**	[benzin dut:u kɔlɔŋka]
parking lot	**дӀахӀоттайойла**	[dəhɔt:ajojla]

80. Signs

sign (on shop, bar etc.)	**гойтург**	[gɔjturg]
inscription (plaque etc.)	**тӏеяздар**	[thejazdar]
poster	**плакат**	[plakat]
direction sign	**гойтург**	[gɔjturg]
arrow (direction sign)	**цамза**	[tsamza]
caution	**лардар**	[lardar]
warning	**дӏахьедар**	[dəahedar]
to warn (of the danger)	**дӏахьедан**	[dəahedan]
day off	**мукъа де**	[muqha de]
timetable (schedule)	**расписани**	[raspisani]
opening hours	**белхан сахьташ**	[belhan sahtaʃ]
WELCOME!	**ДИКАНЦА ДОГӏИЙЛА!**	[dikantsa dɔɣi:la]
ENTRANCE	**ЧУГӏОЙЛА**	[tʃuɣɔjla]
EXIT	**АРАДОЛИЙЛА**	[aradɔli:la]
PUSH	**ШЕГАРА**	[ʃegara]
PULL	**ШЕН ТӏЕ**	[ʃen the]
OPEN	**ДИЛЛИНА**	[dil:ina]
CLOSED	**КЪОВЛИНА**	[qhɔvlina]
WOMEN	**ЗУДАРИЙН**	[zudari:n]
MEN	**БОЖАРИЙН**	[bɔʒari:n]
DISCOUNTS	**МАХ ТӏЕРБАККХАР**	[mah therbak:ar]
SALE	**ДОЬХКИНА**	[døhkina
	ДӏАДАККХАР	deadak:ar]
NEW!	**КЕРЛАНИГ!**	[kerlanig]
FREE	**МАЬХЗА**	[mæhza]
ATTENTION!	**ЛАДОГӏА!**	[ladɔɣa]
NO VACANCIES	**МЕТТИГ ЯЦ**	[met:ig jats]
RESERVED	**ЦХЬАНАН ТӏЕХЬ**	[tshanan theh
	ЧӏАГӏИЙНА	tʃhaɣjina]
ADMINISTRATION	**АДМИНИСТРАЦИ**	[administratsi]
STAFF ONLY	**ПЕРСОНАЛАН БЕ**	[personalan be]
BEWARE OF THE DOG!	**ДЕРА ЖӏАЬЛА**	[dera ʒæla]
NO SMOKING	**ЦИГАЬРКА ОЗА**	[tsigærka ɔza
	МЕГАШ ДАЦ	megaʃ dats]
DO NOT TOUCH!	**КУЬЙГАШ МА ДЕТТА!**	[kyjgaʃ ma det:a]
DANGEROUS	**КХЕРАМЕ**	[qerame]
DANGER	**КХЕРАМ**	[qeram]
HIGH TENSION	**ЛАКХАРЧУ**	[laqartʃu
	БУЛЛАМАН ТОК	bul:aman tɔk]

| NO SWIMMING! | ЛИЙЧА ЦА МЕГА | [liːtʃa tsa mega] |
| OUT OF ORDER | БОЛХ ЦА БО | [bɔlh tsa bɔ] |

FLAMMABLE	ЦIЕ КХЕРАМЕ	[tʃhe qerame]
FORBIDDEN	ЦА МЕГА	[tsa mega]
NO TRESPASSING!	ЧЕКХДАЛАР ЦА МЕГА	[tʃeqdalar tsa mega]
WET PAINT	БАСАР ХЬАЬКХНА	[basar hæqna]

81. Urban transport

bus	автобус	[avtobus]
streetcar	трамвай	[tramvaj]
trolley	троллейбус	[trɔlːejbus]
route (of bus)	маршрут	[marʃrut]
number (e.g., bus ~)	номер	[nɔmer]

to go by ...	даха	[daha]
to get on (~ the bus etc.)	тIехаа	[thehaː]
to get off ...	охьадосса	[ɔhadɔsːa]
to get out (vi)	арадала	[aradala]

stop (e.g., bus ~)	социйла	[sɔtsiːla]
next stop	порlепа социйла	[rɔyera sɔtsiːla]
terminus	тIаьххьара социйла	[thæhara sɔtsiːla]
schedule	расписани	[raspisani]
to wait (vi, vt)	хьежа	[heʒa]

| ticket | билет | [bilet] |
| fare (charge for bus etc.) | билетан мах | [biletan mah] |

cashier	кассир	[kasːir]
ticket inspection	контроль	[kɔntrɔʎ]
conductor	контролёр	[kɔntrɔlɜr]

to be late (for ...)	тIаьхьадиса	[thæhadisa]
to miss ... (the train etc.)	тIаьхьадиса	[thæhadisa]
to be in a hurry	сихадала	[sihadala]

taxi, cab	такси	[taksi]
taxi driver	таксист	[taksist]
by taxi	таксин тIехь	[taksin theh]
taxi stand	такси дIахIоттайойла	[taksi dəahɔtːajɔjla]
to call a taxi	таксига кхайкха	[taksiga qajqa]
to take a taxi	такси лаца	[taksi latsa]

traffic	урамашкахула лелар	[uramaʃkahula lelar]
traffic jam	дIадукъар	[dəaduqhar]
rush hour	юкъъелла хан	[juqhʰelːa han]
to park (vi)	машина дIахIоттар	[maʃina dəahɔtːar]
to park (vt)	машина дIахIотто	[maʃina dəahɔtːɔ]

parking lot	дӀахӀоттайойла	[dəɑhɔt:ɑjojlɑ]
subway	метро	[metrɔ]
station	станци	[stɑnʦi]
to take the subway	метрохь ваха	[metrɔh vɑhɑ]
train	цӀерпошт	[ʦherpɔʃt]
train station	вокзал	[vɔkzɑl]

82. Sightseeing

monument	хӀоллам	[hɔl:ɑm]
fortress	гӀап	[ɣɑp]
palace	гӀала	[ɣɑlɑ]
castle	гӀала	[ɣɑlɑ]
tower	бӀов	[bəɔv]
mausoleum	мавзолей	[mɑvzɔlej]

architecture	архитектура	[ɑrhitekturɑ]
medieval	юккъерчу бӀешерийн	[jukqhertʃu bəeʃəri:n]
ancient	тамашена	[tɑmɑʃənɑ]
national	къаьмнийн	[qhæmni:n]
famous	гӀарадаьлла	[ɣɑrɑdæl:ɑ]

tourist	турист	[turist]
guide (person)	гид	[gid]
excursion (organized trip)	экскурси	[ɛkskursi]
to show (vt)	гайта	[gɑjtɑ]
to tell (vi, vt)	дийца	[di:ʦɑ]

to find (vt)	каро	[kɑrɔ]
to get lost	дан	[dɑn]
map (e.g., subway ~)	схема	[shemɑ]
map (e.g., city ~)	план	[plɑn]

souvenir, gift	совгӀат	[sɔvɣɑt]
gift shop	совгӀатан туька	[sɔvɣɑtɑn tykɑ]
to take pictures	сурт даккха	[surt dɑk:ɑ]
to be photographed	сурт даккхийта	[surt dɑk:i:tɑ]

83. Shopping

to buy (purchase)	эца	[ɛʦɑ]
purchase	эцар	[ɛʦɑr]
to go shopping	хӀуманаш эца	[humɑnɑʃ ɛʦɑ]
shopping	эцар	[ɛʦɑr]

to be open	болх бан	[bɔlh bɑn]
to be closed	дӀакъовла	[dəɑqhɔvlɑ]
footwear	мача	[mɑtʃɑ]

clothes, clothing	бедар	[bedar]
cosmetics	косметика	[kɔsmetika]
food	сурсаташ	[sursataʃ]
gift, present	совгӏат	[sɔvɣat]

| salesman | йохкархо | [jɔhkarhɔ] |
| saleswoman | йохкархо | [jɔhkarhɔ] |

check out, cash desk	касса	[kas:a]
mirror	куьзга	[kyzga]
counter (in shop)	гӏопаста	[ɣɔpasta]
fitting room	примерочни	[primerɔʧni]

to try on	тӏедуьйхина хьажа	[thedyjhina haʒa]
to fit (about dress etc.)	гӏехьа хила	[ɣeha hila]
to like (I like ...)	хазахета	[hazaheta]

price	мах	[mah]
price tag	махло	[mahlɔ]
to cost (vt)	деха	[deha]
How much?	Хӏун доккху?	[hun dɔk:u]
discount	тӏерадаккхар	[theradak:ar]

inexpensive	деза доцу	[deza dɔtsu]
cheap (inexpensive)	дораха	[dɔraha]
expensive	деза	[deza]
It's expensive	Иза механ деза ду.	[iza mehan deza du]

rental (noun)	прокат	[prɔkat]
to rent (~ a tuxedo)	прокатан схьаэца	[prɔkatan shaətsa]
credit	кредит	[kredit]
on credit	кредитан	[kreditan]

84. Money

money	ахча	[ahʧa]
exchange	хийцар	[hi:tsar]
exchange rate	мах	[mah]
ATM	банкомат	[baŋkɔmat]
coin	ахча	[ahʧa]

| dollar | доллар | [dɔl:ar] |
| euro | евро | [evrɔ] |

lira (currency)	лира	[lira]
Deutschmark	марка	[marka]
franc	франк	[fraŋk]
pound sterling	стерлингийн фунт	[sterliŋi:n funt]
yen	йена	[jena]
debt	декхар	[deqar]

debtor	декхархо	[deqarhɔ]
to lend (money)	юхалург дала	[juhalurg dala]
to borrow (vi, vt)	юхалург эца	[juhalurg ɛtsa]

bank	банк	[baŋk]
account	счёт	[stʃɔt]
to make a deposit	счёт тӀедилла	[stʃɔt thedil:a]
to withdraw (vt)	счёт тӀера схьаэца	[stʃɔt thera shaɘtsa]

credit card	кредитан карта	[kreditan karta]
cash	карахь долу ахча	[karah dɔlu ahtʃa]
check	чек	[tʃek]
to write a check	чёт язъян	[tʃɔt jazʰjan]
checkbook	чекан книшка	[tʃekan niʃka]

wallet	бумаьштиг	[bumæʃtig]
change purse	бохча	[bɔhtʃa]
billfold	портмоне	[pɔrtmɔne]
safe	сейф	[sejf]

heir	верас	[weras]
inheritance	диснарг	[disnarg]
fortune (wealth)	бахам	[baham]

lease, rent	аренда	[arenda]
rent money	петаран мах	[petaran mah]
to rent (of a tenant)	лаца	[latsa]

price	мах	[mah]
cost	мах	[mah]
sum (amount of money)	жамӀ	[ʒamə]

to spend (vi, vt)	дайа	[daja]
expenses	харжаш	[harʒaʃ]
to economize (vi, vt)	довзо	[dɔvzɔ]
economical	девзаш долу	[devzaʃ dɔlu]

to pay (vi, vt)	ахча дала	[ahtʃa dala]
payment	алапа далар	[alapa dalar]
change (give the ~)	юхадоӀург	[juhadɔɣurg]

tax	налог	[nalɔg]
fine	гӀуда	[ɣuda]
to fine	гӀуда тоха	[ɣuda tɔha]

85. Post. Postal service

post office	пошт	[pɔʃt]
mail (letters etc.)	пошт	[pɔʃt]
mailman	почтальон	[pɔtʃtaʎɔn]

working hours	**белхан сахьташ**	[belhan sahtaʃ]
letter	**кехат**	[kehat]
registered letter	**заказ дина кехат**	[zakaz dina kehat]
postcard	**открытк**	[ɔtkrɪtk]
telegram	**телеграмма**	[telegram:a]
parcel	**посылка**	[pɔsɪlka]
money transfer	**дӀатесна ахча**	[dəatesna ahʧa]
to receive (vt)	**схьаэца**	[shaeʦa]
to send (vt)	**дӀадахьийта**	[dədahi:ta]
sending	**дӀадахьийтар**	[dədahi:tar]
address	**адрес**	[adres]
ZIP code	**индекс**	[indeks]
addressee	**адресат**	[adresat]
sender	**дӀадахьийтинарг**	[dədahi:tinarg]
receiver, addressee	**схьаэцархо**	[shaeʦarhɔ]
name	**цӀе**	[ʦhe]
family name	**фамили**	[famili]
rate (of postage)	**тариф**	[tarif]
ordinary	**гуттарлера**	[gut:arlera]
standard (adj)	**кхоаме**	[qɔame]
weight	**дозалла**	[dozal:a]
to weigh up (vt)	**оза**	[ɔza]
envelope	**ботт**	[bɔt:]
postage stamp	**марка**	[marka]

Dwelling. House. Home

86. House. Dwelling

house	цІа	[ʦ̊ha]
at home	цІахь	[ʦ̊hah]
courtyard	керт	[kert]
railings (fence)	керт	[kert]
brick (noun)	кибарчиг	[kibarʧig]
brick (building)	кибарчигийн	[kibarʧigi:n]
stone (noun)	тІулг	[thulg]
stone (made of stone)	тІулган	[thulgan]
concrete (noun)	бетон	[betɔn]
concrete (attr)	бетонан	[betɔnan]
new	цІина	[ʦ̊hina]
old	тиша	[tiʃa]
decrepit (house)	тиша	[tiʃa]
modern	вайн хенан	[vajn henan]
multistory	дукхазза тІекІелдина	[duqaz:a thek:eldina]
high	лекха	[leqa]
floor, story	этаж	[ɛtaʒ]
single-story	цхьа этаж йолу	[ʦ̊ha ɛtaʒ jolu]
ground floor	лахара этаж	[lahara ɛtaʒ]
top floor	лакхара этаж	[laqara ɛtaʒ]
roof (of building)	тхов	[thov]
chimney	биргІа	[birɣa]
tiles (for roof)	гериг	[gerig]
tiled	гериган	[gerigan]
loft (attic)	чардакх	[ʧardaq]
window	кор	[kɔr]
glass	ангали	[aŋali]
window ledge	коран у	[kɔran u]
shutters	коран неІараш	[kɔran neəraʃ]
wall	пен	[pen]
balcony	балкон	[balkɔn]
downspout	малхбалехьара биргІа	[malhbalehara birɣa]
upstairs (to be ~)	лакхахь	[laqah]
to go upstairs	тІедала	[thedala]
to come down	охьадан	[ɔhadan]
to move (to new premises)	дІаваха	[dəavaha]

87. House. Entrance. Lift

entrance	тIеводийла	[theʋɔdi:la]
stairs (stairway)	лами	[lami]
stairs (steps)	тIерланаш	[theɣanaʃ]
banisters	перила	[perila]
lobby (e.g., hotel ~)	дуьхьал чоь	[dyhal ʧø]
mailbox	поштан яьшка	[pɔʃtan jaʃka]
trash can	нехаш кхуьйсу бак	[nehaʃ qyjsu bak]
trash chute	нехашдIаузург	[nehaʃdəauzurg]
elevator	лифт	[lift]
freight elevator	киранан лифт	[kiranan lift]
elevator cage	лифтан кабин	[liftan kabin]
to take the elevator	даха	[daha]
apartment	петар	[petar]
tenants	хIусамхой	[husamhoj]
neighbor (man)	лулахо	[lulaho]
neighbor (woman)	лулахо	[lulaho]
neighbors	лулахой	[lulahoj]

88. House. Electricity

electricity	электричество	[ɛlektriʧestvɔ]
light bulb	лампа	[lampa]
switch (for light)	дIаяйоург	[dəajajourg]
fuse	тIус	[thus]
cable, wire (electric ~)	сара	[sara]
wiring	далор	[dalɔr]
electricity meter	лорург	[lɔrurg]
readings	гайтам	[gajtam]

89. House. Doors. Locks

door	нел	[neə]
gate (of villa etc.)	ков	[kɔv]
handle, doorknob	тIам	[tham]
to unlock (unbolt)	дIайела	[dəajela]
to open (vi, vt)	схьайела	[shajela]
to close (vt)	дIакъовла	[dəaqhovla]
key	дорIа	[dɔɣa]
bunch (of keys)	дорIанийн кочар	[dɔɣani:n kɔʧar]
to creak (door hinge)	цIийза	[tshi:za]

creak	цІийзар	[tʃhi:zɑr]
hinge (of door)	кІажа	[k:ɑʒɑ]
doormat	кузан цуьрг	[kuzɑn tsyrg]

lock	дорІа	[dɔɣɑ]
keyhole	дорІанан Іуьрг	[dɔɣɑnɑn əyrg]
bolt (big sliding bar)	гІуй	[ɣuj]
bolt (small latch)	зайл	[zɑjl]
padlock	навесной дорІа	[nɑwesnɔj dɔɣɑ]

to ring (~ the door bell)	детта	[det:ɑ]
ringing (sound)	горгали	[gɔrgɑli]
doorbell	горгали	[gɔrgɑli]
button	кнопка	[knɔpkɑ]
knock (at the door)	тата	[tɑtɑ]
to knock (vi)	детта	[det:ɑ]

code	код	[kɔd]
code lock	кодови дорІа	[kɔdɔwi dɔɣɑ]
door phone	домофон	[dɔmɔfɔn]
number (on the door)	номер	[nɔmer]
nameplate	гойтург	[gɔjturg]
peephole	бІаьрг	[bəærg]

90. Country house

village	юрт	[jurt]
vegetable garden	хасбеш	[hɑsbeʃ]
fence	керт	[kert]

paling	керт	[kert]
wicket gate	ринжа	[rinʒɑ]

granary	амбар	[ɑmbɑr]
cellar	ларма	[lɑrmɑ]

shed (in garden)	божал	[bɔʒɑl]
well (for water)	гІу	[ɣu]

stove (for heating)	пеш	[peʃ]
to stoke	даго	[dɑgɔ]

firewood	дечиг	[detʃig]
log (firewood)	туьппалг	[typ:ɑlg]

veranda, stoop	уче	[utʃe]
terrace (patio)	уче	[utʃe]

front steps	лаба	[lɑbɑ]
swing (hanging seat)	бираьнчик	[biræntʃik]

91. Villa. Mansion

country house	гӀалил ара цӀа	[ɣalil ara tsha]
villa (by sea)	вилла	[wil:a]
wing (of building)	арло	[aɣɔ]

garden	хасбеш	[hasbeʃ]
park	беш	[beʃ]
greenhouse (tropical ~)	оранжерей	[ɔranʒerej]
to look after (garden etc.)	Ӏалашдан	[əalaʃdan]

swimming pool	бассейн	[bas:ejn]
gym	спортан зал	[spɔrtan zal]
tennis court	теннисан корт	[teɲisan kɔrt]
home theater room	кинотеатр	[kinɔteatr]
garage	гараж	[garaʒ]

private property	долара хьал	[dɔlara hal]
private land	долара хьал	[dɔlara hal]

warning (caution)	дӀахьедар	[dəahedar]
warning sign	дӀахьедаран йоза	[dəahedaran joza]

security	ха	[ha]
security guard	хехо	[heho]
burglar alarm	хаамбийриг	[ha:mbi:rig]

92. Castle. Palace

castle	гӀала	[ɣala]
palace	гӀала	[ɣala]
fortress	гӀап	[ɣap]

wall (round castle)	пен	[pen]
tower	бӀов	[bəov]
main tower, donjon	коьрта бӀов	[kørta bəov]

portcullis	хьалаайалун ков	[hala:jalun kɔv]
underground passage	лаьттан бухара чекхдолийла	[læt:an buhara tʃeqdɔli:la]
moat	саьнгар	[sæŋar]
chain	зӀе	[zəe]
arrow loop	бӀарол	[bəarɔl]

magnificent	исбаьхьа	[isbæha]
majestic	инзара-доккха	[inzara dɔk:a]
impregnable	тӀекхачалур воцу	[theqatʃalur vɔtsu]
knight's	къонахчун	[qhonahtʃun]
medieval	юккъерчу бӀешерийн	[jukqhertʃu bəeʃeri:n]

93. Apartment

apartment	петар	[petar]
room	чоь	[ʧø]
bedroom	дуьйшу чоь	[dyjʃu ʧø]
dining room	столови	[stɔlɔwi]
living room	хьешан цӀа	[heʃan ʦha]
study	кабинет	[kabinet]
entry room	сени	[seni]
bathroom	ваннан чоь	[vaŋan ʧø]
half bath	хьаштагӀа	[haʃtaɣa]
ceiling	тхов	[thov]
floor	цӀенкъа	[ʦhenqha]
corner (inside room)	са	[sa]

94. Apartment. Cleaning

to clean (vi, vt)	дӀадаха	[dəadaha]
to put away (vt)	дӀадаха	[dəadaha]
dust	чан	[ʧan]
dusty	ченан	[ʧenan]
to dust (vt)	чан дӀаяккха	[ʧan dəajak:a]
vacuum cleaner	чанъузург	[ʧanʰuzurg]
to vacuum (vt)	чанъузург хьакха	[ʧanʰuzurg haqa]
to sweep (vi, vt)	нуй хьакха	[nuj haqa]
sweepings	нехаш	[nehaʃ]
order	къепе	[qhepe]
disorder, mess	къепе яцар	[qhepe jaʦar]
mop	швабра	[ʃvabra]
dust cloth	горгам	[gorgam]
broom	нуй	[nuj]
dustpan	аьшкал	[æʃkal]

95. Furniture. Interior

furniture (for house)	мебель	[mebeʎ]
table	стол	[stɔl]
chair	гӀант	[ɣant]
bed	маьнга	[mæŋa]
couch, sofa	диван	[divan]
armchair	кресло	[kreslɔ]
bookcase	шкаф	[ʃkaf]

shelf	терхи	[terhi]
set of shelves	книгашйохкург	[knigaʃjohkurg]
wardrobe	шкаф	[ʃkaf]
coat rack	бедаршъухкург	[bedarʃʼuhkurg]
coat stand	бедаршъухкург	[bedarʃʼuhkurg]
chest of drawers	комод	[kɔmɔd]
coffee table	журналан стол	[ʒurnalan stɔl]
mirror	куьзга	[kyzga]
carpet	куз	[kuz]
rug, small carpet	кузан цуьрг	[kuzan tsyrg]
fireplace	товха	[tɔvha]
candle	чIурам	[tʃhuram]
candlestick	чIурамхIотторг	[tʃhuramhɔt:ɔrg]
kitchen curtains	уллург	[ul:urg]
drapes	штораш	[ʃtɔraʃ]
wallpaper	обойш	[ɔbɔjʃ]
blinds (jalousie)	жалюзаш	[ʒalyzaʃ]
table lamp	стоьла тIе хIотто лампа	[støla the hɔt:ɔ lampa]
wall lamp	къуьда	[qhyda]
floor lamp	торшер	[tɔrʃer]
chandelier	люстра	[lystra]
leg (of chair, table)	ког	[kɔg]
armrest	голагIорторг	[gɔlaɣɔrtɔrg]
back	букъ	[buqh]
drawer	яьшка	[jaʃka]

96. Bedding

bedclothes	чухулаюху хIуманаш	[tʃuhulajuhu humanaʃ]
pillow	гIайба	[ɣajba]
pillowcase	лоччар	[lɔtʃar]
blanket (comforter)	юргIа	[jurɣa]
sheet	шаршу	[ʃarʃu]
bedspread	меттан шаршу	[met:an ʃarʃu]

97. Kitchen

kitchen	кухни	[kuhni]
gas	газ	[gaz]
gas stove	газан плита	[gazan plita]
electric stove	электрически плита	[ɛlektritʃeski plita]

oven	духовка	[duhovkɑ]
microwave oven	микроволнови пеш	[mikrɔvɔlnɔwi peʃ]
fridge	шелиг	[ʃəlig]
freezer	морозильник	[mɔrɔziʎnik]
dishwasher	пхьерlаш йулу машина	[pheɣɑʃ julu maʃina]
meat grinder	жижигъохьург	[ʒiʒigʰɔhurg]
juicer	муттадоккхург	[mut:adɔk:urg]
toaster	тостер	[tɔster]
mixer	миксер	[mikser]
coffee maker	къахьокхехкорг	[qhahɔqehkɔrg]
coffee pot	къахьокхехкорг	[qhahɔqehkɔrg]
coffee grinder	къахьоахьарг	[qhahɔaharg]
kettle	чайник	[ʧajnik]
teapot	чайник	[ʧajnik]
lid	неrlап	[neɣɑr]
tea strainer	цаца	[tsatsa]
spoon	lайг	[əɑjg]
teaspoon	стаканан lайг	[stakanan əɑjg]
tablespoon	аьчка lайг	[æʧka əɑjg]
fork	мlара	[məɑrɑ]
knife	урс	[urs]
tableware	пхьерlаш	[pheɣɑʃ]
plate	бошхап	[bɔʃhap]
saucer	бошхап	[bɔʃhap]
small wineglass	рюмка	[rymkɑ]
glass (e.g., ~ of water)	стака	[stakɑ]
cup	кад	[kad]
sugar bowl	шекардухкург	[ʃəkarduhkurg]
salt shaker	туьхадухкург	[tyhaduhkurg]
pepper shaker	бурчъюхкург	[burʧʰjuhkurg]
butter dish	даьттадуьллург	[dæt:adyl:urg]
saucepan	яй	[jɑj]
frying pan	зайла	[zajlɑ]
ladle	чами	[ʧami]
colander	луьттар	[lyt:ar]
tray	хедар	[hedɑr]
bottle	шиша	[ʃiʃa]
jar (glass)	банка	[baŋkɑ]
can	банка	[baŋkɑ]
bottle opener	схьадоьллург	[shadøl:urg]
can opener	схьадоьллург	[shadøl:urg]

corkscrew	штопор	[ʃtɔpɔr]
filter	луьттург	[lyt:urg]
to filter (vt)	литта	[lit:a]
trash	нехаш	[nehaʃ]
trash can	нехийн ведар	[nehi:n wedar]

98. Bathroom

bathroom	ваннан чоь	[vaŋan ʧø]
water	хи	[hi]
tap, faucet	кран	[kran]
hot water	довха хи	[dɔvha hi]
cold water	шийла хи	[ʃi:la hi]
toothpaste	цергийн паста	[tsergi:n pasta]
to brush one's teeth	цергаш цlанъян	[tsergaʃ tshanʰjan]
to shave (vi)	даша	[daʃa]
shaving foam	чопа	[ʧɔpa]
razor	урс	[urs]
to wash (clean)	дила	[dila]
to take a bath	дила	[dila]
shower	душ	[duʃ]
to take a shower	лийча	[li:ʧa]
bathtub	ванна	[vaŋa]
toilet	унитаз	[unitaz]
sink	раковина	[rakɔwina]
soap	саба	[saba]
soap dish	сабадуьллург	[sabadyl:urg]
sponge	худург	[hudurg]
shampoo	шампунь	[ʃampuɲ]
towel	гата	[gata]
bathrobe	оба	[ɔba]
laundry (process)	диттар	[dit:ar]
washing machine	хlуманаш юьтту машина	[humanaʃ jut:u maʃina]
to do the laundry	чухулаюху хlуманаш йитта	[ʧuhulajuhu humanaʃ jit:a]
laundry detergent	хlуманаш юьтту порошок	[humanaʃ jut:u pɔrɔʃɔk]

99. Household appliances

TV set	телевизор	[telewizɔr]
tape recorder	магнитофон	[magnitɔfɔn]
video, VCR	видеомагнитофон	[wideɔmagnitɔfɔn]
radio	приёмник	[priɜmnik]
player (CD, MP3 etc.)	плеер	[ple:r]

video projector	видеопроектор	[wideɔprɔektɔr]
home movie theater	цӀахь лело кинотеатр	[tshah lelɔ kinɔteatr]
DVD player	DVD гойтург	[diwidi gɔjturg]
amplifier	чӀарӀдийриг	[tʃhaɣdi:rig]
video game console	ловзаран приставка	[lɔvzaran pristavka]

video camera	видеокамера	[wideɔkamera]
camera (photo)	фотоаппарат	[fɔtɔap:arat]
digital camera	цифровой фотоаппарат	[tsifrɔvɔj fɔtɔap:arat]

vacuum cleaner	чанъузург	[tʃanʰuzurg]
iron (e.g., steam ~)	иту	[itu]
ironing board	иту хьокху у	[itu hɔqu u]

telephone	телефон	[telefɔn]
mobile phone	мобильни телефон	[mɔbiʎni telefɔn]
typewriter	зорба туху машина	[zɔrba tuhu maʃina]
sewing machine	чарх	[tʃarh]

microphone	микрофон	[mikrɔfɔn]
headphones	ладугӀургаш	[laduɣurgaʃ]
remote control (TV)	пульт	[puʎt]

compact disc, CD	компакт-диск	[kɔmpakt disk]
cassette	кассета	[kas:eta]
record (vinyl LP)	пластинка	[plastiŋka]

100. Repairs. Renovation

renovations	таяр	[tajar]
to renovate (vt)	ремонт яр	[remɔnt jar]
to repair (vt)	ремонт ян	[remɔnt jan]
to put in order	къепе дало	[qhepe dalɔ]
to redo (vt)	юхадан	[juhadan]

paint	басар	[basar]
to paint (e.g., ~ a wall)	басар хьакха	[basar haqa]
house painter	басарча	[basartʃa]
brush	щётка	[ɕɜtka]
whitewash	кир тоха	[kir tɔha]

to whitewash (vt)	кир тоха	[kir tɔha]
wallpaper	обойш	[ɔbɔjʃ]
to put up wallpaper	обойш лато	[ɔbɔjʃ latɔ]
varnish	лак	[lak]
to varnish (vt)	лак хьакха	[lak haqa]

101. Plumbing

water	хи	[hi]
hot water	довха хи	[dɔvha hi]
cold water	шийла хи	[ʃiːla hi]
tap, faucet	кран	[kran]

drop (of water)	тӀадам	[thadam]
to drip (vi)	леда	[leda]
to leak (about pipe)	эха	[ɛha]
leak (in pipe)	дӀаэхар	[dəaəhar]
puddle	Ӏам	[əam]

pipe	бирrӀа	[birɣa]
valve	пиллиг	[pilːig]
to be clogged up	дукъадала	[duqhadala]

tools	гӀирсаш	[ɣirsaʃ]
adjustable wrench	галморзахдоккху догӀа	[galmɔrzahdɔkːu dɔɣa]
to unscrew (vt)	схьахьовзо	[shahɔvzɔ]
to screw (tighten)	хьовзо	[hɔvzɔ]

to unclog (vt)	дӀацӀандан	[dəatʃhandan]
plumber	сантехник	[santehnik]
basement	ор	[ɔr]
sewerage (system)	канализаци	[kanalizatsi]

102. Fire. Conflagration

fire (e.g., to catch ~)	цӀе	[tʃhe]
flame	алу	[alu]
spark	суй	[suj]
smoke (from fire)	кӀур	[kːur]
torch (flaming stick)	хаьштиг	[hæʃtig]
campfire	цӀе	[tʃhe]

gas, gasoline	бензин	[benzin]
kerosene (for aircraft)	мехкадаьтта	[mehkadætːa]
flammable	догу	[dɔgu]
explosive	эккхар кхераме	[ɛkːar qerame]
NO SMOKING	ЦИГАЬРКА ОЗА МЕГАШ ДАЦ!	[tsigærka ɔza megaʃ dats]

safety	кхерамза	[qeramza]
danger	кхерам	[qeram]
dangerous	кхераме	[qerame]
to catch fire	дата	[data]
explosion	эккхар	[ɛk:ar]
to set fire	лато	[latɔ]
incendiary (arsonist)	цӏетасархо	[tshetasarhɔ]
arson	цӏе йиллар	[tshe jıl:ar]
to blaze (vi)	алу тийса	[alu ti:sa]
to burn (be on fire)	догуш хила	[dɔguʃ hila]
to burn down	даьгна дӏадала	[dægna dɔadala]
fireman	цӏе йойу	[tshe joju]
fire truck	цӏе йойу машина	[tshe joju maʃina]
fire department	цӏе йойу орца	[tshe joju ɔrtsa]
fire truck ladder	цӏе йойу лами	[tshe joju lami]
fire hose	марш	[marʃ]
fire extinguisher	цӏейойург	[tshejojurg]
helmet	каска	[kaska]
siren	сирена	[sirena]
to shout (vi)	мохь бетта	[mɔh bet:a]
to call for help	гӏонна кхайкха	[ɣɔŋa qajqa]
rescuer	кӏелхьардакххархо	[k:elhardaqharhɔ]
to rescue (vt)	кӏелхьардаккха	[k:elhardak:a]
to arrive (vi)	дан	[dan]
to extinguish (vt)	дӏадайа	[dɔadaja]
water	хи	[hi]
sand	гӏум	[ɣum]
ruins (destruction)	къапалг	[qhapalg]
to collapse (building, roof)	харца	[hartsa]
to fall down	чухарца	[tʃuhartsa]
to cave in (ceiling, floor)	охьахарца	[ɔhahartsa]
fragment (piece of wall etc.)	кийсиг	[ki:sig]
ash	чим	[tʃim]
to suffocate (die)	садукъадала	[saduqhadala]
to be killed (perish)	хӏаллакьхила	[hal:akʲhila]

HUMAN ACTIVITIES

Job. Business. Part 1

103. Office. Working in the office

office (of firm)	офис	[ɔfis]
office (of director etc.)	кабинет	[kabinet]
front desk (in the office)	ресепшн	[resepʃn]
secretary	секретарь	[sekretarʲ]
director	директор	[direktɔr]
manager (employee)	менеджер	[menedʒer]
accountant	бухгалтер	[buhgalter]
employee	къинхьегамча	[qhinhegamtʃa]
furniture	мебель	[mebeʎ]
desk	стол	[stɔl]
desk chair	кресло	[kreslɔ]
chest of drawers	тумбочка	[tumbɔtʃka]
coat stand	бедаршъухкург	[bedarʃʲuhkurg]
computer	компьютер	[kɔmpjyter]
printer	принтер	[printer]
fax machine	факс	[faks]
photocopier	копи йоккху аппарат	[kɔpi jɔk:u ap:arat]
paper	кехат	[kehat]
office supplies	канцелярин гӀирс	[kantseʎarin ɣirs]
mouse pad	кузан цуьрг	[kuzan tsyrg]
sheet (of paper)	кехат	[kehat]
folder, binder	папка	[papka]
catalog	каталог	[katalɔg]
phone book	справочник	[spravɔtʃnik]
documentation	документаш	[dɔkumentaʃ]
booklet	брошюра	[brɔʃyra]
leaflet	кехат	[kehat]
sample	кеп	[kep]
training meeting	Ӏамор	[əamɔr]
meeting (of managers)	кхеташо	[qetaʃɔ]
lunch time	делкъана садаӀар	[delqhana sadaəar]
to copy (photocopy)	копи яккха	[kɔpi jak:a]
to make copies	даржо	[darʒɔ]

| to receive a fax | факс схьаэца | [faks shaetsa] |
| to send a fax | факс дӀайахьийта | [faks dəajahi:ta] |

to call (telephone)	тоха	[tɔha]
to answer (vi, vt)	жоп дала	[ʒɔp dala]
to put through	зӀе таса	[zəe tasa]

to arrange (organize, plan)	билгалдан	[bilgaldan]
to show (to display)	демонстраци ян	[demɔnstratsi jan]
to be absent	ца хила	[tsa hila]
absence	чекхдалийтар	[tʃeqdali:tar]

104. Business processes. Part 1

occupation	гӀуллакх	[ɣul:aq]
firm	фирма	[firma]
company	компани	[kɔmpani]
corporation	корпораци	[kɔrpɔratsi]
enterprise	предприяти	[predprijati]
agency	агенство	[agenstvɔ]

agreement (contract)	барт	[bart]
contract	чӀарӀам	[tʃhaɣam]
deal	барт	[bart]
order (to place an ~)	заказ	[zakaz]
term (of contract)	биллам	[bil:am]

wholesale (adv)	туьпахь	[typah]
wholesale (adj)	туьпахь	[typah]
wholesale (noun)	туьпахь дохка	[typah dɔhka]
retail (adj)	дустуш духку	[dustuʃ duhku]
retail (noun)	узуш дохка	[uzuʃ dɔhka]

competitor	къийсархо	[qhi:sarhɔ]
competition	къийсам	[qhi:sam]
to compete (vi)	къийса	[qhi:sa]

| partner (associate) | декъашхо | [deqhaʃhɔ] |
| partnership | дакъа лацар | [daqha latsar] |

crisis	кризис	[krizis]
bankruptcy	банкрот хилар	[baŋkrɔt hilar]
to go bankrupt	декхарлахь диса	[deqarlah disa]
difficulty	хало	[halɔ]
problem	проблема	[prɔblema]
catastrophe	ирча бохам	[irtʃa bɔham]

economy	экономика	[ɛkɔnɔmika]
economic (e.g., ~ growth)	экономикин	[ɛkɔnɔmikin]
economic recession	экономикин лахдалар	[ɛkɔnɔmikin lahdalar]

goal (aim)	**lалашо**	[əalaʃɔ]
task	**декхар**	[deqar]
to trade (vi)	**мах лело**	[mah lelɔ]
network (distribution ~)	**туькнаш**	[tyknaʃ]
stock	**склад**	[sklad]
assortment	**ассортимент**	[as:ɔrtiment]
leader	**лидер**	[lider]
big, large	**доккха**	[dɔk:a]
monopoly	**монополи**	[mɔnɔpɔli]
theory	**теори**	[teɔri]
practice	**практика**	[praktika]
experience (in my ~)	**зеделларг**	[zedel:arg]
trend (tendency)	**тенденци**	[tendentsi]
development	**кхиам**	[qiam]

105. Business processes. Part 2

profit (benefit)	**пайда**	[pajda]
profitable	**пайдан**	[pajdan]
delegation (group)	**векалш**	[wekalʃ]
salary	**белхан алапа**	[belhan alapa]
to correct (vt)	**нисдан**	[nisdan]
business trip	**командировка**	[kɔmandirɔvka]
commission	**комисси**	[kɔmis:i]
to control (vt)	**тlехьажа**	[thehaʒa]
conference	**конференци**	[kɔnferentsi]
license	**лицензи**	[litsenzi]
reliable (trustworthy)	**тешаме**	[teʃame]
initiative (new project etc.)	**дlадолор**	[deadɔlɔr]
norm (standard)	**барам**	[baram]
circumstance	**хьал**	[hal]
duty (of employee)	**декхар**	[deqar]
enterprise	**организаци**	[ɔrganizatsi]
organization (process)	**вовшахтохар**	[vɔvʃahtɔhar]
organized	**вовшахкхетта**	[vɔvʃahqet:a]
cancellation (calling off)	**дlадаккхар**	[deadak:ar]
to cancel (call off)	**дlадаккха**	[deadak:a]
report (e.g., official ~)	**отчёт**	[ɔʧɜt]
patent	**патент**	[patent]
to patent (obtain patent)	**патент ян**	[patent jan]
to plan (vi, vt)	**план хlотто**	[plan hɔt:ɔ]
bonus (money)	**совгlат**	[sɔvɣat]

| professional | корматаллин | [kɔrmatal:in] |
| procedure | кеп | [kep] |

to examine (contract etc.)	къасто	[qhastɔ]
calculation	ларар	[larar]
reputation	репутаци	[reputatsi]
risk	кхерам	[qeram]

to manage (business etc.)	куьйгалл3 дан	[kyjgal:z dan]
information	хабар	[habar]
property	долалла	[dɔlal:a]
union (association, group)	барт	[bart]

life insurance	дахаран страховани яр	[daharan strahovani jar]
to insure (vt)	страховани ян	[strahovani jan]
insurance	страховка	[strahovka]

auction	кхайкхош дохкар	[qajqɔʃ dɔhkar]
to notify (inform)	д1ахаийта	[dəahai:ta]
management (process)	лелор	[lelɔr]
service (in shop, hotel)	г1уллакх	[ɣul:aq]

forum	гулам	[gulam]
to function (vi)	болх бан	[bɔlh ban]
stage (phase)	мур	[mur]
legal	юридически	[juriditʃeski]
lawyer (legal expert)	юрист	[jurist]

106. Production. Works

plant	завод	[zavɔd]
factory	фабрика	[fabrika]
workshop	цех	[tseh]
production site	производство	[prɔizvɔdstvɔ]

industry	промышленность	[prɔmɪʃlenɔstʲ]
industrial	промышленни	[prɔmɪʃleɲi]
heavy industry	еза промышленность	[eza prɔmɪʃlenɔstʲ]
light industry	яйн промышленность	[jajn prɔmɪʃlenɔstʲ]

products	сурсат	[sursat]
to produce (vt)	дан	[dan]
raw materials	аьргалла	[ærgal:a]

foreman	бригадир	[brigadir]
workers team	бригада	[brigada]
worker	белхало	[belhalɔ]

| workday | белхан де | [belhan de] |
| pause | сада1ар | [sadaəar] |

| meeting | гулам | [gulam] |
| to discuss (~ a problem) | дийцаре дилла | [di:tsare dil:a] |

plan	план	[plan]
to fulfill the plan	план кхочушян	[plan qotʃuʃan]
rate (of output)	барам	[baram]
quality	дикалла	[dikal:a]
checking (control)	контроль	[kontroʎ]
quality control	дикаллан контроль	[dikal:an kontroʎ]

| safety of work | белхан кхерамзалла | [belhan qeramzal:a] |
| discipline | низам | [nizam] |

| violation (of rules) | дохор | [dohor] |
| to violate (vt) | дохо | [doho] |

| strike | забастовка | [zabastovka] |
| striker | забастовкахо | [zabastovkaho] |

| to be on strike | забастовка ян | [zabastovka jan] |
| labor union | профсоюз | [profsojuz] |

to invent (machine etc.)	кхолла	[qol:a]
invention	кхоллар	[qol:ar]
research	таллар	[tal:ar]
to improve (make better)	тадан	[tadan]

| technology | технологи | [tehnologi] |
| technical drawing | чертёж | [tʃertɜʒ] |

load, cargo	мохь	[moh]
loader (person)	киранча	[kirantʃa]
to load (vehicle etc.)	тӏедотта	[thedot:a]
loading (process)	тӏедоттар	[thedot:ar]

| to unload (vi, vt) | дассо | [das:ɔ] |
| unloading | дассор | [das:ɔr] |

transportation	транспорт	[transport]
transportation company	транспортан компани	[transportan kompani]
to transport (vt)	дӏакхехьа	[dəaqeha]

freight car	вагон	[vagon]
cistern	цистерна	[tsisterna]
truck	киранийн машина	[kirani:n maʃina]

| machine tool | станок | [stanɔk] |
| mechanism | механизм | [mehanizm] |

industrial waste	даххаш	[dahaʃ]
packing (process)	дӏахьарчор	[dəahartʃɔr]
to pack (vt)	дӏахьарчо	[dəahartʃɔ]

107. Contract. Agreement

contract	чIарlам	[tʃhaɣam]
agreement	барт	[bart]
addendum	тIедалар	[thedalar]

to sign a contract	чIарlам бан	[tʃhaɣam ban]
signature	куьг	[kyg]
to sign (vt)	куьг таlо	[kyg taəɔ]
stamp (on document)	мухlар	[muhar]

subject (of contract)	договаран хlума	[dɔgɔvaran huma]
clause	пункт	[puŋkt]
parties (in contract)	аrlонаш	[aɣɔnaʃ]
legal address	юридически адрес	[juriditʃeski adres]

to break the contract	контракт дохо	[kɔntrakt dɔho]
commitment	тlелацам	[thelatsam]
responsibility	жоьпалла	[ʒøpal:a]
force majeure	форс-мажор	[fɔrs maʒɔr]
dispute	къовсам	[qhɔvsam]
penalties	гlуданан санкциш	[ɣudanan saŋktsiʃ]

108. Import & Export

import (activity)	импорт	[impɔrt]
importer	импортхо	[impɔrtho]
to import (vt)	импорт ян	[impɔrt jan]
import (e.g., ~ goods)	импортан	[impɔrtan]

exporter	экспортхо	[ɛkspɔrtho]
to export (vi, vt)	экспорт ян	[ɛkspɔrt jan]

goods	товар	[tɔvar]
load (e.g., carload)	жут	[ʒut]
weight	дозалла	[dɔzal:a]
volume	дукхалла	[duqal:a]
cubic meter	кубически метр	[kubitʃeski metr]

manufacturer	арахоьцург	[arahøtsurg]
transportation company	транспортан компани	[transpɔrtan kɔmpani]
container (for cargo)	контейнер	[kɔntejner]

border (boundary)	доза	[dɔza]
customs	таможни	[tamɔʒni]
customs duty	таможнин ял	[tamɔʒnin jal]
customs officer	таможхо	[tamɔʒho]
smuggling	контрабанда	[kɔntrabanda]
contraband (goods)	контрабанда	[kɔntrabanda]

109. Finances

share, stock	акци	[aktsi]
bond (certificate)	облигаци	[ɔbligatsi]
bill of exchange	вексель	[wekseʎ]
stock exchange	биржа	[birʒa]
stock price	акцин мах	[aktsin mah]
to become cheaper	дайдала	[dajdala]
to rise in price	даздала	[dazdala]
controlling interest	контролан пакет	[kɔntrɔlan paket]
investment	инвестици	[inwestitsi]
to invest (vi, vt)	инвестици ян	[inwestitsi jan]
percent	процент	[prɔtsent]
interest (on investment)	ял	[jal]
profit	пайда	[pajda]
profitable	пайде	[pajde]
tax	налог	[nalɔg]
currency (foreign ~)	валюта	[valyta]
national	къаьмнийн	[qhæmni:n]
exchange (of currency)	хийцар	[hi:tsar]
accountant	бухгалтер	[buhgalter]
accounts department	бухгалтери	[buhgalteri]
bankruptcy	банкрот хилар	[baŋkrɔt hilar]
collapse, crash	хӀаллакъхилар	[hal:aqhilar]
ruin	даькъаздаккхар	[dæqhazdak:ar]
to be ruined	даькъаздала	[dæqhazdala]
inflation	инфляци	[infʎatsi]
devaluation	девальваци	[devaʎvatsi]
capital	капитал	[kapital]
income	пайда	[pajda]
turnover	го баккхар	[gɔ bak:ar]
resources	тӀаьхьалонаш	[thæhalɔnaʃ]
monetary resources	ахча	[ahtʃa]
to reduce (expenses)	жимдан	[ʒimdan]

110. Marketing

marketing	маркетинг	[marketiŋ]
market	рынок	[rɪnɔk]
market segment	рынкан сегмент	[rɪŋkan segment]
product	сурсат	[sursat]

goods	товар	[tɔvar]
brand	механ марка, бренд	[mehan marka], [brend]
logotype	фирмин хьаьрк	[firmin hærk]
logo	логотип	[lɔgɔtip]

demand	хьашт хилар	[haʃt hilar]
offer	предложени	[predlɔʒeni]
need	хьашто	[haʃtɔ]
consumer	хьаштхо	[haʃtho]

analysis	анализ	[analiz]
to analyze (vt)	анализ ян	[analiz jan]
positioning	позиционировани	[pɔzitsiɔnirɔvani]
to position (product)	позиционировать ян	[pɔzitsiɔnirɔvatʲ jan]

price	мах	[mah]
pricing policy	механ политика	[mehan pɔlitika]
pricing	мах хилар	[mah hilar]

111. Advertising

advertising	реклама	[reklama]
to advertise (vt)	реклама ян	[reklama jan]
budget	бюджет	[bydʒet]

ad, advertisement	кхайкхор	[qajqɔr]
TV advertising	телереклама	[telereklama]
radio advertising	радион реклама	[radiɔn reklama]
outdoor advertising	арахьара реклама	[arahara reklama]

mass media	массийн хааман гӏирс	[mas:i:n ha:man ɣirs]
periodical (noun)	муьран арахецнарг	[myran arahetsnarg]
image (public appearance)	имидж	[imidʒ]

slogan	лозунг	[lɔzuŋ]
motto (maxim)	девиз	[dewiz]

campaign	кампани	[kampani]
advertising campaign	рекламан кампани	[reklaman kampani]
target group	Ӏалашонан аудитори	[ʔalaʃɔnan auditɔri]

business card	визитан карта	[wizitan karta]
leaflet	кехат	[kehat]
brochure	брошюра	[brɔʃyra]
pamphlet	буклет	[buklet]
newsletter	бюллетень	[byl:eteɲ]

sign (on shop, bar etc.)	гойтург	[gɔjturg]
poster	плакат	[plakat]
billboard	рекламан у	[reklaman u]

112. Banking

bank	банк	[baŋk]
branch (of bank etc.)	отделени	[ɔtdeleni]
consultant	консультант	[kɔnsuʌtant]
manager (boss)	урхалхо	[urhalho]
banking account	счёт	[stʃɔt]
account number	чотан номер	[tʃɔtan nɔmer]
checking account	карара чот	[karara tʃɔt]
savings account	накопительни чот	[nakɔpiteʌni tʃɔt]
to open an account	чот схьайелла	[tʃɔt shajel:a]
to close the account	чот дӀакъовла	[tʃɔt dəqhɔvla]
to deposit (vt)	счёт тӀедилла	[stʃɔt thedil:a]
to withdraw (vt)	счёт тӀера схьаэца	[stʃɔt thera shaetsa]
deposit	диллар	[dil:ar]
to make a deposit	дилла	[dil:a]
wire transfer	дахьийтар	[dahi:tar]
to wire (money)	дахьийта	[dahi:ta]
sum (amount of money)	жамӀ	[ʒamə]
How much?	Мел?	[mel]
signature	куьг	[kyg]
to sign (vt)	куьг тӀало	[kyg taəɔ]
credit card	кредитан карта	[kreditan karta]
code	код	[kɔd]
credit card number	кредитан картан номер	[kreditan kartan nɔmer]
ATM	банкомат	[baŋkɔmat]
check	чек	[tʃek]
to write a check	чек язъян	[tʃek jazʰjan]
checkbook	чекан книшка	[tʃekan kniʃka]
loan (bank ~)	кредит	[kredit]
to ask for a loan	кредит дехар	[kredit dehar]
to take a loan	кредит эца	[kredit ɛtsa]
to grant a credit	кредит далар	[kredit dalar]
guarantee	юкъархилар	[juqharhilar]

113. Telephone. Phone conversation

telephone	телефон	[telefɔn]
mobile phone	мобильни телефон	[mɔbiʌni telefɔn]
answering machine	автоответчик	[avto:twetʃik]

| to call (telephone) | детта | [det:a] |
| phone call | горгали | [gɔrgali] |

to dial a number	номер эца	[nɔmer ɛtsa]
Hello!	Алло!	[al:ɔ]
to ask (vi, vt)	хатта	[hat:a]
to answer (vi, vt)	жоп дала	[ʒɔp dala]

to hear (vi, vt)	хаза	[haza]
well	дика ду	[dika du]
not good, bad (adv)	вон ду	[vɔn du]
noises	новкъарлонаш	[nɔvqharlɔnaʃ]

receiver	луьлла	[lyl:a]
to pick up (~ the phone)	луьлла эца	[lyl:a ɛtsa]
to hang up (~ the phone)	луьлла охьайилла	[lyl:a ɔhajıl:a]

busy	мукъа доцу	[muqha dɔtsu]
to ring (about phone)	етта	[et:a]
telephone book	телефонан книга	[telefɔnan kniga]

local call	меттигара	[met:igara]
international call	гӏаланашна юккъера горгали	[ɣalanaʃna jukqhera gɔrgali]
international	гӏаланашна юккъера	[ɣalanaʃna jukqhera]

114. Mobile telephone

mobile phone	мобильни телефон	[mɔbiʎni telefɔn]
display	дисплей	[displej]
button	кнопка	[knɔpka]
SIM card	SIM-карта	[sim karta]

battery	батарей	[batarej]
to be dead (battery)	кхачадала	[qatʃadala]
charger	юзаран гӏирс	[juzaran ɣirs]

menu	меню	[meny]
settings	настройкаш	[nastrɔjkaʃ]
tune (melody)	мукъам	[muqham]
to choose (select)	харжа	[harʒa]

| calculator | калькулятор | [kaʎkuʎatɔr] |
| answering machine | автоответчик | [avto:twetʃik] |

| alarm clock | сомавоккху сахьт | [sɔmavɔk:u saht] |
| contacts | телефонан книга | [telefɔnan kniga] |

| SMS (text message) | SMS-хаам | [ɛsɛmɛs ha:m] |
| subscriber | абонент | [abɔnent] |

115. Stationery

ballpoint pen	авторучка	[avtɔrutʃka]
fountain pen	перо	[perɔ]
pencil	къолам	[qhɔlam]
highlighter	маркер	[marker]
felt-tip pen	фломастер	[flɔmaster]
notepad	блокнот	[blɔknɔt]
datebook	ежедневник	[eʒednevnik]
ruler	линейка	[linejka]
calculator	калькулятор	[kaʎkuʎatɔr]
eraser	лаьстиг	[læstig]
thumbtack	кнопка	[knɔpka]
paper clip	маlap	[maɵar]
glue	клей	[klej]
stapler	степлер	[stepler]
hole punch	lуьргашдохург	[əyrgaʃdɔhurg]
pencil sharpener	точилк	[tɔtʃilk]
pointer	гайтаргlа	[gajtarɣa]
card index	картотека	[kartɔteka]
label	этикетка	[ɛtiketka]

116. Various kinds of documents

account (report)	отчёт	[ɔtʃət]
agreement	барт	[bart]
application form	дlахьедар	[dəahedar]
authentic	бакъ долу	[baqh dɔlu]
badge (identity tag)	бэдж	[bɛdʒ]
business card	визитан карта	[wizitan karta]
certificate (~ of quality)	сертификат	[sertifikat]
check (e.g., draw a ~)	чек	[tʃek]
check (in restaurant)	счёт	[stʃɔt]
constitution	конституци	[kɔnstitutsi]
contract	чlарlам	[tʃhaɣam]
copy	копи	[kɔpi]
copy (of contract etc.)	экземпляр	[ɛkzempʎar]
declaration	деклараци	[deklaratsi]
document	документ	[dɔkument]
driver's license	лелорхочун бакъонаш	[lelɔrhɔtʃun baqhɔnaʃ]
attachment (to the contract)	тlедалар	[thedalar]

form	анкета	[aŋketa]
identity card, ID	тешалла	[teʃal:a]
inquiry (request)	жоп дехар	[ʒɔp dehar]
invitation	кхойкху билет	[qɔjqu bilet]
invoice	чот	[tʃ̇ot]

law	закон	[zakɔn]
letter (mail)	кехат	[kehat]
letterhead	бланк	[blaŋk]
list (of names etc.)	список	[spisɔk]
manuscript	куьйгайоза	[kyjgajoza]
newsletter	бюллетень	[byl:eteɲ]
note (short letter)	кехат	[kehat]

pass (for worker, visitor)	пропуск	[prɔpusk]
passport	паспорт	[paspɔrt]
permit	бакъо	[baqhɔ]
résumé	резюме	[rezyme]
debt note, iou	куьг яздар	[kyg jazdar]
receipt (for purchase etc.)	квитанци	[kwitantsi]
sales slip (receipt)	чек	[tʃ̇ek]
report	рапорт	[rapɔrt]

to show (ID etc.)	дІакховдо	[deaqovdɔ]
to sign (vt)	куьг таІо	[kyg taeɔ]
signature	куьг	[kyg]
stamp (on document)	мухІар	[muhar]
text	текст	[tekst]
ticket (for entry)	билет	[bilet]

| to cross out | дІадайа | [deadaja] |
| to fill out (~ a form etc.) | яздан | [jazdan] |

| waybill | накладной | [nakladnɔj] |
| will | весет | [weset] |

117. Kinds of business

accounting services	бухгалтерин гІуллакхаш	[buhgalterin ɣul:aqaʃ]
advertising	реклама	[reklama]
advertising agency	рекламан агенталла	[reklaman agental:a]
air-conditioners	кондиционераш	[kɔnditsiɔneraʃ]
airline	авиакомпани	[awiakɔmpani]

alcoholic drinks	спиртан маларш	[spirtan malarʃ]
antiques	антиквариат	[antikvariat]
art gallery	галерей	[galerej]
audit services	аудитаран гІуллакхаш	[auditaran ɣul:aqaʃ]
banks	банкан бизнес	[baŋkan biznes]

bar	**бар**	[bar]
beauty parlor	**хазаллан салон**	[hazal:an salɔn]
bookstore	**книшкийн туька**	[kniʃki:n tyka]
brewery	**йийн доккху меттиг**	[ji:n dɔk:u met:ig]
business center	**бизнес-центр**	[biznes tsentr]
business school	**бизнес-школа**	[biznes ʃkɔla]
casino	**казино**	[kazinɔ]
construction	**гӀишло яр**	[ɣiʃlɔ jar]
consulting	**консалтинг**	[kɔnsaltiŋ]
dentistry	**стоматологи**	[stɔmatɔlɔgi]
design	**дизайн**	[dizajn]
drugstore, pharmacy	**аптека**	[apteka]
dry cleaners	**химцӀандар**	[himtʃhandar]
employment agency	**кадрашха агенталла**	[kadraʃha agental:a]
financial services	**финансийн гӀуллакхаш**	[finansi:n ɣul:aqaʃ]
food (industry)	**сурсаташ**	[sursataʃ]
funeral home	**велчан ламаста ден бюро**	[weltʃan lamasta den byrɔ]
furniture (for house)	**мебель**	[mebeʎ]
garment	**бедар**	[bedar]
hotel	**хьешийн цӀа**	[heʃi:n tsha]
ice-cream	**морожени**	[mɔrɔʒeni]
industry	**промышленность**	[prɔmɪʃleŋɔstʲ]
insurance	**страхована**	[strahovana]
Internet	**интернет**	[internet]
investment	**инвестици**	[inwestitsi]
jeweler	**ювелир**	[juwelir]
jewelry	**ювелиран хӀуманаш**	[juweliran humanaʃ]
laundry (room, shop)	**прачечни**	[pratʃetʃni]
legal advisor	**юридически гӀуллакхаш**	[juriditʃeski ɣul:aqaʃ]
light industry	**яйн промышленность**	[jajn prɔmɪʃleŋɔstʲ]
magazine	**журнал**	[ʒurnal]
mail-order selling	**каталог тӀехула махлелор**	[katalog thehula mahlelɔr]
medicine	**медицина**	[meditsina]
movie theater	**кинотеатр**	[kinɔteatr]
museum	**музей**	[muzej]
news agency	**информацин агенталла**	[infɔrmatsin agental:a]
newspaper	**газета**	[gazeta]
nightclub	**буьйсанан клуб**	[byjsanan klub]
oil (petroleum)	**нефть**	[neftʲ]
parcels service	**курьеран гӀуллакх**	[kurjeran ɣul:aq]
pharmaceuticals	**фармацевтика**	[farmatsevtika]

| printing (industry) | полиграфи | [poligrafi] |
| publishing house | издательство | [izdateʌstvɔ] |

radio	радио	[radiɔ]
real estate	ара-чу ца баккхалун бахам	[ara ʧu tsa bak:alun baham]
restaurant	ресторан	[restɔran]

security agency	ха ден агенталла	[ha den agental:a]
sports	спорт	[spɔrt]
stock exchange	биржа	[birʒa]
store	туька	[tyka]
supermarket	супермаркет	[supermarket]
swimming pool	бассейн	[bas:ejn]

tailors	ателье	[ateʌje]
television	телевидени	[telewideni]
theater	театр	[teatr]
trade	махлелор	[mahlelor]
transportation	дӏадахьарш	[dəadaharʃ]
travel	туризм	[turizm]

veterinarian	ветеринар	[weterinar]
warehouse	склад	[sklad]
waste management	нехаш аракхехьар	[nehaʃ araqehar]

Job. Business. Part 2

118. Show. Exhibition

exhibition, show	гайтам	[gajtam]
trade show	махбаран гайта хӏоттор	[mahbaran gajta hɔt:ɔr]
participation	дакъа лацар	[daqha latsar]
to participate (vi)	дакъа лаца	[daqha latsa]
participant	декъашхо	[deqhaʃho]
director	директор	[direktɔr]
organizer's office	дирекци, оргкомитет	[direktsi], [ɔrgkɔmitet]
organizer	вовшахтохархо	[vɔvʃahtɔharhɔ]
to organize (vt)	вовшахтоха	[vɔvʃahtɔha]
participation form	дакъа лацар дӏахьедан	[daqha latsar dɘahedan]
to fill out (vt)	яздан	[jazdan]
details	деталаш	[detalaʃ]
information	хаам	[ha:m]
price	мах	[mah]
including	тӏехь	[theh]
to include (vt)	юкъадало	[juqhadalɔ]
to pay (vi, vt)	ахча дала	[ahtʃa dala]
registration fee	регистрацин ахча далар	[registratsin ahtʃa dalar]
entrance	чуглойла	[tʃuɣɔjla]
pavilion, hall	павильон	[pawiʎɔn]
to register (vt)	регистраци ян	[registratsi jan]
badge (identity tag)	бэдж	[bɛdʒ]
booth, stand	гайтаман стенд	[gajtaman stend]
to reserve, to book	бронь ян	[brɔɲ jan]
display case	витрина	[witrina]
spotlight	къуьда	[qhyda]
design	дизайн	[dizajn]
to place (put, set)	хила	[hila]
distributor	дистрибьютор	[distribjytɔr]
supplier	латторг	[lat:ɔrg]
country	мохк	[mɔhk]
foreign	кхечу мехкан	[qetʃu mehkan]

product	сурсат	[sursat]
association (grouping)	цхьаьнакхетар	[tshænaqetar]
conference hall	конференц-зал	[kɔnferents zal]
congress	конгресс	[kɔŋres:]
contest (competition)	конкурс	[kɔŋkurs]
visitor	оьхург	[øhurg]
to visit (vi, vt)	хьажа даха	[haʒa daha]
customer	заказхо	[zakazho]

119. Mass Media

newspaper	газета	[gazeta]
magazine	журнал	[ʒurnal]
press (printed media)	пресса	[pres:a]
radio	радио	[radiɔ]
radio station	радиостанци	[radiɔstantsi]
television	телевидени	[telewideni]
anchorman	телевиденин ведущий	[telewidenin weduçi:]
newscaster	дитктор	[ditktɔr]
commentator	комментархо	[kɔm:entarhɔ]
journalist	журналист	[ʒurnalist]
correspondent (reporter)	корреспондент	[kor:espɔndent]
press photographer	фотокорреспондент	[fɔtɔkor:espɔndent]
reporter	репортёр	[repɔrtɜr]
editor	редактор	[redaktɔr]
editor-in-chief	коьрта редактор	[kørta redaktɔr]
to subscribe to …	яздала	[jazdala]
subscription	яздар	[jazdar]
subscriber	язвалархо	[jazvalarhɔ]
to read (vi, vt)	еша	[eʃa]
reader	ешархо	[eʃarhɔ]
circulation (of newspaper)	тираж	[tiraʒ]
monthly	хlоп беттан	[hɔr bet:an]
weekly (adj)	хlоп кlиранан	[hɔr k:iranan]
issue (edition)	номер	[nɔmer]
recent (new)	керла	[kerla]
headline	корта	[kɔrta]
short article	билгало	[bilgalɔ]
column (regular article)	рубрика	[rubrika]
article	статья	[statja]
page	аrlо	[aɣɔ]
reportage, report	репортаж	[repɔrtaʒ]
event	хилларг	[hil:arg]

sensation (news)	сенсаци	[sensatsi]
scandal	дов	[dɔv]
scandalous	девне	[devne]
great (e.g., ~ scandal)	чlорla	[ʧhɔɣa]

program	передача	[peredatʃa]
interview	интервью	[intervjy]
live broadcast	дуьххьал трансляци	[dyhal transʌatsi]
channel	канал	[kanal]

120. Agriculture

agriculture	юртан бахам	[jurtan baham]
peasant (man)	ахархо	[aharhɔ]
peasant (woman)	ахархо	[aharhɔ]
farmer	фермер	[fermer]

| tractor | трактор | [traktɔr] |
| combine, harvester | комбайн | [kɔmbajn] |

plow	гота	[gɔta]
to plow (vi, vt)	аха	[aha]
plowland	охана	[ɔhana]
furrow (in field)	харш	[harʃ]

to sow (vi, vt)	ден	[den]
seeder	хlутосург	[hutɔsurg]
sowing (process)	дlадер	[dəader]

| scythe | мангал | [maɳal] |
| to mow, to scythe | мангал хьакха | [maɳal haqa] |

| shovel (tool) | бел | [bel] |
| to dig (vi, vt) | ахка | [ahka] |

hoe	метиг	[metig]
to hoe, to weed	асар дан	[asar dan]
weed (plant)	асар	[asar]

watering can	хитухург	[hituhurg]
to water (plants)	хи тоха	[hi tɔha]
watering (act)	хи тохар	[hi tɔhar]

| pitchfork | шада | [ʃada] |
| rake | кагтуха | [kagtuha] |

fertilizer	удобрени	[udɔbreni]
to fertilize (vt)	удобрени тасар	[udɔbreni tasar]
manure (fertilizer)	кхелли	[qel:i]
field	аре	[are]

meadow	бай	[baj]
vegetable garden	хасбеш	[hasbeʃ]
orchard (e.g., apple ~)	хасбеш	[hasbeʃ]

to herd (livestock)	дажо	[daʒɔ]
herdsman	ly	[əu]
pastureland	дежийла	[deʒi:la]

| cattle breeding | даьхнилелор | [dæhnilelɔr] |
| sheep farming | жалелор | [ʒalelɔr] |

plantation	плантаци	[plantatsi]
row (garden bed ~s)	хесалг	[hesalg]
greenhouse	парник	[parnik]
hothouse	теплица	[teplitsa]

| drought (lack of rain) | йокъо | [jɔqhɔ] |
| dry (~ summer) | йокъо хӀутту | [jɔqhɔ hut:u] |

| cereal plants | буьртиган | [byrtigan] |
| to harvest, to gather | буьртигаш долу | [byrtigaʃ dɔlu] |

miller (person)	хьархо	[harhɔ]
mill (e.g., gristmill)	хьера	[hera]
to grind (grain)	ахьа	[aha]
flour	дама	[dama]
straw	ча	[ʧa]

121. Building. Building process

construction site	гӀишлош йойла	[ɣiʃloʃ jojla]
to build (vt)	дан	[dan]
construction worker	гӀишлошъярхо	[ɣiʃloʃjarhɔ]

project	проект	[prɔekt]
architect	архитектор	[arhitektɔr]
worker	белхало	[belhalɔ]

foundation (of building)	бух	[buh]
roof	тхов	[thov]
pile (foundation ~)	бӀорлам	[bəɣam]
wall	пен	[pen]

| reinforcing bars | арматура | [armatura] |
| scaffolding | гӀоьнан ламеш | [ɣønan lameʃ] |

concrete	бетон	[betɔn]
granite	гранит	[granit]
stone	тӀулг	[thulg]
brick	кибарчиг	[kibarʧig]

sand	гIум	[ɣum]
cement	цемент	[ʦement]
plaster (for walls)	хьахар	[hahar]
to plaster (vt)	хьаха	[haha]
paint	басар	[basar]
to paint (e.g., ~ a wall)	басар хьакха	[basar haqa]
barrel	боьшка	[bøʃka]

crane	чIинт	[ʧhint]
to lift (vt)	хьалаайар	[hala:jar]
to lower (vt)	дIахеца	[dəahetsa]

bulldozer	бульдозер	[buʎdozer]
excavator	экскаватор	[ɛkskavator]
scoop, bucket	кхимар	[qimar]
to dig (excavate)	ахка	[ahka]
hard hat	каска	[kaska]

122. Science. Research. Scientists

science	Iилма	[əilma]
scientific	Iилманан	[əilmanan]
scientist	дешна	[deʃna]
theory	теори	[teori]

axiom	аксиома	[aksioma]
analysis	анализ	[analiz]
to analyze (vt)	анализ ян	[analiz jan]
argument (reasoning)	аргумент	[argument]
substance (matter)	хIума	[huma]

hypothesis	гипотеза	[gipoteza]
dilemma	дилемма	[dilem:a]
dissertation	диссертаци	[dis:ertaʦi]
dogma	догма	[dogma]

doctrine	доктрина	[doktrina]
research	таллар	[tal:ar]
to do research	талла	[tal:a]
testing	контроль	[kontroʎ]
laboratory	лаборатори	[laboratori]

method	некъ	[neqh]
molecule	молекула	[molekula]
monitoring	мониторинг	[monitoriŋ]
discovery (act, event)	гучудаккхар	[guʧudak:ar]

postulate	постулат	[postulat]
principle	принцип	[prinʦip]
forecast	прогноз	[prognoz]

to forecast (vt)	прогноз ян	[prɔgnɔz jan]
synthesis	синтез	[sintez]
trend (tendency)	тенденци	[tendentsi]
theorem	теорема	[teɔrema]
teachings	хьехар	[hehar]
fact	хилларг	[hilːarg]
expedition (to go on an ~)	экспедици	[ɛkspeditsi]
experiment	эксперимент	[ɛksperiment]
academician	академик	[akademik]
bachelor (e.g., ~ of Arts)	бакалавр	[bakalavr]
doctor (PhD)	доктор	[dɔktɔr]
Associate Professor	доцент	[dɔtsent]
Master (e.g., ~ of Arts)	магистр	[magistr]
professor	профессор	[prɔfesːɔr]

Professions and occupations

123. Job search. Dismissal

job	болх	[bɔlh]
personnel, staff	персонал	[persɔnal]
career	карьера	[karjera]
prospect	перспектива	[perspektiva]
skills (expertise)	говзалла	[gɔvzal:a]
selection (for job)	харжар	[harʒar]
employment agency	кадрашха агенталла	[kadraʃha agental:a]
résumé	резюме	[rezyme]
interview (for job)	къамел дар	[qhamel dar]
vacancy, opening	ваканси	[vakansi]
salary, pay	алапа	[alapa]
fixed pay	алапа	[alapa]
pay, compensation	алапа далар	[alapa dalar]
position (job)	гӀуллакх	[ɣul:aq]
duty (of employee)	декхар	[deqar]
range of duties	нах	[nah]
busy	мукъаза	[muqhaza]
to fire (dismiss)	дӀадаккха	[dəadak:a]
dismissal	дӀадаккхар	[dəadak:ar]
unemployment	белхазалла	[belhazal:a]
unemployed (noun)	белхазхо	[belhazho]
retirement	пенси	[pensi]
to retire (from job)	пенси ваха	[pensi vaha]

124. Business people

director	директор	[direktɔr]
manager (director)	урхалхо	[urhalho]
boss	куьйгалхо, шеф	[kyjgalho], [ʃef]
superior	хьаькам	[hækam]
management	хьаькамаш	[hækamaʃ]
president	паччахь	[patʃah]
chairman	председатель	[predsedateʎ]
deputy (substitute)	когаметтаниг	[kɔgamet:anig]

assistant	гӀоьнча	[ɣønʧa]
secretary	секретарь	[sekretarʲ]
personal assistant	долахь волу секретарь	[dɔlah vɔlu sekretarʲ]
businessman	бизнесхо	[biznesho]
entrepreneur	хьуьнарча	[hynarʧa]
founder	диллинарг	[dil:inarg]
to found (vt)	дилла	[dil:a]
associate	кхолларохо	[qɔl:arhɔ]
partner	декъашхо	[deqhaʃho]
shareholder	акци ерг	[aktsi erg]
millionaire	миллионхо	[mil:iɔnho]
billionaire	миллиардхо	[mil:iardho]
owner	да	[da]
landowner	лаьттада	[læt:ada]
customer	заказхо	[zakazho]
client	клиент	[klient]
regular client	даимлера клиент	[daimlera klient]
buyer (customer)	эцархо	[ɛtsarhɔ]
visitor	оьхург	[øhurg]
professional (noun)	говзанча	[gɔvzanʧa]
expert	эксперт	[ɛkspert]
specialist	говзанча	[gɔvzanʧa]
banker	банкир	[baŋkir]
broker	брокер	[brɔker]
cashier, teller	кассир	[kas:ir]
accountant	бухгалтер	[buhgalter]
security guard	хехо	[heho]
investor	инвестор	[inwestɔr]
debtor	декхархо	[deqarhɔ]
creditor	кредитор	[kreditɔr]
borrower	декхархо	[deqarhɔ]
importer	импортхо	[impɔrtho]
exporter	экспортхо	[ɛkspɔrtho]
manufacturer	арахоьцург	[arahøtsurg]
distributor	дистрибьютор	[distribjytɔr]
middleman	юкъарлонча	[juqharlɔnʧa]
consultant	консультант	[kɔnsuʎtant]
representative	векал	[wekal]
agent	агент	[agent]
insurance agent	страховкин агент	[strahovkin agent]

125. Service professions

cook	кхачанхо	[qatʃanho]
chef	шеф-кхачанхо	[ʃəf qatʃanho]
baker	пурнхо	[purnho]
bartender	бармен	[barmen]
waiter	официант	[ɔfitsiant]
waitress	официантка	[ɔfitsiantka]
lawyer, attorney	хьехамча	[hehamtʃa]
lawyer (legal expert)	юрист	[jurist]
notary	нотариус	[nɔtarius]
electrician	монтер	[mɔnter]
plumber	сантехник	[santehnik]
carpenter	дечиг-пхьар	[detʃig phar]
masseur	массажхо	[mas:aʒho]
masseuse	массажхо	[mas:aʒho]
doctor	лор	[lɔr]
taxi driver	таксист	[taksist]
driver	шофер	[ʃɔfer]
courier	курьер	[kurjer]
chambermaid	хlусамча	[husamtʃa]
security guard	хехо	[heho]
flight attendant	стюардесса	[styardes:a]
teacher (in primary school)	хьехархо	[heharhɔ]
librarian	библиотекахо	[bibliɔtekaho]
translator	талмаж	[talmaʒ]
interpreter	талмаж	[talmaʒ]
guide (person)	гид	[gid]
hairdresser	парикмахер	[parikmaher]
mailman	почтальон	[pɔtʃtaʎɔn]
salesman	йохкархо	[johkarhɔ]
gardener	бешахо	[beʃaho]
servant (in household)	ялхо	[jalho]
maid	ялхо	[jalho]
cleaner (cleaning lady)	цlанонча	[tshanɔntʃa]

126. Military professions and ranks

private	могlарера	[mɔɣarera]
sergeant	сержант	[serʒant]

lieutenant	лейтенант	[lejtenant]
captain	капитан	[kapitan]
major	майор	[major]
colonel	полковник	[pɔlkovnik]
general	инарла	[inarla]
marshal	маршал	[marʃal]
admiral	адмирал	[admiral]
military man	тӏеман	[theman]
soldier	салти	[salti]
officer	эпсар	[ɛpsar]
commander	командир	[kɔmandir]
border guard	дозанхо	[dɔzanhо]
radio operator	радиохаамхо	[radioha:mho]
scout (searcher)	талламхо	[tal:amho]
pioneer (sapper)	сапёр	[sapɔr]
marksman	кхоссархо	[qɔs:arhɔ]
navigator	штурман	[ʃturman]

127. Officials. Priests

king	паччахь	[patʃah]
queen	зуда-паччахь	[zuda patʃah]
prince	принц	[prints]
princess	принцесса	[printses:a]
tsar, czar	паччахь	[patʃah]
czarina	зуда-паччахь	[zuda patʃah]
president	паччахь	[patʃah]
Secretary (~ of State)	министр	[ministr]
prime minister	примьер-министр	[primjer ministr]
senator	сенатхо	[senatho]
diplomat	дипломат	[diplɔmat]
consul	консул	[kɔnsul]
ambassador	векал	[wekal]
councelor, advisor	хьехамча	[hehamtʃa]
official (civil servant)	чиновник	[tʃinɔvnik]
prefect	префект	[prefekt]
mayor	мэр	[mɛr]
judge	суьдхо	[sydho]
district attorney	прокурор	[prɔkurɔr]
missionary	миссионер	[mis:iɔner]
monk	монах	[mɔnah]

abbot	аббат	[ab:at]
rabbi	равин	[rawin]
vizier	визирь	[wizirʲ]
shah	шах	[ʃah]
sheikh	шайх	[ʃajh]

128. Agricultural professions

beekeeper	накхарамозийлелорхо	[naqaramɔzi:lelɔrhɔ]
herdsman	ly	[əu]
agronomist	агроном	[agrɔnɔm]
cattle breeder	даьхнийлелорхо	[dæhni:lelɔrhɔ]
veterinarian	ветеринар	[weterinar]
farmer	фермер	[fermer]
winemaker	чаӀардоккхург	[ʧaɣardɔk:urg]
potter	куьпчи	[kypʧi]
zoologist	зоолог	[zo:lɔg]
cowboy	ковбой	[kɔvbɔj]

129. Art professions

actor	актёр	[aktɜr]
actress	актриса	[aktrisa]
singer (man)	эшархо	[ɛʃarhɔ]
singer (woman)	эшархо	[ɛʃarhɔ]
dancer (man)	хелхархо	[helharhɔ]
dancer (woman)	хелхархо	[helharhɔ]
performing artist (masc.)	артист	[artist]
performing artist (fem.)	артист	[artist]
musician	музыкант	[muzɪkant]
pianist	пианист	[pianist]
guitar player	гитарча	[gitarʧa]
conductor (of musicians)	дирижёр	[diriʒɜr]
composer	композитор	[kɔmpɔzitɔr]
impresario	импресарио	[impresariɔ]
movie director	режиссёр	[reʒis:ɜr]
producer	продюсер	[prɔdyser]
scriptwriter	сценарихо	[stsenariho]
critic	критик	[kritik]
writer	яздархо	[jazdarhɔ]

poet	илланча	[ilːantʃa]
sculptor	скульптор	[skuʌptor]
artist (painter)	исбаьхьалча	[isbæhaltʃa]

juggler	жонглёр	[ʒoŋlɜr]
clown	жухарг	[ʒuharg]
acrobat	пелхьо	[pelhɔ]
magician	бозбуунча	[bɔzbuːntʃa]

130. Various professions

doctor	лор	[lɔr]
nurse (in hospital)	лорйиша	[lɔrjɪʃa]
psychiatrist	психиатр	[psihiatr]
dentist	цергийн лор	[tsergiːn lɔr]
surgeon	хирург	[hirurg]

astronaut	астронавт	[astrɔnavt]
astronomer	астроном	[astrɔnɔm]
pilot	кеманхо	[kemanho]

driver (of car, taxi etc.)	лелорхо	[lelɔrhɔ]
engineer (train driver)	машинхо	[maʃinho]
mechanic	механик	[mehanik]

miner	кӏорабаккхархо	[kːɔrabakːarhɔ]
worker	белхало	[belhalɔ]
metalworker	слесарь	[slesarʲ]
joiner, carpenter	дечка пхьар	[detʃka phar]
turner	токарь	[tɔkarʲ]
construction worker	гӏишлошъярхо	[ɣiʃloʃʲjarhɔ]
welder	латорхо	[latɔrhɔ]

professor	профессор	[prɔfesːɔr]
architect	архитектор	[arhitektɔr]
historian	историк	[istɔrik]
scientist	дешна	[deʃna]
physicist	физик	[fizik]
chemist (scientist)	химик	[himik]

archeologist	археолог	[arheolɔg]
geologist	геолог	[geɔlɔg]
researcher	талламхо	[talːamhɔ]

| babysitter | баба | [baba] |
| teacher | хьехархо | [heharhɔ] |

editor	редактор	[redaktɔr]
editor-in-chief	коьрта редактор	[kørta redaktɔr]
correspondent	корреспондент	[kɔrːespɔndent]

typist (woman)	машинхо	[maʃinho]
designer	дизайнер	[dizajner]
computer expert	компьютерхо	[kɔmpjyterhɔ]
programmer	программист	[prɔgram:ist]
engineer (designer)	инженер	[inʒener]

seaman	хӀордахо	[hɔrdaho]
sailor	хӀордахо	[hɔrdaho]
rescuer	кӀелхьардакххархо	[k:elhardaqharhɔ]

fireman	цӀе йойу	[tshe joju]
policeman	полици	[pɔlitsi]
watchman	хехо	[heho]
detective	лахарча	[lahartʃa]

customs officer	таможхо	[tamɔʒho]
bodyguard	ларвархо	[larvarhɔ]
prison guard	набахтхо	[nabahtho]
inspector	инспектор	[inspektɔr]

sportsman	спортхо	[spɔrtho]
trainer, coach	тренер	[trener]
butcher	хасапхо	[hasapho]
cobbler	эткийн пхьар	[ɛtki:n phar]
businessman	совдегар	[sɔvdegar]
loader (person)	киранча	[kirantʃa]

| fashion designer | модельхо | [mɔdeʎho] |
| model (woman) | модель | [mɔdeʎ] |

131. Occupations. Social status

| schoolboy | школахо | [ʃkɔlaho] |
| student (college ~) | студент | [student] |

philosopher	философ	[filɔsɔf]
economist	экономист	[ɛkɔnɔmist]
inventor	кхоллархо	[qɔl:arhɔ]

unemployed (noun)	белхазхо	[belhazho]
retiree	пенсионер	[pensiɔner]
spy, secret agent	шпион	[ʃpiɔn]

prisoner	лаьцна стаг	[lætsna stag]
striker	забастовкахо	[zabastɔvkaho]
bureaucrat	бюрократ	[byrɔkrat]
traveler	некъахо	[neqhaho]

| homosexual | гомосексуализмхо | [gɔmɔseksualizmho] |
| hacker | хакер | [haker] |

bandit	**талорхо**	[talɔrhɔ]
hit man, killer	**йолах дийнарг**	[jolah di:narg]
drug addict	**наркоман**	[narkɔman]
drug dealer	**наркотикаш йохкархо**	[narkɔtikaʃ johkarhɔ]
prostitute (woman)	**кхахьпа**	[qahpa]
pimp	**сутенёр**	[sutenɜr]
sorcerer	**холмачхо**	[holmaʧho]
sorceress	**холмачхо**	[holmaʧho]
pirate	**пират**	[pirat]
slave	**лай**	[laj]
samurai	**самурай**	[samuraj]
savage (primitive)	**акха адам**	[aqa adam]

Sports

132. Kinds of sports. Sportspersons

sportsman	спортхо	[sportho]
kind of sports	спортан кеп	[sportan kep]
basketball	баскетбол	[basketbol]
basketball player	баскетболхо	[basketbolho]
baseball	бейсбол	[bejsbol]
baseball player	бейсболхо	[bejsbolho]
soccer	футбол	[futbol]
soccer player	футболхо	[futbolho]
goalkeeper	кевнахо	[kevnaho]
hockey	хоккей	[hok:ej]
hockey player	хоккейхо	[hok:ejho]
volleyball	волейбол	[volejbol]
volleyball player	волейболхо	[volejbolho]
boxing	бокс	[boks]
boxer	боксёр	[boksɜr]
wrestling	латар	[latar]
wrestler	латархо	[latarho]
karate	карате	[karate]
karate fighter	каратист	[karatist]
judo	дзюдо	[dʑydo]
judo athlete	дзюдоист	[dʑydoist]
tennis	теннис	[teɲis]
tennis player	теннисхо	[teɲisho]
swimming	нека	[neka]
swimmer	неканча	[nekantʃa]
fencing	фехтовани	[fehtovani]
fencer	фехтовальщик	[fehtovaʎɕik]
chess	шахматаш	[ʃahmataʃ]
chess player	шахматхо	[ʃahmatho]

| alpinism | альпинизм | [aʎpinizm] |
| alpinist | альпинист | [aʎpinist] |

| running | дадар | [dadar] |
| runner | идархо | [idarhɔ] |

| athletics | яйн атлетика | [jajn atletika] |
| athlete | атлет | [atlet] |

| horseback riding | говрийн спорт | [gɔvri:n spɔrt] |
| rider | бере | [bere] |

figure skating	куьцара хехкар	[kytsara hehkar]
figure skater (man)	фигурахо	[figuraho]
figure skater (woman)	фигурахо	[figuraho]

weightlifting	еза атлетика	[eza atletika]
car racing	автомобилаш хахкар	[avtɔmɔbilaʃ hahkar]
racing driver	хахкархо	[hahkarhɔ]

| cycling | вилиспетан спорт | [wilispetan spɔrt] |
| cyclist | вилиспетхо | [wilispetho] |

broad jump	дохалла	[dɔhal:a
	кхийссаваларш	qi:s:avalarʃ]
pole vault	хьокханца кхоссавалар	[hɔqantsa qɔs:avalar]
jumper	кхоссавалархо	[qɔs:avalarhɔ]

133. Kinds of sports. Miscellaneous

football	америкин футбол	[amerikin futbɔl]
badminton	бадминтон	[badmintɔn]
biathlon	биатлон	[biatlɔn]
billiards	биллиард	[bil:iard]

bobsled	бобслей	[bɔbslej]
bodybuilding	бодибилдинг	[bɔdibildiŋ]
water polo	хин поло	[hin pɔlɔ]
handball	гандбол	[gandbɔl]
golf	гольф	[gɔʎf]
rowing	пийсиг хьакхар	[pi:sig haqar]
diving	дайвинг	[dajwiŋ]
cross-country skiing	лыжийн хахкар	[lɪʒi:n hahkar]
ping-pong	стоьлан тенис	[stølan tenis]

sailing	гатанан спорт	[gatanan spɔrt]
rally	ралли	[ral:i]
rugby	регби	[regbi]
snowboarding	сноуборд	[snɔubɔrd]
archery	секхlад кхоссар	[sekhad qɔs:ar]

134. Gym

barbell	штанга	[ʃtaŋa]
dumbbells	гантелаш	[gantelaʃ]
training machine	тренажёр	[trenaʒʒr]
bicycle trainer	вилиспетан тренажёр	[wilispetan trenaʒʒr]
treadmill	бовду некъ	[bɔvdu neqh]
horizontal bar	васхал	[vashal]
parallel bars	брусаш	[brusaʃ]
vaulting horse	конь	[kɔŋ]
mat (in gym)	мат	[mat]
aerobics	аэробика	[aərɔbika]
yoga	йогалла	[jogal:a]

135. Hockey

hockey	хоккей	[hok:ej]
hockey player	хоккейхо	[hok:ejho]
to play hockey	хоккейх ловза	[hok:ejh lɔvza]
ice	ша	[ʃa]
puck	шайба	[ʃajba]
hockey stick	клюшка	[klyʃka]
ice skates	канкеш	[kaŋkeʃ]
board	arlo	[aɣɔ]
shot	кхоссар	[qɔs:ar]
goaltender	кевнахо	[kevnaho]
goal (score)	гол	[gɔl]
to score a goal	гол чутоха	[gɔl tʃutɔha]
period	мур	[mur]
substitutes bench	сов ловзархочуна гӏант	[sɔv lɔvzarhɔtʃuna ɣant]

136. Football

soccer	футбол	[futbɔl]
soccer player	футболхо	[futbɔlho]
to play soccer	футболах ловза	[futbɔlah lɔvza]
major league	уггар лакхара лига	[ug:ar laqara liga]
soccer club	футболан клуб	[futbɔlan klub]
coach	тренер	[trener]

owner	да	[da]
team	команда	[komanda]
team captain	командин капитан	[komandin kapitan]
player	ловзархо	[lovzarhɔ]
substitute	сов ловзархо	[sɔv lɔvzarhɔ]

forward	тӀелетарг	[theletarg]
center forward	юккъера тӀелетарг	[jukqhera theletarg]
striker, scorer	бомбардир	[bombardir]
defender, back	лардархо	[lardarhɔ]
halfback	полузащитник	[poluzaɕitnik]

match	матч	[matʃ]
to meet (vi, vt)	вовшахкхета	[vɔvʃahqeta]
final	финал	[final]
semi-final	ахфинал	[ahfinal]
championship	чемпионат	[tʃempiɔnat]

period, half	тайм	[tajm]
first period	I-ра тайм	[ə ra tajm]
half-time	садаӀар	[sadaəar]

goal	ков	[kɔv]
goalkeeper	кевнахо	[kevnahɔ]
goalpost	штанга	[ʃtaŋa]
crossbar	васхал	[vashal]
net	бой	[bɔj]
to miss (fail to catch)	чекхдалийта	[tʃeqdali:ta]
to miss the ball	чекхдалийта	[tʃeqdali:ta]

ball	буьрка	[byrka]
pass	пас, дӀадалар	[pas], [dəadalar]
kick	тохар	[tɔhar]
to kick (~ the ball)	тоха	[tɔha]
free kick	штрафан тохар	[ʃtrafan tɔhar]
corner kick	агӀонгара тохар	[aɣɔŋara tɔhar]

attack	атака	[ataka]
counterattack	контратака	[kontrataka]
combination	комбинаци	[kombinatsi]

referee	арбитр	[arbitr]
to whistle (vi)	шок етта	[ʃɔk et:a]
whistle (sound)	шок	[ʃɔk]
foul, misconduct	дохор	[dohor]
to commit a foul	дохо	[doho]
to send off	майдан тӀера дӀаваккха	[majdan thera dəavak:a]

yellow card	можа карточка	[mɔʒa kartɔtʃka]
red card	цӀе карточка	[tshe kartɔtʃka]
disqualification	дисквалификаци	[diskvalifikatsi]
to disqualify (vt)	дисквалификаци ян	[diskvalifikatsi jan]

penalty kick	пенальти	[penaʎti]
wall	пен	[pen]
to score (vi, vt)	чутоха	[tʃutɔha]
goal (score)	гол	[gɔl]
to score a goal	гол чутоха	[gɔl tʃutɔha]

replacement	хийцар	[hi:tsar]
to replace (vt)	хийца	[hi:tsa]
rules	бакъонаш	[baqhɔnaʃ]
tactics	тактика	[taktika]

stadium	стадион	[stadiɔn]
stand (at stadium)	трибуна	[tribuna]
fan, supporter	фан, хьажархо	[fan], [haʒarhɔ]
to shout (vi, vt)	мохь бетта	[mɔh bet:a]

| scoreboard | табло | [tablɔ] |
| score | чот | [tʃot] |

defeat	эшар	[ɛʃar]
to lose (not win)	эша	[ɛʃa]
draw	ничьья	[nitʃja]
to draw (vi)	ничьях ловза	[nitʃjah lɔvza]

victory	толам	[tɔlam]
to win (vi, vt)	тола	[tɔla]
champion	тоьлларг	[tøl:arg]
the best	уггар дикаха	[ug:ar dikaha]
to congratulate (vt)	декъалдан	[deqhaldan]

commentator	комментархо	[kɔm:entarhɔ]
to commentate (vi, vt)	комментареш яла	[kɔm:entareʃ jala]
broadcast	трансляци	[transʎatsi]

137. Alpine skiing

skis	когсалазаш	[kɔgsalazaʃ]
to ski (vi)	лыжаш хехка	[lɪʒaʃ hehka]
mountain-ski resort	горнолыжни курорт	[gɔrnɔlɪʒni kurɔrt]
ski lift	хьалаойург	[halaɔjurg]
ski poles	гӀажаш	[ɣaʒaʃ]
slope	басе	[base]
slalom	слалом	[slalɔm]

138. Tennis. Golf

| golf | гольф | [gɔʎf] |
| golf club | гольфан-клуб | [gɔʎfan klub] |

golfer	гольфан ловзархо	[gоʌfɑn lɔvzɑrhɔ]
hole	кlаг	[k:ɑg]
club	клюшка	[klyʃkɑ]
golf trolley	клюшкийн гlудалкх	[klyʃki:n ɣudɑlq]

tennis	теннис	[teɲis]
court (for tennis)	корт	[kɔrt]
serve	далар	[dɑlɑr]
to serve (vt)	дала	[dɑlɑ]
racket	ракетка	[rɑketkɑ]
net	бой	[bɔj]
ball	буьрка	[byrkɑ]

139. Chess

chess	шахматаш	[ʃɑhmɑtɑʃ]
chessmen	шахматаш	[ʃɑhmɑtɑʃ]
chess player	шахматхо	[ʃɑhmɑtho]
chessboard	шахматийн у	[ʃɑhmɑti:n u]
chessman	фигура	[figurɑ]

| White (white pieces) | кlайн | [k:ɑjn] |
| Black (black pieces) | lаьржа | [əærʒɑ] |

pawn	жlакки	[ʒəɑk:i]
bishop	пийл	[pi:l]
knight	говр	[gɔvr]
castle	бlов	[bəɔv]
queen	ферзь	[ferzʲ]
king	паччахь	[pɑtʃah]

move	лелар	[lelɑr]
to move (vi, vt)	лела	[lelɑ]
to sacrifice	таса	[tɑsɑ]
castling	паччахь хийцар	[pɑtʃah hi:tsɑr]
check	шах	[ʃɑh]
checkmate	мат	[mɑt]

chess tournament	шахматийн турнир	[ʃɑhmɑti:n turnir]
Grand Master	гроссмейстер	[grɔs:mejster]
combination	комбинаци	[kɔmbinɑtsi]
game (in chess)	парти	[pɑrti]
checkers	шашкаш	[ʃɑʃkɑʃ]

140. Boxing

| boxing | бокс | [bɔks] |
| fight | латар | [lɑtɑr] |

| boxing match | латар | [latar] |
| round (in boxing) | раунд | [raund] |

| ring | ринг | [riŋ] |
| gong | жиргӀа | [ʒirɣa] |

punch	тохар	[tɔhar]
knock-down	нокдаун	[nɔkdaun]
knockout	нокаут	[nɔkaut]
to knock out	нокаут дан	[nɔkaut dan]

| boxing glove | боксерски каран | [bɔkserski karan] |
| referee | рефери | [referi] |

lightweight	дайн дозалла	[dajn dɔzal:a]
middleweight	юккъера дозалла	[jukqhera dɔzal:a]
heavyweight	деза дозалла	[deza dɔzal:a]

141. Sports. Miscellaneous

Olympic Games	олимпан ловзараш	[ɔlimpan lɔvzaraʃ]
winner	толамхо	[tɔlamho]
to be winning	эшо	[ɛʃɔ]
to win (vi)	тола	[tɔla]

| leader | лидер | [lider] |
| to lead (vi) | лидер хила | [lider hila] |

first place	хьалхара меттиг	[halhara met:ig]
second place	шолгӀа меттиг	[ʃɔlɣa met:ig]
third place	кхоалгӀа меттиг	[qɔalɣa met:ig]

medal	мидал	[midal]
trophy	хӀонс	[hɔns]
cup (trophy)	кубок	[kubɔk]
prize (in game)	совгӀат	[sɔvɣat]
main prize	коьрта совгӀат	[kørta sɔvɣat]

| record | рекорд | [rekɔrd] |
| to set a record | рекорд хӀотто | [rekɔrd hɔt:ɔ] |

| final | финал | [final] |
| final (adj) | финалан | [finalan] |

| champion | тоьлларг | [tøl:arg] |
| championship | чемпионат | [ʧempiɔnat] |

stadium	стадион	[stadiɔn]
stand (at stadium)	трибуна	[tribuna]
fan, supporter	фан, хьажархо	[fan], [haʒarhɔ]

opponent, rival	мостагӀ	[mɔstaɣ]
start	старт	[start]
finish	финиш	[finiʃ]
defeat	эшор	[ɛʃɔr]
to lose (not win)	эша	[ɛʃa]
referee	суьдхо	[sydhɔ]
judges	жюри	[ʒyri]
score	счёт	[stʃɔt]
draw	ничья	[nitʃja]
to draw (vi)	ничьях ловза	[nitʃjah lɔvza]
point	очко	[ɔtʃkɔ]
result (of match)	хилам	[hilam]
half-time	садаӀар	[sadaəar]
dope (for athlete, horse)	допинг	[dɔpiŋ]
to penalize (vt)	гӀуда тоха	[ɣuda tɔha]
to disqualify (vt)	дисквалификаци ян	[diskvalifikatsi jan]
apparatus	гӀирс	[ɣirs]
javelin	гоьмукъ	[gɵmuqh]
shot (metal ball)	хӀоъ	[hɔ]
ball (in snooker, croquet)	горгал	[gɔrgal]
target (objective)	Ӏалашо	[əalaʃɔ]
target (e.g., for archery)	гӀакх	[ɣaq]
to shoot (vi)	кхийса	[qi:sa]
precise (shot)	нийса	[ni:sa]
trainer, coach	тренер	[trener]
to train sb	Ӏамо	[əamɔ]
to train (vi)	Ӏама	[əama]
training	Ӏамор	[əamɔr]
gym	спортзал	[sportzal]
exercise (physical)	упражнени	[upraʒneni]
warm-up (of athlete)	дегӀ хецадалийтар	[deɣ hetsadali:tar]

Education

142. School

school	школа	[ʃkɔla]
headmaster	директор	[direktɔr]
pupil (boy)	дешархо	[deʃarhɔ]
pupil (girl)	дешархо	[deʃarhɔ]
schoolboy	школахо	[ʃkɔlahɔ]
schoolgirl	школахо	[ʃkɔlahɔ]
to teach (sb)	хьеха	[heha]
to learn (language etc.)	Iамо	[əamɔ]
to learn by heart	дагахь Iамо	[dagah əamɔ]
to study (vi)	Iама	[əama]
to be in school	Iама	[əama]
to go to school	школе ваха	[ʃkɔle vaha]
alphabet	абат	[abat]
subject (at school)	предмет	[predmet]
classroom	класс	[klas:]
classes	дешар	[deʃar]
lesson	урок	[urɔk]
school bell	горгали	[gɔrgali]
desk (for pupil)	парта	[parta]
chalkboard	классан у	[klas:an u]
grade	отметка	[ɔtmetka]
good grade	дика отметка	[dika ɔtmetka]
bad grade	вон отметка	[vɔn ɔtmetka]
to give a grade	отметка хIотто	[ɔtmetka hɔt:ɔ]
mistake	гIалат	[ɣalat]
to make mistakes	гIалат дан	[ɣalat dan]
to correct (vt)	нисдан	[nisdan]
cheat sheet	шпаргалка	[ʃpargalka]
homework	цIера тIедиллар	[tsʰera thedil:ar]
exercise (in education)	упражнени	[upraʒneni]
to be present	хила	[hila]
to be absent	ца хила	[tsa hila]
to punish (vt)	тaIзар дан	[taəzar dan]

| punishment | та1зар | [taezɑr] |
| conduct (behavior) | лелар | [lelɑr] |

report card	дневник	[dnevnik]
pencil	къолам	[qhɔlɑm]
eraser	лаьстиг	[læstig]
chalk	мел	[mel]
pencil case	г1утакх	[ɣutɑq]

schoolbag	портфель	[pɔrtfeʎ]
pen	ручка	[ruʧkɑ]
school notebook	тетрадь	[tetrɑdʲ]
textbook	учебник	[uʧebnik]
compasses	циркуль	[ʦirkuʎ]

| to draw (a blueprint etc.) | дилла | [dil:ɑ] |
| technical drawing | чертёж | [ʧertɜʒ] |

poem	байт	[bɑjt]
by heart	дагахь	[dɑgɑh]
to learn by heart	дагахь 1амо	[dɑgɑh əɑmɔ]

| school vacation | каникулаш | [kɑnikulɑʃ] |
| to be on vacation | каникулашт хилар | [kɑnikulɑʃt hilɑr] |

quiz (at school)	талламан болх	[tɑl:ɑmɑn bɔlh]
essay (composition)	сочинени	[sɔʧineni]
dictation	диктант	[diktɑnt]
exam	экзамен	[ɛkzɑmen]
to take an exam	экзамен д1аялар	[ɛkzɑmen dəɑjɑlɑr]
experiment (chemical ~)	г1улч	[ɣulʧ]

143. College. University

academy	академи	[ɑkɑdemi]
university	университет	[uniwersitet]
faculty (section)	факультет	[fɑkuʎtet]

student (man)	студент	[student]
student (woman)	студентка	[studentkɑ]
lecturer (teacher)	хьехархо	[heharhɔ]
professor	профессор	[prɔfes:ɔr]

lecture hall, room	аудитори	[ɑuditɔri]
graduate (of high school)	дешна ваьлларг	[deʃnɑ væl:ɑrg]
diploma	диплом	[diplɔm]
dissertation	диссертаци	[dis:ertɑtsi]

| study (report) | таллар | [tɑl:ɑr] |
| laboratory | лаборатори | [lɑbɔrɑtɔri] |

lecture	лекци	[lekʦi]
schoolmate	курсахо	[kursaho]
stipend	стипенди	[stipendi]
academic degree	Іилманан дарж	[əilmanan darʒ]

144. Sciences. Disciplines

mathematics	математика	[matematika]
algebra	алгебра	[algebra]
geometry	геометри	[geɔmetri]

astronomy	астрономи	[astrɔnɔmi]
biology	биологи	[biɔlɔgi]
geography	географи	[geɔgrafi]
geology	геологи	[geɔlɔgi]
history	истори	[istɔri]

medicine	медицина	[meditsina]
pedagogy	педагогика	[pedagɔgika]
law (e.g., student of ~)	бакъо	[baqhɔ]

physics	физика	[fizika]
chemistry	хими	[himi]
philosophy	философи	[filɔsɔfi]
psychology	психологи	[psihɔlɔgi]

145. Writing system. Orthography

grammar	грамматика	[gram:atika]
vocabulary	лексика	[leksika]
phonetics	фонетика	[fɔnetika]

noun	цІердош	[ʦherdɔʃ]
adjective	билгалдош	[bilgaldɔʃ]
verb	хандош	[handɔʃ]
adverb	куцдош	[kuʦdɔʃ]

pronoun	цІерметдош	[ʦhermetdɔʃ]
interjection	айдардош	[ajdardɔʃ]
preposition	предлог	[predlɔg]

root (base form)	дешан орам	[deʃan ɔram]
ending	чаккхе	[ʧak:e]
prefix	дешхьалхе	[deʃhalhe]
syllable	дешдакъа	[deʃdaqha]
suffix	суффикс	[suf:iks]
stress mark	тохар	[tɔhar]
apostrophe	апостроф	[apɔstrɔf]

period, dot	тӀадам	[thadam]
comma	цӀоьмалг	[tshømalg]
semicolon	тӀадамца цӀоьмалг	[thadamtsa tshømalg]
colon	ши тӀадам	[ʃi thadam]
ellipsis	тӀадамаш	[thadamaʃ]

| question mark | хаттаран хьаьрк | [hat:aran hærk] |
| exclamation point | айдаран хьаьрк | [ajdaran hærk] |

quotation marks	кавычкаш	[kavɪtʃkaʃ]
in quotation marks	кавычкаш юккъе	[kavɪtʃkaʃ jukqhe]
parenthesis	къовларш	[qhovlarʃ]
in parenthesis	къовларш юккъе	[qhovlarʃ jukqhe]

| hyphen | сизалг | [sizalg] |
| dash | тиз | [tiz] |

| space (between words) | юкъ | [juqh] |
| hyphen (end of a line) | сехьадаккхар | [sehadak:ar] |

| letter | элп | [ɛlp] |
| capital letter | доккха элп | [dɔk:a ɛlp] |

| vowel (noun) | мукъа аз | [muqha az] |
| consonant (noun) | мукъаза аз | [muqhaza az] |

sentence	предложени	[predlɔʒeni]
subject	подлежащи	[pɔdleʒaɕi]
predicate	сказуеми	[skazuemi]

line (in writing)	моӀа	[mɔɣa]
on a new line	керлачу моӀарера	[kerlatʃu mɔɣarera]
paragraph	абзац	[abzats]

word	дош	[dɔʃ]
word group	дешнийн цхьаьнакхетар	[deʃni:n tshænaqetar]
expression	алар	[alar]

| synonym | синоним | [sinɔnim] |
| antonym | антоним | [antɔnim] |

rule	бакъо	[baqhɔ]
exception	юкъарадаккхар	[juqharadak:ar]
right (correct)	нийса	[ni:sa]

conjugation	хийцар	[hi:tsar]
declension	легар	[legar]
nominal case	дожар	[dɔʒar]
question	хаттар	[hat:ar]
to underline (vt)	билгалдаккха	[bilgaldak:a]
dotted line	пунктир	[puŋktir]

146. Foreign languages

language	мотт	[mɔt:]
foreign language	кхечу мехкийн мотт	[qetʃu mehki:n mɔt:]
to study (vt)	lамо	[əamɔ]
to learn (language etc.)	lамо	[əamɔ]
to read (vi, vt)	еша	[eʃa]
to speak (vi, vt)	дийца	[di:tsa]
to understand (vt)	кхета	[qeta]
to write (vi, vt)	яздан	[jazdan]
fast	сиха	[siha]
slowly	меллаша	[mel:aʃa]
fluently	паргlат	[parɣat]
rules	бакъонаш	[baqhɔnaʃ]
grammar	грамматика	[gram:atika]
vocabulary	лексика	[leksika]
phonetics	фонетика	[fɔnetika]
textbook	учебник	[utʃebnik]
dictionary	дошам, словарь	[dɔʃam], [slɔvarʲ]
teach-yourself book	lамалург	[əamalurg]
phrasebook	къамелlаморг	[qhameləamɔrg]
cassette	кассета	[kas:eta]
videotape	видеокассета	[widəɔkas:eta]
CD (compact disc)	CD	[sidi]
DVD	DVD	[diwidi]
alphabet	алфавит	[alfawit]
to spell (vt)	элпашц мотт бийца	[ɛlpaʃts mɔt: bi:tsa]
pronunciation	алар	[alar]
accent	акцент	[aktsent]
with an accent	акцент	[aktsent]
without an accent	акцент ца хила	[aktsent tsa hila]
word	дош	[dɔʃ]
meaning	маьlна	[mæəna]
course (e.g., a French ~)	курсаш	[kursaʃ]
to sign up	дlаяздала	[dəajazdala]
teacher	хьехархо	[heharhɔ]
translation (process)	дахьийтар	[dahi:tar]
translation (text etc.)	гоч дар	[gɔtʃ dar]
translator	талмаж	[talmaʒ]
interpreter	талмаж	[talmaʒ]
polyglot	полиглот	[pɔliglɔt]
memory	эс	[ɛs]

147. Fairy tale characters

| Santa Claus | Санта Клаус | [santa klaus] |
| mermaid | хи-аьзни | [hi æzni] |

magician, wizard	бозбуунча	[bɔzbu:nʧa]
good witch	бозбуунча	[bɔzbu:nʧa]
magic	бозбуунчаллин	[bɔzbu:nʧal:in]
magic wand	шайтӀанан гӀаж	[ʃajthanan ɣaʒ]

fairy tale	туьйра	[tyjra]
miracle	Ӏаламат	[əalamat]
dwarf	буьйдолг	[byjdɔlg]
to turn into …	дерза	[derza]

ghost	гӀаларт	[ɣalart]
phantom	бӀарлагӀа	[bəarlaɣa]
monster	Ӏаламат	[əalamat]
dragon	саьрмик	[særmik]
giant	дӀуьтӀа	[dəytha]

148. Zodiac Signs

Aries	Овен	[ɔwen]
Taurus	Телец	[telets]
Gemini	Близнецы	[bliznetsɪ]
Cancer	Рак	[rak]
Leo	Лев	[lev]
Virgo	Дева	[deva]

Libra	Весы	[wesɪ]
Scorpio	Скорпион	[skɔrpiɔn]
Sagittarius	Стрелец	[strelets]
Capricorn	Козерог	[kɔzerɔg]
Aquarius	Водолей	[vodɔlej]
Pisces	Рыбы	[rɪbɪ]

character	амал	[amal]
features of character	амаллин башхала	[amal:in baʃhala]
behavior	лелар	[lelar]
to tell fortunes	пал тийса	[pal ti:sa]
fortune-teller	палтуьйсург	[paltyjsurg]
horoscope	гороскоп	[gɔrɔskɔp]

Arts

149. Theater

theater	театр	[teɑtr]
opera	опера	[ɔperɑ]
operetta	оперетта	[ɔperet:ɑ]
ballet	балет	[bɑlet]
playbill	афиша	[afiʃɑ]
company	труппа	[trup:ɑ]
tour	гастролаш	[gɑstrɔlɑʃ]
to be on tour	гастролаш яла	[gɑstrɔlɑʃ jɑlɑ]
to rehearse (vi, vt)	репетици ян	[repetitsi jɑn]
rehearsal	репетици	[repetitsi]
repertoire	репертуар	[repertuɑr]
performance	хьожийла	[hɔʒi:lɑ]
show, play	спектакль	[spektɑkʎ]
play	пьеса	[pjesɑ]
ticket	билет	[bilet]
ticket office	билетан касса	[biletɑn kɑs:ɑ]
lobby, foyer	чоь	[ʧø]
coat check	гардероб	[gɑrderɔb]
coat check tag	номер	[nɔmer]
binoculars	турмал	[turmɑl]
usher	контролёр	[kɔntrɔlɜr]
orchestra seats	партер	[pɑrter]
balcony	балкон	[bɑlkɔn]
dress circle	бельэтаж	[beʎætɑʒ]
box	ложа	[lɔʒɑ]
row	морла	[mɔɣɑ]
seat	меттиг	[met:ig]
audience	гулбелларш	[gulbel:ɑrʃ]
spectator	хьажархо	[hɑʒɑrhɔ]
to clap (vi, vt)	тӏараш детта	[tharɑʃ det:ɑ]
applause	аплодисменташ	[aplɔdismentɑʃ]
ovation	оваци	[ɔvɑtsi]
stage	сцена	[stsenɑ]
curtain	кирхьа	[kirhɑ]
scenery	декорации	[dekɔrɑtsi]
backstage	кулисаш	[kulisɑʃ]

scene (e.g., the last ~)	сурт	[surt]
act	дакъа	[daqha]
intermission	антракт	[antrakt]

150. Cinema

| actor | актёр | [aktзr] |
| actress | актриса | [aktrisa] |

| movies (industry) | кино | [kinɔ] |
| episode | сери | [seri] |

detective	детектив	[detektiv]
action movie	боевик	[bɔewik]
adventure movie	хиллачеран фильм	[hil:aʧeran fiʌm]
science fiction movie	фонтазин фильм	[fɔntazin fiʌm]
horror movie	къематин фильм	[qhematin fiʌm]

comedy movie	кинокомеди	[kinɔkɔmedi]
melodrama	мелодрама	[melɔdrama]
drama	драма	[drama]

fictional movie	исбаьхьаллин фильм	[isbæhal:in fiʌm]
documentary	бакъдолчуна тɪера фильм	[baqhdɔlʧuna thera fiʌm]
cartoon	мультфильм	[muʌtfiʌm]
silent movies	аз доцу кино	[az dɔtsu kinɔ]

role	роль	[rɔʌ]
leading role	коьрта роль	[kørta rɔʌ]
to play (vi, vt)	лело	[lelɔ]

movie star	кинозвезда	[kinɔzwezda]
well-known	гɪарадаьлла	[ɣaradæl:a]
famous	гɪарадаьлла	[ɣaradæl:a]
popular	гɪраваьлла	[ɣravæl:a]

script (screenplay)	сценари	[stsenari]
scriptwriter	сценарихо	[stsenarihɔ]
movie director	режиссёр	[reʒis:зr]
producer	продюсер	[prɔdyser]
assistant	ассистент	[as:istent]
cameraman	оператор	[ɔperatɔr]
stuntman	каскадёр	[kaskadзr]

to shoot a movie	фильм яккха	[fiʌm jak:a]
audition, screen test	хьажар	[haʒar]
shooting	яккхар	[jak:ar]
movie crew	кино йоккху группа	[kinɔ jok:u grup:a]
movie set	кино йоккху майда	[kinɔ jok:u majda]

camera	кинокамера	[kinɔkamera]
movie theater	кинотеатр	[kinɔteatr]
screen (e.g., big ~)	экран	[ɛkran]
to show a movie	фильм гайта	[fiʎm gajta]

soundtrack	аьзнийн дорожк	[æzni:n dɔrɔʒk]
special effects	леррина эффекташ	[ler:ina ɛf:ektaʃ]
subtitles	субтитраш	[subtitraʃ]
credits	титраш	[titraʃ]
translation	гоч дар	[gɔtʃ dar]

151. Painting

art	исбаьхьалла	[isbæhɑl:a]
fine arts	исбаьхьаллин говзалла	[isbæhɑl:in gɔvzɑl:a]
art gallery	галерей	[galerej]
art exhibition	сурташ гайтар	[surtaʃ gajtar]

painting	суьрташ дахкар	[syrtaʃ dahkar]
graphic art	графика	[grafika]
abstract art	абстракционизм	[abstraktsiɔnizm]
impressionism	импрессионизм	[impres:iɔnizm]

picture (painting)	суьрт	[syrt]
drawing	сурт	[surt]
poster	плакат	[plakat]

illustration (picture)	иллюстраци	[il:ystratsi]
miniature	миниатюра	[miniatyra]
copy (of painting etc.)	копи	[kɔpi]
reproduction	репродукци	[reprɔduktsi]

mosaic	мозаика	[mɔzaika]
stained glass	витраж	[witraʒ]
fresco	фреска	[freska]
engraving	огана	[ɔgana]

bust (sculpture)	бюст	[byst]
sculpture	скульптура	[skuʎptura]
statue	статуя	[statuja]
plaster of Paris	гипс	[gips]
plaster (e.g., ~ statue)	гипсехь	[gipseh]

portrait	портрет	[pɔrtret]
self-portrait	автопортрет	[avtɔpɔrtret]
landscape	сурт	[surt]
still life	натюрморт	[natyrmɔrt]
caricature	карикатура	[karikatura]
sketch	сурт	[surt]

paint	басар	[basar]
watercolor	акварель	[akvareʎ]
oil (paint)	даьтта	[dæt:a]
pencil	къолам	[qholam]
Indian ink	шекъа	[ʃeqha]
charcoal	кӏора	[k:ora]
to draw (vi, vt)	сурт дилла	[surt dil:a]
to pose (vi)	позе хӏотта	[poze hot:a]
artist's model (man)	натурахо	[naturaho]
artist's model (woman)	натурахо	[naturaho]
artist (painter)	исбаьхьалча	[isbæhaltʃa]
work of art	произведени	[proizwedeni]
masterpiece	шедевр	[ʃədevr]
workshop (of artist)	пхьалгӏа	[phalɣa]
canvas (cloth)	гата	[gata]
easel	мольберт	[moʎbert]
palette	палитра	[palitra]
frame (of picture etc.)	гур	[gur]
restoration	реставраци	[restavratsi]
to restore (vt)	реставраци ян	[restavratsi jan]

152. Literature & Poetry

literature	литература	[literatura]
author (writer)	автор	[avtor]
pseudonym	псевдоним	[psevdonim]
book	книшка	[kniʃka]
volume	том	[tom]
contents list	чулацам	[tʃulatsam]
page	агӏо	[aɣo]
main character	коьрта турпалхо	[kørta turpalho]
autograph	автограф	[avtograf]
short story	дийцар	[di:tsar]
story (novella)	повесть	[powestʲ]
novel	роман	[roman]
work (writing)	сочинени	[sotʃineni]
fable	басни	[basni]
detective novel	детектив	[detektiv]
poem (verse)	байт	[bajt]
poetry	поэзи	[poɛzi]
poem (epic, ballad)	поэма	[poɛma]
poet	илланча	[il:antʃa]
fiction	беллетристика	[bel:etristika]

science fiction	Ӏилманан фантастика	[əilmanan fantastika]
adventures	хилларг	[hil:arg]
educational literature	дешаран литература	[deʃaran literatura]
children's literature	берийн литература	[beri:n literatura]

153. Circus

circus	цирк	[tsirk]
big top (circus)	цирк-шапито	[tsirk ʃapitɔ]
program	программа	[prɔgram:a]
performance	хьожийла	[hɔʒi:la]

| act (circus ~) | номер | [nɔmer] |
| circus ring | майда | [majda] |

| pantomime (act) | пантомима | [pantɔmima] |
| clown | жухарг | [ʒuharg] |

acrobat	пелхьо	[pelhɔ]
acrobatics	пелхьолла	[pelhɔl:a]
gymnast	гимнастхо	[gimnastho]
gymnastics	гимнастика	[gimnastika]
somersault	сальто	[saʌtɔ]

athlete	атлет	[atlet]
animal-tamer	караламорхо	[karaөamɔrhɔ]
rider	бере	[bere]
assistant	ассистент	[as:istent]

stunt	трюк	[tryk]
conjuring trick	бозбуунчалла	[bɔzbu:ntʃal:a]
conjurer, magician	бозбуунча	[bɔzbu:ntʃa]

juggler	жонглёр	[ʒɔŋlɔr]
to juggle (vi, vt)	жонглировать дан	[ʒɔŋlirɔvatʲ dan]
animal trainer	караламорг	[karaөamɔrg]
animal training	караламор	[karaөamɔr]
to train (animals)	караламо	[karaөamɔ]

154. Music. Pop music

music	музыка	[muzika]
musician	музыкант	[muzikant]
musical instrument	музыкин гӀирс	[muzikin ɣirs]
to play ...	лакха	[laqa]

| guitar | гитара | [gitara] |
| violin | чӀондарг | [tʃʲhɔndarg] |

cello	виолончель	[wiolontʃeʌ]
double bass	контрабас	[kontrabas]
harp	арфа	[arfa]
piano	пианино	[pianinɔ]
grand piano	рояль	[rɔjaʌ]
organ	орган	[ɔrgan]
wind instruments	зурманийн гӀирсаш	[zurmani:n ɣirsaʃ]
oboe	гобой	[gɔbɔj]
saxophone	саксофон	[saksɔfɔn]
clarinet	кларнет	[klarnet]
flute	флейта	[flejta]
trumpet	зурма	[zurma]
accordion	кехатпондар	[kehatpɔndar]
drum	вота	[vɔta]
duo	дуэт	[duɛt]
trio	трио	[triɔ]
quartet	квартет	[kvartet]
choir	хор	[hɔr]
orchestra	оркестр	[ɔrkestr]
pop music	рок-музыка	[rɔk muzɪka]
rock music	рок-музыка	[rɔk muzɪka]
rock group	рок-группа	[rɔk grup:a]
jazz	джаз	[dʒaz]
idol	цӀу	[tshu]
admirer, fan	ларамхо	[laramhɔ]
concert	концерт	[kɔntsert]
symphony	симфони	[simfɔni]
composition	сочинени	[sɔtʃineni]
to compose (write)	кхолла	[qɔl:a]
singing	лакхар	[laqar]
song	илли	[il:i]
tune (melody)	мукъам	[muqham]
rhythm	ритм	[ritm]
blues	блюз	[blyz]
sheet music	ноташ	[nɔtaʃ]
baton	гӀаж	[ɣaʒ]
bow	чӀондаргӀа	[tʃhɔndarɣa]
string	мерз	[merz]
case (e.g., for guitar)	ботт	[bɔt:]

Rest. Entertainment. Travel

155. Trip. Travel

tourism	туризм	[turizm]
tourist	турист	[turist]
trip, voyage	араваьлла лелар	[aravæl:a lelar]
adventure	хилларг	[hil:arg]
trip, journey	дахар	[dahar]
vacation	отпуск	[ɔtpusk]
to be on vacation	отпускехь хилар	[ɔtpuskeh hilar]
rest	садаlар	[sadaɐar]
train	цlерпошт	[tsherpɔʃt]
by train	цlерпоштахь	[tsherpɔʃtah]
airplane	кема	[kema]
by airplane	кеманца	[kemantsa]
by car	машина тlехь	[maʃina theh]
by ship	кеманца	[kemantsa]
luggage	кира	[kira]
suitcase, luggage	чамда	[ʧamda]
luggage cart	киран гlудакх	[kiran ɣudaq]
passport	паспорт	[paspɔrt]
visa	виза	[wiza]
ticket	билет	[bilet]
air ticket	авиабилет	[awiabilet]
guidebook	некъгойтург	[neqhgɔjturg]
map	карта	[karta]
area (place)	меттиг	[met:ig]
place, site	меттиг	[met:ig]
exotica	экзотика	[ɛkzɔtika]
exotic	экзотикин	[ɛkzɔtikin]
amazing	тамашена	[tamaʃəna]
group	группа	[grup:a]
excursion	экскурси	[ɛkskursi]
guide (person)	экскурсилелорхо	[ɛkskursilelɔrhɔ]

156. Hotel

hotel, inn	хьешийн цIа, отель	[heʃiːn tʃha], [ɔteʎ]
hotel	хьешийн цIа	[heʃiːn tʃha]
motel	мотель	[mɔteʎ]
three-star	кхо седа	[qø seda]
five-star	пхи седа	[phi seda]
to stay (in hotel etc.)	саца	[satsa]
room	номер	[nɔmer]
single room	цхьа меттиг йолу номер	[tʃha metːig jolu nɔmer]
double room	шиъ меттиг йолу номер	[ʃi metːig jolu nɔmer]
to book a room	номер бронь ян	[nɔmer brɔɲ jan]
half board	полупансион	[pɔlupansiɔn]
full board	йиззина пансион	[jɪzːina pansiɔn]
with bath	ваннер	[vaɳer]
with shower	душер	[duʃer]
satellite television	спутникови телевидени	[sputnikɔwi telewideni]
air-conditioner	кондиционер	[kɔnditsiɔner]
towel	гата	[gata]
key	догIа	[dɔɣa]
administrator	администратор	[administratɔr]
chambermaid	хIусамча	[husamtʃa]
porter, bellboy	киранхо	[kiranho]
doorman	портье	[pɔrtje]
restaurant	ресторан	[restɔran]
pub, bar	бар	[bar]
café	кафе	[kafe]
breakfast	марта	[marta]
dinner	пхьор	[phɔr]
buffet	шведийн стоьл	[ʃwediːn støl]
lobby	вестибюль	[westibyʎ]
elevator	лифт	[lift]
DO NOT DISTURB	МА ХЬЕВЕ	[ma hewe]
NO SMOKING	ЦИГАЬРКА ОЗА МЕГАШ ДАЦ!	[tsigærka oza megaʃ dats]

157. Books. Reading

book	книшка	[kniʃka]
author	автор	[avtɔr]

writer	яздархо	[jazdarhɔ]
to write (e.g., ~ a book)	язъян	[jazʰjan]
reader	ешархо	[eʃarhɔ]
to read (vi, vt)	еша	[eʃa]
reading (activity)	ешар	[eʃar]
silently	дагахь	[dagah]
aloud	хезаш	[hezaʃ]
to publish (vt)	арахеца	[arahetsa]
publication	арахецар	[arahetsar]
publisher	арахецархо	[arahetsarhɔ]
publishing house	издательство	[izdateʎstvɔ]
to come out	арадала	[aradala]
publication	арадалар	[aradalar]
print run	тираж	[tiraʒ]
bookstore	книшкийн туька	[kniʃki:n tyka]
library	библиотека	[bibliɔteka]
story (novella)	повесть	[pɔwestʲ]
short story	дийцар	[di:tsar]
novel	роман	[rɔman]
detective novel	детектив	[detektiv]
memoirs	мемуараш	[memuaraʃ]
legend	дийцар	[di:tsar]
myth	миф	[mif]
poetry, poems	байташ	[bajtaʃ]
autobiography	автобиографи	[avtɔbiɔgrafi]
collected works	хаьржина	[hærʒina]
science fiction	фантастика	[fantastika]
title	цIе	[tshe]
introduction	чудалор	[tʃudalɔr]
title page	титулан арло	[titulan aɣɔ]
chapter	корта	[kɔrta]
extract	дакъа	[daqha]
episode	эпизод	[ɛpizɔd]
thread (of story)	сюжет	[syʒet]
contents	чулацам	[tʃulatsam]
table of contents	чулацам	[tʃulatsam]
main character	коьрта турпалхо	[kørta turpalhɔ]
volume	том	[tɔm]
cover	мужалт	[muʒalt]
binding	мужалт яр	[muʒalt jar]

154

bookmark	юкъаюьллург	[juqhajul:urg]
page	арло	[aɣɔ]
to flick through	херца	[hertsa]
margins	йистош	[jɪstɔʃ]
note (in margins)	билгало	[bilgalɔ]
annotation	билгалдаккхар	[bilgaldak:ar]

text	текст	[tekst]
type, font	зорба	[zɔrba]
misprint, typo	гӏалат кхетар	[ɣalat qetar]

translation	гоч	[gɔtʃ]
to translate (vi, vt)	гочдинарг	[gɔtʃdinarg]
original (read in the ~)	бакъдерг	[baqhderg]

famous	гӏарадаьлла	[ɣaradæl:a]
unknown	девзаш доцу	[devzaʃ dɔtsu]
interesting	самукъане	[samuqhane]
bestseller	бестселлер	[bestsel:er]

dictionary	дошам, словарь	[dɔʃam], [slɔvarʲ]
textbook	учебник	[utʃebnik]
encyclopedia	энциклопеди	[ɛntsiklɔpedi]

158. Hunting. Fishing

hunt (of animal)	таллар	[tal:ar]
to hunt (vi, vt)	талла эха	[tal:a ɛha]
hunter	тallapхо	[tal:arhɔ]

to shoot (vi)	кхийса	[qi:sa]
rifle	топ	[tɔp]
bullet (cartridge)	патарма	[patarma]
shotgun pellets	дробь	[drɔbʲ]

trap (e.g., bear ~)	гура	[gura]
snare (for birds etc.)	речӏа	[retʃha]
to lay a trap	гура боӏла	[gura bɔɣa]

poacher	браконьер	[brakɔnjer]
game (in hunting)	экха	[ɛqa]
hound	таллархойн жӏаьла	[tal:arhɔjn ʒeæla]
safari	сафари	[safari]
mounted animal	мунда	[munda]

fisherman	чӏерийлецархо	[tʃheri:letsarhɔ]
fishing	чӏерийлецар	[tʃheri:letsar]
to fish (vi)	чӏерий леца	[tʃheri: letsa]
fishing rod	мӏара	[meara]
fishing line	леска	[leska]

hook	мӀара	[məara]
float	тӀус	[thus]
bait	кхоллург	[qɔl:urg]

to cast a line	къийдамаш бан	[qhi:damaʃ ban]
to bite (about fish)	муьрг етта	[myrg et:a]
catch (of fish)	лецна	[letsna]
ice-hole	Ӏуьрг	[əyrg]

net	бой	[bɔj]
boat	кема	[kema]
to net (catch with net)	бойца леца	[bɔjtsa letsa]
to cast the net	бой чукхосса	[bɔj tʃuqɔs:a]
to haul in the net	бой аратакхо	[bɔj arataqɔ]

whaler (person)	китобой	[kitɔbɔj]
whaleboat	китобойни кема	[kitɔbɔjni kema]
harpoon	чаьнчакх	[tʃæntʃaq]

159. Games. Billiards

billiards	биллиард	[bil:iard]
billiard room, hall	биллиардан	[bil:iardan]
ball	биллиардан шар	[bil:iardan ʃar]

to pocket a ball	шар чутоха	[ʃar tʃutɔha]
cue	кий	[ki:]
pocket	луза	[luza]

160. Games. Playing cards

diamonds	черо	[tʃerɔ]
spades	ӀаьржбӀаьрг	[əærʒbəærg]
hearts	черви	[tʃerwi]
clubs	ӀаьржабӀаьргаш	[əærʒabəærgaʃ]

ace	тӀуз	[thuz]
king	паччахь	[patʃah]
queen	йол	[joə]
jack, knave	салти	[salti]

playing card	ловзо кехат	[lɔvzɔ kehat]
cards	кехаташ	[kehataʃ]
trump	козар	[kɔzar]
deck of cards	туп	[tup]

| to deal (vi, vt) | декъа | [deqha] |
| to shuffle (in card games) | эдан | [ɛdan] |

| lead, turn (noun) | дахар | [dahar] |
| card sharp | хьарамча | [haramtʃa] |

161. Casino. Roulette

casino	казино	[kazinɔ]
roulette (game)	рулетка	[ruletka]
bet, stake	диллар	[dil:ar]
to place bets	дилла	[dil:a]

red (in roulette)	цlен	[tʃhen]
black	lаьржа	[əærʒa]
to bet on red	цlенчун тlе дилла	[tʃhentʃun the dil:a]
to bet on black	lаьржчун тlе дилла	[əærʒtʃun the dil:a]

croupier	крупье	[krupje]
to turn the wheel	бера хьийзо	[bera hi:zɔ]
rules (of game)	ловзаран бакъонаш	[lɔvzaran baqhɔnaʃ]
chip	фишка	[fiʃka]

| to win (vi, vt) | даккха | [dak:a] |
| winnings | даккхар | [dak:ar] |

| to lose (not win) | эша | [ɛʃa] |
| loss | эшар | [ɛʃar] |

player	ловзархо	[lɔvzarhɔ]
blackjack (card game)	блэк джэк	[blɛk dʒɛk]
game of dice	даьлахках ловзар	[dæəahkah lɔvzar]
slot machine	ловзо автомат	[lɔvzɔ avtɔmat]

162. Rest. Games. Miscellaneous

to walk, to stroll (vi)	доладала	[dɔladala]
walk, stroll	доладалар	[dɔladalar]
pleasure-ride, trip	доладалар	[dɔladalar]
adventure	хилларг	[hil:arg]
picnic	пикник	[piknik]

game (chess etc.)	ловзар	[lɔvzar]
player	ловзархо	[lɔvzarhɔ]
game (one ~ of chess)	парти	[parti]

collector (e.g., philatelist)	гулдархо	[guldarhɔ]
to collect (vt)	гулъян	[gulʰjan]
collection	гулдар	[guldar]
crossword	кроссворд	[krɔs:vɔrd]
racecourse (for horses)	ипподром	[ip:ɔdrɔm]

disco (place)	дискотека	[diskɔteka]
sauna	сауна	[sɑuna]
lottery	лотерей	[lɔterej]

camping trip	поход	[pɔhod]
camp	лагерь	[lager']
tent (for camping)	четар	[ʧetar]
compass	къилба	[qhilba]
camper	турист	[turist]

to watch (movie etc.)	хьежа	[heʒa]
viewer	телехьажархо	[telehaʒarhɔ]
TV show	телепередача	[teleperedaʧa]

163. Photography

| camera (photo) | фотоаппарат | [fɔtɔap:arat] |
| photo, picture | фото, сурт | [fɔtɔ], [surt] |

photographer	суьрташдохург	[syrtaʃdohurg]
photo studio	фотостуди	[fɔtɔstudi]
photo album	фотоальбом	[fɔtɔaʎbɔm]

camera lens	объектив	[ɔbʰektiv]
telephoto lens	телеобъектив	[teleɔbʰektiv]
filter	фильтр	[fiʎtr]
lens	линза	[linza]

set of lenses	оптика	[ɔptika]
diaphragm (aperture)	диафрагма	[diafragma]
exposure time	выдержка	[vɪderʒka]
viewfinder	видоискатель	[widɔiskateʎ]

digital camera	цифрийн камера	[ʦifri:n kamera]
tripod	штатив	[ʃtativ]
flash	эккхар	[ɛk:ar]

to photograph (vt)	сурт даккха	[surt dak:a]
to take pictures	даккха	[dak:a]
to be photographed	сурт даккхийта	[surt dak:i:ta]

focus	резкость	[rezkɔst']
to adjust the focus	резкостан тӏедало	[rezkɔstan thedalɔ]
sharp, in focus	чӏоарла	[ʧhɔaɣa]
sharpness	чӏоарла хилар	[ʧhɔaɣa hilar]

contrast	къастам	[qhastam]
contrasty	къастаме	[qhastame]
picture (photo)	сурт	[surt]
negative (noun)	негатив	[negativ]

film (e.g., a roll of ~)	фотоплёнка	[fɔtɔplзŋka]
shot, frame	кадр	[kadr]
to print (photos)	зорба тоха	[zɔrba tɔha]

164. Beach. Swimming

beach	пляж	[pʌaʒ]
sand	гӀум	[ɣum]
deserted (beach)	гӀум-аренан	[ɣum arenan]

suntan	кхарзавалар	[qarzavalar]
to get a tan	вага	[vaga]
tan (adj)	маьлхо дагийна	[mælho dagi:na]
sunscreen	кхарзваларан дуьхьал крем	[qarzvalaran dyhal krem]

bikini	бикини	[bikini]
bathing suit	луьйчушъюхург	[lyjʧuʃʲjuhurg]
swim briefs	плавкаш	[plavkaʃ]

swimming pool	бассейн	[bas:ejn]
to swim (vi)	нека дан	[neka dan]
shower	душ	[duʃ]
to change (one's clothes)	бедар хийца	[bedar hi:tsa]
towel	гата	[gata]

| boat | кема | [kema] |
| motorboat | катер | [kater] |

water ski	хин лыжаш	[hin lıʒaʃ]
pedal boat	хин вилиспет	[hin wilispet]
surfing	серфинг	[serfiŋ]
surfer	серфингхо	[serfinhɔ]

scuba set	акваланг	[akvalaŋ]
flippers	пиллигаш	[pil:igaʃ]
mask	маска	[maska]
diver, snorkeler	чулелхархо	[ʧulelharhɔ]
to dive (vi)	чулелха	[ʧulelha]
underwater (adv)	хин кӀел	[hin k:el]

beach umbrella	зонтик	[zɔntik]
beach chair	шезлонг	[ʃezlɔŋ]
sunglasses	куьзганаш	[kyzganaʃ]
air mattress	нека дан гоь	[neka dan gø]

to play (amuse oneself)	ловза	[lɔvza]
to go for a swim	лийча	[li:ʧa]
beach ball	буьрка	[byrka]
to inflate (vt)	дуса	[dusa]

inflatable, air	дусу	[dusu]
wave	тулгle	[tulɣe]
buoy	буй	[buj]
to drown (ab. person)	бухадаха	[buhadɑha]
to save, to rescue	кlелхьардакхха	[k:elhɑrdɑqha]
life vest	кlелхьарвокхху жилет	[k:elhɑrvɔqhu ʒilet]
to observe, to watch	тергам бан	[tergɑm bɑn]
lifeguard	кlелхьардакххархо	[k:elhɑrdɑqharhɔ]

TECHNICAL EQUIPMENT. TRANSPORT

Technical equipment

165. Computer

computer	компьютер	[kɔmpjyter]
notebook, laptop	ноутбук	[noutbuk]
to switch on (vt)	лато	[latɔ]
to turn off	дӏадайа	[dəadaja]
keyboard	клавиатура	[klawiatura]
key	пиллиг	[pil:ig]
mouse	мышь	[mɪʃ]
mouse pad	кузан цуьрг	[kuzan tsyrg]
button	кнопка	[knɔpka]
cursor	курсор	[kursɔr]
monitor	монитор	[mɔnitɔr]
screen	экран	[ɛkran]
hard disk	жёстки диск	[ʒɜstki disk]
hard disk volume	жестки дискан барам	[ʒestki diskan baram]
memory	эс	[ɛs]
random access memory	оперативни эс	[ɔperativni ɛs]
file	файл	[fajl]
folder	папка	[papka]
to open (a file)	схьаделла	[shadel:a]
to close (vt)	дӏакъовла	[dəaqhɔvla]
to save (vt)	ӏалашдан	[əalaʃdan]
to delete (vt)	дӏадаккха	[dəadak:a]
to copy (vt)	копи яккха	[kɔpi jak:a]
to sort (vt)	сорташ дан	[sɔrtaʃ dan]
to copy (vt)	схьаяздан	[shajazdan]
program	программа	[prɔgram:a]
software	программни кхачам	[prɔgram:ni qatʃam]
programmer	программист	[prɔgram:ist]
to program (vi)	программа хӏотто	[prɔgram:a hɔt:ɔ]
hacker	хакер	[haker]
password	пароль	[parɔʎ]

| virus | вирус | [wirus] |
| to find, to detect | каро | [karɔ] |

| byte | байт | [bajt] |
| megabyte | мегабайт | [megabajt] |

| data | хаамаш | [ha:maʃ] |
| database | хаамашан база | [ha:maʃan baza] |

cable (wire)	кабель	[kabeʎ]
to disconnect (vt)	дӀадаккха	[dədak:a]
to connect (sth to sth)	вовшахтаса	[vɔvʃahtasa]

166. Internet. E-mail

Internet	интернет	[internet]
browser	браузер	[brauzer]
search engine	лехамийн ресурс	[lehami:n resurs]
provider	провайдер	[prɔvajder]

web master	веб-мастер	[web master]
website	веб-сайт	[web sajt]
web page	веб-arlo	[web aɣɔ]

| address | адрес | [adres] |
| address book | адресийн книга | [adresi:n kniga] |

| mailbox | поштан яьшка | [pɔʃtan jaʃka] |
| mail | пошт | [pɔʃt] |

message	хаам	[ha:m]
sender	дӀадахьийтинарг	[dədahi:tinarg]
to send (vt)	дӀадахьийта	[dədahi:ta]
sending (of mail)	дӀадахьийтар	[dədahi:tar]

| receiver | схьаэцархо | [shaetsarhɔ] |
| to receive (vt) | зхьаэца | [zhaetsa] |

| correspondence | кехаташ дӀасакхехьийтар | [kehataʃ dəsaqehi:tar] |
| to correspond (vi) | кехаташ дӀасакхехьийта | [kehataʃ dəsaqehi:ta] |

file	файл	[fajl]
to download (vt)	чудаккха	[tʃudak:a]
to create (vt)	кхолла	[qɔl:a]
to delete (vt)	дӀадаккха	[dədak:a]
deleted	дӀадаьккхнарг	[dədæk:narg]
connection (good, bad ~)	дазар	[dazar]
speed	сихалла	[sihal:a]

modem	модем	[mɔdem]
access	тlекхочийла	[theqɔtʃi:la]
port (e.g., input ~)	порт	[pɔrt]

| connection | дlатасар | [dəatasar] |
| to connect to ... (vi) | дlатаса | [dəatasa] |

| to choose (vt) | харжа | [harʒa] |
| to search for ... | леха | [leha] |

167. Electricity

electricity	электричество	[ɛlektritʃestvɔ]
electrical	электрически	[ɛlektritʃeski]
electric power station	электростанци	[ɛlektrɔstantsi]
energy	ницкъ	[nitsqh]
electric power	электроницкъ	[ɛlektrɔnitsqh]

light bulb	лампа	[lampa]
flashlight	фонарик	[fɔnarik]
street light	фонарь	[fɔnarʲ]

light	серло	[serlɔ]
to turn on	лато	[latɔ]
to turn off	дlадайа	[dəadaja]
to turn off the light	серло дlайа	[serlɔ dəajaja]

to burn out (vi)	дага	[daga]
short circuit	электрически серий вовшахкхетар	[ɛlektritʃeski seri: vɔvʃahqetar]
broken wire	хадор	[hadɔr]
contact	хьакхадалар	[haqadalar]

switch (for light)	дlайайоург	[dəajajourg]
wall socket	розетка	[rɔzetka]
plug	мlара	[məara]
extension cord	удлинитель	[udliniteʎ]

fuse	предохранитель	[predɔhraniteʎ]
cable, wire	сара	[sara]
wiring	далор	[dalɔr]

ampere	ампер	[amper]
amperage	токан ицкъ	[tɔkan itsqh]
volt	вольт	[vɔʎt]
voltage	булам	[bulam]

electrical device	электроприбор	[ɛlektrɔpribɔr]
indicator	индикатор	[indikatɔr]
electrician	электрик	[ɛlektrik]

to solder (vt)	лато	[latɔ]
soldering iron	латорг	[latɔrg]
current	ток	[tɔk]

168. Tools

tool, instrument	гӏирс	[ɣirs]
tools	гӏирсаш	[ɣirsaʃ]
equipment (factory ~)	гӏирс хӏоттор	[ɣirs hɔtɔr]

hammer	жӏов	[ʒəov]
screwdriver	сетал	[setal]
ax	диг	[dig]

saw	херх	[herh]
to saw (vt)	хьакха	[haqa]
plane (tool)	воттан	[vɔt:an]
to plane (vt)	хьекха	[heqa]
soldering iron	латорг	[latɔrg]
to solder (vt)	лато	[latɔ]

file (for metal)	ков	[kɔv]
carpenter pincers	морзах	[mɔrzah]
lineman's pliers	чӏапморзах	[ʧhapmɔrzah]
chisel	сто	[stɔ]

drill bit	буру	[buru]
electric drill	буру	[buru]
to drill (vi, vt)	буру хьовзо	[buru hɔvzɔ]

knife	урс	[urs]
pocket knife	кисанахь лело урс	[kisanah lelɔ urs]
folding (knife etc.)	мокъара туху	[mɔqara tuhu]
blade	дитт	[dit:]

sharp (knife)	ира	[ira]
blunt	аьрта	[ærta]
to become blunt	аьртадала	[ærtadala]
to sharpen (vt)	ирдан	[irdan]

bolt	болт	[bɔlt]
nut	гайка	[gajka]
thread (of a screw)	агар	[agar]
screw (for wood)	шуруп	[ʃurup]

| nail | хьостам | [hɔstam] |
| nailhead | кӏуж | [k:uʒ] |

| ruler (for measuring) | линейка | [linejka] |
| tape measure | рулетка | [ruletka] |

level (tool)	тӏадам	[thɑdɑm]
magnifying glass	бӏаьрг	[bəærg]
measuring instrument	юсту прибор	[justu pribɔr]
to measure (vt)	дуста	[dustɑ]
scale (of thermometer etc.)	шкала	[ʃkɑlɑ]
readings	гайтам	[gɑjtɑm]
compressor	компрессор	[kɔmpres:ɔr]
microscope	микроскоп	[mikrɔskɔp]
pump (e.g., water ~)	насос	[nɑsɔs]
robot	робот	[rɔbɔt]
laser	лазер	[lɑzer]
wrench	гайкин догӏа	[gɑjkin dɔɣɑ]
adhesive tape	скоч	[skɔtʃ]
glue	клей	[klej]
emery paper	ялпаран кехат	[jɑlpɑrɑn kehɑt]
spring	пружина	[pruʒinɑ]
magnet	магнит	[mɑgnit]
gloves	карнаш	[kɑrnɑʃ]
rope	чуха	[tʃuhɑ]
cord	тӏийриг	[thi:rig]
wire (e.g., telephone ~)	сара	[sɑrɑ]
cable	кабель	[kɑbeʎ]
sledgehammer	варзап	[vɑrzɑp]
crowbar	ваба	[vɑbɑ]
ladder	лами	[lɑmi]
stepladder	лами	[lɑmi]
to screw (tighten)	хьовзо	[hɔvzɔ]
to unscrew (vt)	схьахьовзо	[shɑhɔvzɔ]
to tighten (vt)	юкъакъовла	[juqhɑqhɔvlɑ]
to glue, to stick	тӏелато	[thelɑtɔ]
to cut (vt)	хедо	[hedɔ]
malfunction (fault)	доьхнарг	[døhnɑrg]
fault, problems	тайна цахилар	[tɑjnɑ tsɑhilɑr]
repair (mending)	тадар	[tɑdɑr]
to repair, to mend (vt)	тадан	[tɑdɑn]
to adjust (machine etc.)	нисдан	[nisdɑn]
to check (to examine)	хьажа	[hɑʒɑ]
checking	хьажар	[hɑʒɑr]
readings	гайтам	[gɑjtɑm]
reliable (machine)	тешаме	[teʃɑme]
complicated	чолхе	[tʃɔlhe]

to rust (vi)	**мекхадола**	[meqadɔla]
rusty, rusted	**мекхадоьлла**	[meqadøl:a]
rust	**мекха**	[meqa]

Transport

169. Airplane

airplane	кема	[kema]
air ticket	авиабилет	[awiabilet]
airline	авиакомпани	[awiakɔmpani]
airport	аэропорт	[aerɔpɔrt]
supersonic	озал тӀехь	[ɔzal theh]
captain	кеман командир	[keman kɔmandir]
crew	экипаж	[ɛkipaʒ]
pilot	кеманхо	[kemanho]
flight attendant	стюардесса	[styardes:a]
navigator	штурман	[ʃturman]
wings	тӀемаш	[themaʃ]
tail	цӀога	[tshɔga]
cockpit	кабина	[kabina]
engine	двигатель	[dwigateʎ]
undercarriage	шасси	[ʃas:i]
turbine	бера	[bera]
propeller	бера	[bera]
black box	Ӏаьржа яьшка	[əærʒa jaʃka]
control column	штурвал	[ʃturval]
fuel	ягорг	[jagɔrg]
instructions	инструкци	[instruktsi]
oxygen mask	кислородан маска	[kislɔrɔdan maska]
uniform	униформа	[uniforma]
life vest	кӀелхьарвоккху жилет	[k:elharvɔqhu ʒilet]
parachute	четар	[tʃetar]
takeoff	хьалагӀаттар	[halaɣat:ar]
to take off (vi)	хьалагӀатта	[halaɣat:a]
runway	хьалагӀотту аса	[halaɣɔt:u asa]
visibility	гуш хилар	[guʃ hilar]
flight (act of flying)	дахар	[dahar]
altitude	лакхалла	[laqal:a]
air pocket	хӀаваъан ор	[hava:n ɔr]
seat	меттиг	[met:ig]
headphones	ладугӀургаш	[laduɣurgaʃ]
folding tray	цхьалха стол	[tshalha stɔl]

window (in plane)	**иллюминатор**	[il:yminatɔr]
aisle	**чекхдолийла**	[ʧeqdɔli:la]

170. Train

train	**цӏерпошт**	[ʦherpɔʃt]
suburban train	**электричка**	[ɛlektriʧka]
fast train	**чехка цӏерпошт**	[ʧehka ʦherpɔʃt]
diesel locomotive	**тепловоз**	[teplɔvɔz]
steam engine	**цӏермашен**	[ʦhermaʃen]

passenger car	**вагон**	[vagɔn]
dining car	**вагон-ресторан**	[vagɔn restɔran]

rails	**рельсаш**	[reʌsaʃ]
railroad	**аьчка некъ**	[æʧka neqh]
railway tie	**шпала**	[ʃpala]

platform (railway ~)	**платформа**	[platfɔrma]
track (e.g., ~ 1, 2 etc.)	**некъ**	[neqh]
semaphore	**семафор**	[semafɔr]
station	**станци**	[stanʦi]

engineer	**машинхо**	[maʃinhɔ]
porter (of luggage)	**киранхо**	[kiranhɔ]
train steward	**проводник**	[prɔvɔdnik]
passenger	**пассажир**	[pas:aʒir]
conductor	**контролёр**	[kɔntrɔlɔr]

corridor (in train)	**уче**	[uʧe]
emergency break	**стоп-кран**	[stɔp kran]

compartment	**купе**	[kupe]
berth	**терхи**	[terhi]
upper berth	**лакхара терхи**	[laqara terhi]
lower berth	**лахара терхи**	[lahara terhi]
linen	**меттан лоччарш**	[met:an lɔʧarʃ]

ticket	**билет**	[bilet]
schedule	**расписани**	[raspisani]
timetable	**хаамийн у**	[ha:mi:n u]

to leave, to depart	**дӏадаха**	[dəadaha]
departure	**дӏадахар**	[dəadahar]
to arrive (about train)	**схьакхача**	[shaqaʧa]
arrival	**схьакхачар**	[shaqaʧar]

to be late (about train)	**тӏаьхьадиса**	[thæhadisa]
to arrive by train	**цӏерпошташь ван**	[ʦherpɔʃtah van]
to get on the train	**цӏерпошта тӏе хаа**	[ʦherpɔʃta the ha:]

to get off the train	цӏерпошта тӏера охьадосса	[tsherpɔʃta thera ɔhadɔs:a]
train wreck	харцар	[hartsar]
steam engine	цӏермашен	[tshermaʃən]
stoker, fireman	кочегар	[kotʃegar]
firebox	дагор	[dagɔr]
coal	кӏора	[k:ɔra]

171. Ship

ship	кема	[kema]
vessel	кема	[kema]
steamship	цӏеркема	[tsherkema]
riverboat	теплоход	[teplɔhod]
ocean liner	лайнер	[lajner]
cruiser	крейсер	[krejser]
yacht	яхта	[jahta]
tug	буксир	[buksir]
barge	баржа	[barʒa]
ferry	бурам	[buram]
sailing ship	гатанан кема	[gatanan kema]
brigantine	бригантина	[brigantina]
ice breaker	ша-кема	[ʃa kema]
submarine	хи бухахула лела кема	[hi buhahula lela kema]
boat	кема	[kema]
dinghy	шлюпка	[ʃlypka]
lifeboat	кӏелхьарвоккху шлюпка	[k:elharvɔk:u ʃlypka]
motorboat	катер	[kater]
captain	капитан	[kapitan]
seaman	хӏордахо	[hɔrdaho]
sailor	хӏордахо	[hɔrdaho]
crew	экипаж	[ɛkipaʒ]
boatswain	боцман	[botsman]
ship's boy	юнга	[juŋa]
cook	кок	[kɔk]
ship's doctor	хи кеман лор	[hi keman lɔr]
deck	палуба	[paluba]
mast	мачта	[matʃta]
sail	гата	[gata]
hold	трюм	[trym]
bow	кеман мара	[keman mara]

stern	кеман цlога	[keman tshɔga]
oar	пийсиг	[pi:sig]
propeller	винт	[wint]
cabin	каюта	[kajuta]
wardroom	кают-компани	[kajut kɔmpani]
engine room	машинийн отделени	[maʃini:n ɔtdeleni]
the bridge	капитанан тlай	[kapitanan thaj]
radio room	радиотрубка	[radiɔtrubka]
wave (radio)	тулгlе	[tulɣe]
logbook	кеман журнал	[keman ʒurnal]

spyglass	турмал	[turmal]
bell	горгал	[gɔrgal]
flag	байракх	[bajraq]

| rope (mooring ~) | муш | [muʃ] |
| knot (bowline etc.) | шад | [ʃad] |

| handrail | тlам | [tham] |
| gangway | лами | [lami] |

anchor	якорь	[jakɔrʲ]
to weigh anchor	якорь хьалаайа	[jakɔrʲ hala:ja]
to drop anchor	якорь кхосса	[jakɔrʲ qɔs:a]
anchor chain	якоран зlе	[jakɔran zee]

port (harbor)	порт	[pɔrt]
wharf, quay	дlатосийла	[dəatɔsi:la]
to berth (moor)	йистедало	[jistedalɔ]
to cast off	дlадаха	[dəadaha]

trip (voyage)	араваьлла лелар	[aravæl:a lelar]
cruise (sea trip)	круиз	[kruiz]
course (route)	курс	[kurs]
route (itinerary)	маршрут	[marʃrut]

fairway	фарватер	[farvater]
shallows (shoal)	гомхалла	[gɔmhal:a]
to run aground	гlамарла даха	[ɣamarla daha]

storm	дарц	[darts]
signal	сигнал	[signal]
to sink (about boat)	бухадаха	[buhadaha]
SOS	SOS	[sɔs]
life buoy	кlелхьарвоккху го	[k:elharvɔk:u gɔ]

172. Airport

| airport | аэропорт | [aərɔpɔrt] |
| airplane | кема | [kema] |

airline	авиакомпани	[awiakɔmpani]
air-traffic controller	диспетчер	[dispetʃer]
departure	дӏадахар	[dəadahar]
arrival	схьакхачар	[shaqatʃar]
to arrive (vi)	схьакхача	[shaqatʃa]
departure time	гӏовтаран хан	[ɣɔvtaran han]
arrival time	схьакхачаран хан	[shaqatʃaran han]
to be delayed	хьедала	[hedala]
flight delay	хьедар	[hedar]
information board	хаамийн табло	[haːmiːn tablɔ]
information	хаам	[haːm]
to announce (vt)	кхайкхо	[qajqɔ]
flight (e.g., next ~)	рейс	[rejs]
customs	таможни	[tamɔʒni]
customs officer	таможхо	[tamɔʒhɔ]
declaration	декларци	[deklaratsi]
to fill out a declaration	декларци язъян	[deklaratsi jazʰjan]
passport control	пастпортан контроль	[pastpɔrtan kɔntrɔʎ]
luggage	кира	[kira]
hand luggage	куьйга леладен кира	[kyjga leladen kira]
LOST-AND-FOUND	багаж лахар	[baɡaʒ lahar]
luggage cart	гӏудалкх	[ɣudalq]
landing	охьахаар	[ɔhahaːr]
runway	охьахааден аса	[ɔhahaːden asa]
to land (vi)	охьахаа	[ɔhahaː]
airstairs	лами	[lami]
check-in	регистраци	[registratsi]
check-in desk	регистрацин гӏопаста	[registratsin ɣɔpasta]
to check-in (vi)	регистраци ян	[registratsi jan]
boarding pass	тӏехааден талон	[thehaːden talɔn]
departure gate	арадалар	[aradalar]
transit	транзит	[tranzit]
to wait (vi, vt)	хьежа	[heʒa]
departure lounge	хьежаран зал	[heʒaran zal]
to see off	новкъадаккха	[nɔvqhadak:a]
to say goodbye	ӏодика ян	[əɔdika jan]

173. Bicycle. Motorcycle

bicycle	велиспет	[welispet]
scooter	моторoллер	[mɔtɔrɔl:er]

motorcycle, bike	мотоцикл	[mɔtɔʦikl]
to go by bicycle	велиспетехь ваха	[welispeteh vɑha]
handlebars	тӀам	[thɑm]
pedal	педаль	[pedɑʎ]
brake	тормозаш	[tɔrmɔzɑʃ]
bicycle seat	нуьйр	[nyjr]
pump	насос	[nasɔs]
rack	багажник	[bagaʒnik]
front lamp	фонарь	[fɔnɑrʲ]
helmet	гӀем	[ɣem]
wheel	чкъург	[ʧqhurg]
mudguard	тӀам	[thɑm]
rim	туре	[ture]
spoke	чӀу	[ʧhu]

Cars

174. Types of cars

automobile, car	автомобиль	[avtɔmɔbiʎ]
sports car	спортивни автомобиль	[spɔrtivni avtɔmɔbiʎ]
limousine	лимузин	[limuzin]
off-road vehicle	внедорожник, джип	[vnedɔrɔʒnik], [dʒip]
convertible	кабриолет	[kabriɔlet]
minibus	микроавтобус	[mikrɔavtɔbus]
ambulance	сихонан гlо	[sihɔnan ɣɔ]
snowplow	ло дlадоккху машина	[lɔ dəadɔk:u maʃina]
truck	киранийн машина	[kirani:n maʃina]
tank truck	бензовоз	[benzɔvɔz]
van	хlургон	[hurgɔn]
road tractor	озорг	[ɔzɔrg]
trailer	тlаьхьатосург	[thæhatɔsurg]
comfortable	комфорт йолу	[kɔmfɔrt jolu]
second hand	лелийна	[leli:na]

175. Cars. Bodywork

hood	капот	[kapɔt]
fender	тlам	[tham]
roof	тхов	[thov]
windshield	хьалхара ангали	[halhara aɲali]
rear-view mirror	тlехьара сурт гайта ангали	[thehara surt gajta aɲali]
windshield washer	дилар	[dilar]
windshield wipers	ангалицlандийригаш	[aɲalitshandi:rigaʃ]
side window	арlонгара ангали	[aɣɔɲara aɲali]
window crank	ангалихьалаойург	[aɲalihalaɔjurg]
antenna	антенна	[anteɲa]
sun roof	люк	[lyk]
bumper	бампер	[bamper]
trunk	багажник	[bagaʒnik]
door	неl	[neə]

| door handle | тӀам | [tham] |
| door lock | доргӀа | [dɔɣa] |

license plate	номер	[nɔmer]
muffler	лагӀийӀриг	[laɣjiːrig]
gas tank	бензинан бак	[benzinan bak]
tail pipe	выхлопни турба	[vɪhlɔpni turba]

gas, accelerator	газ	[gaz]
pedal	педаль	[pedaʎ]
gas pedal	газан педаль	[gazan pedaʎ]

brake	тормоз	[tɔrmɔz]
brake pedal	тормозан педаль	[tɔrmɔzan pedaʎ]
to slow down (to brake)	тормоз таса	[tɔrmɔz tasa]
parking brake	дӀахӀоттайойларан тормоз	[dɛahɔt:ajojlaran tɔrmɔz]

clutch	вовшахтасар	[vɔvʃahtasar]
clutch pedal	вовшахтасаран педаль	[vɔvʃahtasaran pedaʎ]
clutch plate	вовшахтасаран диск	[vɔvʃahtasaran disk]
shock absorber	амортизатор	[amɔrtizatɔr]

wheel	чкъург	[ʧqhurg]
spare tire	тӀаьхьалонан чкъург	[thæhalɔnan ʧqhurg]
wheel cover (hubcap)	кад	[kad]

driving wheels	лело чкъургаш	[lelɔ ʧqhurgaʃ]
front-wheel drive	хьалхараприводан	[halharaprivɔdan]
rear-wheel drive	тӀехьараприводан	[theharaprivɔdan]
all-wheel drive	дуьззинаприводан	[dyz:inaprivɔdan]

| gearbox | передачан гӀутакх | [peredaʧan ɣutaq] |
| automatic | автоматически | [avtɔmatiʧeski] |

| mechanical | механически | [mehaniʧeski] |
| gear shift | передачан гӀутакхан зеразакъ | [peredaʧan ɣutaqan zerazaqh] |

| headlight | фара | [fara] |
| headlights | фараш | [faraʃ] |

low beam	гергара серло	[gergara serlɔ]
high beam	генара серло	[genara serlɔ]
brake light	собар-хаам	[sɔbar haːm]

parking lights	габаритам серло	[gabaritam serlɔ]
hazard lights	аварии серло	[avari: serlɔ]
fog lights	дахкарна дуьхьалара фараш	[dahkarna dyhalara faraʃ]

| turn signal | «поворотник» | [pɔvɔrɔtnik] |
| back-up light | юханехьа дахар | [juhaneha dahar] |

176. Cars. Passenger compartment

car inside	салон	[salɔn]
leather (attr)	тlаьрсиган	[thærsigan]
velour (attr)	велюран	[welyran]
upholstery	тlетухург	[thetuhurg]
instrument (gage)	прибор	[pribɔr]
dashboard	приборийн у	[pribɔri:n u]
speedometer	спидометр	[spidɔmetr]
needle (pointer)	цамза	[tsamza]
odometer	лолург	[lɔlurg]
indicator	гойтург	[gɔjturg]
level	барам	[baram]
indicator light	лампа	[lampa]
steering wheel	тlам, тlоман чкъург	[tham], [thɔman ʧqhurg]
horn	сигнал	[signal]
button	кнопка	[knɔpka]
switch	лакъорг	[laqhɔrg]
seat	охьахойла	[ɔhahoi:la]
seat back	букъ	[buqh]
headrest	гlовла	[ɣɔvla]
seat belt	доьхка	[døhka]
to fasten the belt	доьхка тlедолла	[døhka thedɔl:a]
adjustment (of seats)	нисдар	[nisdar]
airbag	хlаваан гlайба	[hava:n ɣajba]
air-conditioner	кондиционер	[kɔnditsiɔner]
radio	радио	[radiɔ]
CD player	CD-проигрыватель	[sidi prɔigrıvateʎ]
to turn on	йолаялийта	[jɔlajali:ta]
antenna	антенна	[anteŋa]
glove box	бардачок	[bardaʧok]
ashtray	чимтосург	[ʧimtɔsurg]

177. Cars. Engine

engine	двигатель	[dwigateʎ]
motor	мотор	[mɔtɔr]
diesel (e.g., ~ engine)	дизелан	[dizelan]
gasoline (e.g., ~ engine)	бензинан	[benzinan]
engine volume	двигателан чухоам	[dwigatelan ʧuhoam]
power	нуьцкъалла	[nytsqhal:a]
horsepower	говран ницкъ	[gɔvran nitsqh]

piston	поршень	[pɔrʃən]
cylinder	цилиндр	[tsilindr]
valve	клапан	[klapan]

injector	инжектор	[inʒektɔr]
generator	генератор	[generatɔr]
carburetor	карбюратор	[karbyratɔr]
engine oil	моторан даьтта	[mɔtɔran dæt:a]

radiator	радиатор	[radiatɔr]
cooling liquid	шело туху кочалла	[ʃelɔ tuhu kɔtʃal:a]
cooling fan	мохтухург	[mɔhtuhurg]

battery (accumulator)	аккумулятор	[ak:umuʌatɔr]
starter	стартер	[starter]
ignition	зажигани	[zaʒigani]
spark plug	латаен свеча	[lataen swetʃa]

terminal (of battery)	клемма	[klem:a]
plus (positive terminal)	плюс	[plys]
minus (negative terminal)	минус	[minus]
fuse	предохранитель	[predɔhraniteʌ]

air filter	хӀаваан фильтр	[hava:n fiʌtr]
oil filter	даьттан фильтр	[dæt:an fiʌtr]
fuel filter	ягоран фильтр	[jagɔran fiʌtr]

178. Cars. Crash. Repair

car accident	авари	[avari]
road accident	некъан хилларг	[neqhan hil:arg]
to run into …	кхета	[qeta]
to have an accident	доха	[dɔha]
damage	лазор	[lazɔr]
intact	могуш-маьрша	[mɔguʃ mærʃa]

| to break down (vi) | доха | [dɔha] |
| towrope | буксиран трос | [buksiran trɔs] |

puncture	чеккхдаккхар	[tʃek:dak:ar]
to be flat	дассадала	[das:adala]
to pump up	дуса	[dusa]
pressure	таӀам	[taəam]
to check (to examine)	хьажа	[haʒa]

repair	таяр	[tajar]
auto repair shop	таяран пхьалгӀа	[tajaran phalɣa]
spare part	запчасть	[zaptʃastʲ]
part	деталь	[detaʌ]
bolt	болт	[bɔlt]

screw bolt	винт	[wint]
nut	гайка	[gajka]
washer	шайба	[ʃajba]
bearing	подшипник	[pɔdʃipnik]
tube	турба	[turba]
gasket, washer	прокладка	[prɔkladka]
cable, wire	сара	[sara]
jack	домкрат	[dɔmkrat]
wrench	гайкин догӀа	[gajkin dɔɣa]
hammer	жӀов	[ʒəov]
pump	насос	[nasɔs]
screwdriver	сетал	[setal]
fire extinguisher	цӀайойург	[tshajojurg]
warning triangle	аварии кхосаберг	[avari: qɔsaberg]
to stall (vi)	дӀайов	[dəajov]
stall	сацор	[satsɔr]
to be broken	дохо	[dɔhɔ]
to overheat (vi)	тӀех дохдала	[theh dɔhdala]
to be clogged up	дукъадала	[duqhadala]
to freeze (about pipe etc.)	гӀоро	[ɣɔrɔ]
to burst (vi)	эккха	[ɛk:a]
pressure	тӀалам	[taəam]
level	барам	[baram]
slack (e.g., ~ belt)	гӀийла	[ɣi:la]
dent	ведйина меттиг	[wedjɪna met:ig]
knock (in motor)	тата	[tata]
crack	датӀар	[dathar]
scratch	мацхар	[matshar]

179. Cars. Road

road	некъ	[neqh]
highway, freeway	автонекъ	[avtɔneqh]
freeway	силам-некъ	[silam neqh]
direction (way)	арло, тӀедерзор	[aɣɔ], [thederzɔr]
distance	некъан бохалла	[neqhan bɔhal:a]
bridge	тӀай	[thaj]
parking lot	паркинг	[parkiɲ]
square	майда	[majda]
interchange	гӀонжарӀа	[ɣɔnʒaɣa]
tunnel	туннель	[tuɲeʎ]
gas station	автозаправка	[avtɔzapravka]

parking lot	машинаш дIахІиттайойла	[maʃinaʃ dəahit:ajojla]
gas pump	бензоколонка	[benzɔkɔlɔŋka]
auto repair shop	гараж	[garaʒ]
to get gas	дотта	[dɔt:a]
fuel	ягорг	[jagɔrg]
jerrycan	канистр	[kanistr]

asphalt	асфальт	[asfaʌt]
road markings	билгало	[bilgalɔ]
curb	дийна дист	[di:na dist]
guardrail	керт	[kert]
ditch	кювет	[kywet]
roadside	некъан йист	[neqhan jist]
street light	боrlam	[bɔɣam]

to drive (a car)	лело	[lelɔ]
to turn (steering wheel)	хьийзо	[hi:zɔ]
to turn (left, right etc.)	дIадерза	[dəaderza]
to make a U-turn	духадерзар	[duhaderzar]
reverse	юханехьа дахар	[juhaneha dahar]

to honk (about car)	сигнал етта	[signal et:a]
honk (sound)	аьзнийн сигнал	[æzni:n signal]
to get stuck	диса	[disa]
to spin (in the mud)	хьийзаш латта	[hi:zaʃ lat:a]
to cut, to turn off	дIадайа	[dəadaja]

speed	сихалла	[sihal:a]
to exceed the speed limit	сихалла тIехьа йаккха	[sihal:a theha jak:a]
to give sb a ticket	гIуда тоха	[ɣuda tɔha]
traffic lights	светофор	[swetɔfɔr]
driver's license	лелорхочун бакъонаш	[lelɔrhɔtʃun baqhɔnaʃ]

grade crossing	дехьаволийла	[dehavɔli:la]
intersection	галморзе	[galmɔrze]
crosswalk	гIашлойн дехьаволийла	[ɣaʃlojn dehavɔli:la]
turn (curve in road)	гола	[gɔla]
pedestrian zone	гIашлойн зона	[ɣaʃlojn zɔna]

180. Traffic signs

rules of the road	некъантIехула лела ран бакъонаш	[neqhanthehula lelaran baqhɔnaʃ]
traffic sign	билгало	[bilgalɔ]
passing (overtaking)	хьалхадалар	[halhadalar]
curve	го	[gɔ]
U-turn	духадерзор	[duhaderzɔr]
traffic circle	хьинзаме болам	[hinzame bɔlam]

No entry	чувар дихкина ду	[tʃuːar dihkina du]
No vehicles allowed	лелар дихкина ду	[lelar dihkina du]
No passing	хьалхадалар дихкина ду	[halhadalar dihkina du]
No parking	дlахlуттийла дихкина ду	[dəahutːiːla dihkina du]
No stopping	social дихкина ду	[sotsiːla dihkina du]

dangerous turn	цlеххьашха дlаверзар	[tshehaʃha dəawerzar]
steep descent	цlеххьашха басе	[tshehaʃha base]
one-way traffic	цхьана аrlорхьа лелар	[tshana aɣorha lelar]
pedestrian crossing	гlашлойн дехьаволийла	[ɣaʃlojn dehavoliːla]

slippery road	шера некъ	[ʃera neqh]
YIELD	некъ бита	[neqh bita]

PEOPLE. LIFE EVENTS

Life events

181. Holidays. Event

celebration, holiday	дезде	[dezde]
national day	къаьмнийн дезде	[qhæmni:n dezde]
public holiday	деза де	[deza de]
to celebrate (vi, vt)	даздан	[dazdan]
event (happening)	хилларг	[hil:arg]
event (organized activity)	мероприяти	[merɔprijati]
banquet (party)	той	[tɔj]
reception (formal party)	тlэцар	[thætsar]
feast	той	[tɔj]
anniversary	шо кхачар	[ʃɔ qatʃar]
jubilee	юбилей	[jubilej]
to celebrate (jubilee etc.)	билгалдаккха	[bilgaldak:a]
New Year	Керла шо	[kerla ʃɔ]
Happy New Year!	Керлачу шарца декъал дойла шу!	[kerlatʃu ʃartsa deqhal dɔjla ʃu]
Christmas tree	Ёлка	[ɜlka]
Christmas	Рождество	[rɔʒdestvɔ]
Merry Christmas!	Рождествоца декъал дойла шу!	[rɔʒdestvɔtsa deqhal dɔjla ʃu]
fireworks	салют	[salyt]
wedding	ловзар	[lɔvzar]
groom	зуда ехна стаг	[zuda ehna stag]
bride	нускал	[nuskal]
to invite (vt)	схьакхайкха	[shaqajqa]
invitation	кхайкхар	[qajqar]
guest	хьаша	[haʃa]
to visit with sb	хьошалгlа ваха	[hɔʃalɣa vaha]
to greet the guests	хьешашна дуьхьалвоха	[heʃaʃna dyhalvaha]
gift, present	совгlат	[sɔvɣat]
to give (sth as present)	совгlатна дала	[sɔvɣatna dala]
to receive gifts	совгlаташ схьаэца	[sɔvɣataʃ shaetsa]

bouquet (of flowers)	курс	[kurs]
congratulations	декъалдар	[deqhaldar]
to congratulate (vt)	декъалдан	[deqhaldan]
greeting card	декъалден открытка	[deqhalden ɔtkrɪtka]
to send a postcard	открытка дӀадахьийта	[ɔtkrɪtka dəadahi:ta]
to get a postcard	открытка схьаэца	[ɔtkrɪtka shaəʦa]
toast	кад	[kad]
to offer (a drink etc.)	дала	[dala]
champagne	шампански	[ʃampanski]
to have fun	сакъера	[saqhera]
fun, merriment	сакъерар	[saqherar]
joy	хазахетар	[hazahetar]
dance	хелхар	[helhar]
to dance (vi, vt)	хелхадала	[helhadala]
waltz	вальс	[vaʎs]
tango	танго	[taŋɔ]

182. Funerals. Burial

cemetery	кешнаш	[keʃnaʃ]
grave, tomb	каш	[kaʃ]
gravestone	чурт	[ʧurt]
fence	керт	[kert]
chapel	килс	[kils]
death	далар	[dalar]
to die (vi, vt)	дала	[dala]
the deceased	велларг	[wel:arg]
mourning	Ӏаьржа	[əærʒa]
to bury (vt)	дӀадолла	[dəadɔl:a]
funeral home	велчан ламаста ден бюро	[welʧan lamasta den byrɔ]
funeral	тезет	[tezet]
wreath	кочар	[kɔʧar]
casket	гроб	[grɔb]
hearse	катафалк	[katafalk]
shroud	марчо	[marʧɔ]
procession	процесси	[prɔʦes:i]
cremation urn	урна	[urna]
crematory	крематорий	[krematɔri]
obituary	некролог	[nekrɔlɔg]
to cry (weep)	делха	[delha]
to sob (vi)	делха	[delha]

183. War. Soldiers

platoon	завод	[zavɔd]
company	рота	[rɔta]
regiment	полк	[pɔlk]
army	эскар	[ɛskar]
division	дивизи	[diwizi]

detachment	тоба	[tɔba]
host (army)	эскар	[ɛskar]

soldier	салти	[salti]
officer	эпсар	[ɛpsar]

private	моrlapepa	[mɔɣarera]
sergeant	сержант	[serʒant]
lieutenant	лейтенант	[lejtenant]
captain	капитан	[kapitan]
major	майор	[major]
colonel	полковник	[pɔlkɔvnik]
general	инарла	[inarla]

sailor	хlордахо	[hɔrdaho]
captain	капитан	[kapitan]
boatswain	боцман	[bɔtsman]

artilleryman	артиллерист	[artil:erist]
paratrooper	десантхо	[desantho]
pilot	кеманхо	[kemanho]
navigator	штурман	[ʃturman]
mechanic	механик	[mehanik]

pioneer (sapper)	сапёр	[sapɔr]
parachutist	парашютхо	[paraʃytho]
scout	талламхо	[tal:amho]
sniper	иччархо	[itʃarhɔ]

patrol (group)	патруль	[patruʎ]
to patrol (vi, vt)	rlapoлла дан	[ɣarɔl:a dan]
sentry, guard	rlapoл	[ɣarɔl]

warrior	эскархо	[ɛskarhɔ]
hero	турпалхо	[turpalho]
heroine	турпалхо	[turpalho]
patriot	патриот	[patriot]

traitor	ямартхо	[jamartho]
to betray (vt)	ямартдала	[jamartdala]
betrayer	ямартхо	[jamartho]
deserter	деддарг	[ded:arg]
to desert (vi)	дада	[dada]

mercenary	ялхо	[jalho]
recruit	керла блахо	[kerla bəaho]
volunteer	лаамерниг	[la:mernig]

dead	дийнарг	[di:narg]
wounded	чов хилла	[tʃov hil:a]
prisoner of war	йийсархо	[ji:sarho]

184. War. Military actions. Part 1

war	тӀом	[thɔm]
to be at war	тӀом бан	[thɔm ban]
civil war	граждански тӀом	[graʒdanski thɔm]

treacherously	тешнабехкехь	[teʃnabehkeh]
declaration (~ of war)	дӀахьебан	[dəaheban]
to declare (~ war)	хьебан	[heban]
aggression	агресси	[agres:i]
to attack (invade)	тӀелата	[thelata]

to invade (vt)	дӀалаца	[dəalatsa]
invader	дӀалецархо	[dəaletsarho]
conqueror	даккхархо	[dak:arhɔ]

defense	дуьхьало, лардар	[dyhalɔ], [lardar]
to defend (a country etc.)	дуьхьало ян, лардан	[dyhalɔ jan], [lardan]
to defend oneself	дуьхьало ян	[dyhalɔ jan]

| enemy, hostile | мостаӀ | [mɔstaɣ] |
| hostile (attr) | мостаӀийн | [mɔstaɣi:n] |

| strategy | стратеги | [strategi] |
| tactics | тактика | [taktika] |

order	омра	[ɔmra]
command (order)	буьйр	[byjr]
to order (vi, vt)	омра дан	[ɔmra dan]
mission	тӀедиллар	[thedil:ar]
secret (adj)	къайлаха	[qhajlaha]

| battle | тӀом | [thɔm] |
| combat | тӀом | [thɔm] |

attack	атака	[ataka]
storming (assault)	штурм	[ʃturm]
to storm (vt)	штурм ян	[ʃturm jan]
siege (to be under ~)	лацар	[latsar]

| offensive (noun) | тӀелатар | [thelatar] |
| to go on the offensive | тӀелета | [theleta] |

retreat	юхадалар	[juhadalar]
to retreat (vi)	юхадала	[juhadala]
encirclement	го бар	[gɔ bar]
to encircle (vt)	го бан	[gɔ ban]
bombing (by aircraft)	бомбанаш еттар	[bɔmbanaʃ et:ar]
to drop a bomb	бомб чукхосса	[bɔmb tʃuqɔs:a]
to bomb (vt)	бомбанаш етта	[bɔmbanaʃ et:a]
explosion	эккхар	[ɛk:ar]
shot	ялар	[jalar]
to fire a shot	кхосса	[qɔs:a]
shooting	кхийсар	[qi:sar]
to take aim (at …)	хьежо	[heʒɔ]
to point (a gun)	тӀехьажо	[thehaʒɔ]
to hit (the target)	кхета	[qeta]
to sink (e.g., ~ a ship)	хи бухадахийта	[hi buhadahi:ta]
hole (in a ship)	Ӏуьрг	[əyrg]
to founder, to sink	хи буха даха	[hi buha daha]
front (at war)	фронт	[frɔnt]
rear (noun)	тӀехье	[thehe]
evacuation	эвакуаци	[ɛvakuatsi]
to evacuate (vt)	эвакуаци ян	[ɛvakuatsi jan]
trench	окоп, траншей	[ɔkɔp], [tranʃej]
barbwire	кӀохцал-сара	[k:ɔhtsal sara]
barrier	дуьхьало	[dyhalɔ]
watchtower	чардакх	[tʃardaq]
hospital	госпиталь	[gɔspitaʎ]
to wound (vi, vt)	чов ян	[tʃɔv jan]
wound	чов	[tʃɔv]
wounded (noun)	чов хилла	[tʃɔv hil:a]
to be injured	чов хила	[tʃɔv hila]
serious	хала	[hala]

185. War. Military actions. Part 2

captivity	йийсарехь хилар	[ji:sareh hilar]
to take sb captive	йийсар дан	[ji:sar dan]
to be in captivity	йийсарехь хила	[ji:sareh hila]
to be taken prisoner	йийсарехь кхача	[ji:sareh qatʃa]
concentration camp	концлагерь	[kɔntslagerʲ]
prisoner of war	йийсархо	[ji:sarhɔ]
to escape (vi)	дада	[dada]

to betray (vt)	ямартдала	[jamartdala]
betrayer	ямартхо	[jamartho]
betrayal	ямартло	[jamartlɔ]
to execute (shoot)	тоьпаш тоха	[tøpaʃ tɔha]
execution (shooting)	тоьпаш тохар	[tøpaʃ tɔhar]
uniform	духар	[duhar]
shoulder board	погон	[pɔgɔn]
gas mask	противогаз	[prɔtivɔgaz]
radio transmitter	раци	[ratsi]
cipher, code	шифр	[ʃifr]
conspiracy	конспираци	[kɔnspiratsi]
password	пароль	[parɔʎ]
mine (explosive)	мина	[mina]
to mine (road etc.)	минаш яхка	[minaʃ jahka]
minefield	минийн аре	[mini:n are]
air-raid warning	хӀаваан орца	[hava:n ɔrtsa]
alarm (warning)	орца	[ɔrtsa]
signal	сигнал	[signal]
signal flare	хааман ракета	[ha:man raketa]
headquarters	штаб	[ʃtab]
reconnaissance	разведка	[razwedka]
situation	хьал	[hal]
report	рапорт	[rapɔrt]
ambush	кӀело	[k:elɔ]
reinforcement (of army)	рӀо	[ɣɔ]
target	гӀакх	[ɣaq]
shooting ground	полигон	[pɔligɔn]
military exercise	манёвраш	[manɜvraʃ]
panic	дохар	[dɔhar]
devastation	бохор	[bɔhɔr]
destruction, ruins	дохор	[dɔhɔr]
to destroy (vt)	дохо	[dɔhɔ]
to survive (vi, vt)	дийна диса	[di:na disa]
to disarm (vt)	герз схьадаккха	[gerz shadak:a]
to handle (e.g., ~ a gun)	лело	[lelɔ]
Attention!	Тийна!	[ti:na]
At ease!	ПаргӀат!	[parɣat]
feat (of courage)	хьуьнар	[hynar]
oath (vow)	дуй	[duj]
to swear (an oath)	дуй баа	[duj ba:]
decoration (medal etc.)	совгӀат	[sɔvɣat]

to award (give medal to)	совгӏат дала	[sɔvɣat dala]
medal	мидал	[midal]
order (e.g., ~ of Merit)	орден	[ɔrden]

victory	толам	[tɔlam]
defeat	эшар	[ɛʃar]
armistice	маслаӏат	[maslaəat]

banner (flag)	байракх	[bajraq]
glory (honor, fame)	гӏардалар	[ɣardalar]
parade	парад	[parad]
to march (on parade)	марш-болар дан	[marʃ bɔlar dan]

186. Weapons

weapons	герз	[gerz]
firearm	долу герз	[dɔlu gerz]
cold weapons (knives etc.)	шийла герз	[ʃiːla gerz]

chemical weapons	химически герз	[himitʃeski gerz]
nuclear	ядеран	[jaderan]
nuclear weapons	ядеран герз	[jaderan gerz]

| bomb | бомба | [bɔmba] |
| atomic bomb | атоман бомба | [atɔman bɔmba] |

pistol (gun)	тапча	[taptʃa]
rifle	топ	[tɔp]
submachine gun	автомат	[avtɔmat]
machine gun	пулемёт	[pulemɔt]

muzzle	Iуьрг	[əyrg]
barrel	чӏижаргӏа	[tʃhiӡarɣa]
caliber	калибр	[kalibr]

trigger	лаг	[lag]
sight (aiming device)	лалашо	[əalaʃɔ]
magazine	гӏутакх	[ɣutaq]
butt (of rifle)	хен	[hen]

| hand grenade | гранат | [granat] |
| explosive | оьккхург | [økːurg] |

bullet	даьндарг	[dændarg]
cartridge	патарма	[patarma]
charge	бустам	[bustam]
ammunition	тӏеман гӏирс	[təeman ɣirs]

| bomber (aircraft) | бомбардировщик | [bɔmbardirɔvɕik] |
| fighter | истребитель | [istrebiteʎ] |

helicopter	вертолёт	[wertɔlɜt]
anti-aircraft gun	зенитка	[zenitka]
tank	танк	[taŋk]
tank gun	йоккха топ	[jok:a tɔp]

| artillery | артиллери | [artil:eri] |
| to take aim (at ...) | тӀехьажо | [thehaʒɔ] |

shell (projectile)	снаряд	[snarʲad]
mortar bomb	мина	[mina]
mortar	миномёт	[minɔmɜt]
splinter (of shell)	гериг	[gerig]

submarine	хи буха лела кема	[hi buha lela kema]
torpedo	торпеда	[tɔrpeda]
missile	ракета	[raketa]

to load (gun)	дуза	[duza]
to shoot (vi)	кхийса	[qi:sa]
to take aim (at ...)	хьежо	[heʒɔ]
bayonet	цхьамза	[tshamza]

epee	шпага	[ʃpaga]
saber (e.g., cavalry ~)	тур	[tur]
spear (weapon)	гоьмукъ	[gømuqh]
bow	секха Ӏад	[seqa əad]
arrow	пха	[pha]
musket	мушкет	[muʃket]
crossbow	арбалет	[arbalet]

187. Ancient people

primitive (prehistoric)	духхьарлера	[duharlera]
prehistoric	историл хьалхара	[istoril halhara]
ancient (civilization etc.)	мацахлера	[matsahlera]

Stone Age	Тӏулган оьмар	[thulgan ømar]
Bronze Age	бронзанан оьмар	[brɔnzanan ømar]
Ice Age	шен зама	[ʃen zama]

tribe	туккхам	[tuqam]
cannibal	нахбуург	[nahbu:rg]
hunter	таллархо	[tal:arhɔ]
to hunt (vi, vt)	талла эха	[tal:a ɛha]
mammoth	мамонт	[mamɔnt]

cave	хьех	[heh]
fire	цӀе	[tshe]
campfire	цӀе	[tshe]
rock painting	тархаш тӀера суьрташ	[tarhaʃ thera syrtaʃ]

tool (e.g., stone ax)	къинхьегаман гӀирс	[qhinhegaman ɣirs]
spear	гоьмукъ	[gømuqh]
stone ax	тӀулгийн диг	[thulgi:n dig]
to be at war	тӀом бан	[thɔm ban]
to domesticate (tame)	караламо	[karaəamɔ]

idol	цӀу	[ʦhu]
to worship (vt)	текъа	[teqha]
superstition	доьгӀначух тешар	[døɣnaʧuh teʃar]
rite	Ӏадат	[əadat]

evolution	эволюци	[ɛvɔlyʦi]
development	кхиам	[qiam]
disappearance	дӀадалар	[dəadalar]
to adapt oneself	дӀадола	[dəadɔla]

archeology	археологи	[arheolɔgi]
archeologist	археолог	[arheolɔg]
archeological	археологин	[arheolɔgin]

excavation site	ахкар	[ahkar]
excavations	ахкар	[ahkar]
find (object)	карийнарг	[kari:narg]
fragment	дакъа	[daqha]

188. Middle Ages

people (nation)	халкъ	[halqh]
peoples	адамаш	[adamaʃ]
tribe	тукхам	[tuqam]
tribes	тукхамаш	[tuqamaʃ]

barbarians	варварш	[varvarʃ]
Gauls	галлаш	[gal:aʃ]
Goths	готаш	[gɔtaʃ]
Slavs	славянаш	[slavʲanaʃ]
Vikings	викинг	[wikiŋ]

| Romans | римлянаш | [rimʎanaʃ] |
| Roman | римски | [rimski] |

Byzantines	византийцаш	[wizanti:ʦaʃ]
Byzantium	Византи	[wizanti]
Byzantine	византийн	[wizanti:n]

emperor	император	[imperatɔr]
leader, chief	баьчча	[bæʧa]
powerful (e.g., ~ king)	нуьцкъала	[nyʦqhala]
king	паччахь	[paʧah]
ruler (sovereign)	урхалча	[urhalʧa]

knight	къонах	[qhɔnah]
knightly	къонахчун	[qhɔnahtʃun]
feudal lord	феодал	[feɔdal]
feudal (adj)	феодалийн	[feɔdali:n]
vassal	вассал	[vas:al]

duke	герцог	[gertsɔg]
earl	граф	[graf]
baron	барон	[barɔn]
bishop	епископ	[episkɔp]

armor	гӀарӀ	[ɣaɣ]
shield	турс	[turs]
sword	гӀалакх	[ɣalaq]
visor	цхар	[tshar]
chain armor	гӀарӀ	[ɣaɣ]

| crusade | жӀаран тӀом | [ʒəaran thɔm] |
| crusader | жӀархо | [ʒəarhɔ] |

territory	латта	[lat:a]
to attack (invade)	тӀелата	[thelata]
to conquer (vt)	даккха	[dak:a]
to occupy (invade)	дӀалаца	[dəalatsa]

siege (to be under ~)	лацар	[latsar]
besieged	лаьцна	[lætsna]
to besiege (vt)	лаца	[latsa]

inquisition	Ӏазап латтор	[əazap lat:ɔr]
inquisitor	Ӏазап латторхо	[əazap lat:ɔrhɔ]
torture	Ӏазап	[əazap]
cruel	къиза	[qhiza]
heretic	мунепакъ	[munepaqh]
heresy	мунепакъ-Ӏилма	[munepaqh əilma]

seafaring	хикема лелор	[hikema lelɔr]
pirate	пират	[pirat]
piracy	пираталла	[piratal:a]
boarding (attack)	абордаж	[abɔrdaʒ]

| loot | хӀонц | [hɔnts] |
| treasures | хазна | [hazna] |

discovery	гучудаккхар	[gutʃudak:ar]
to discover (new land etc.)	гучудаккха	[gutʃudak:a]
expedition (noun)	экспедици	[ɛkspeditsi]

musketeer	мушкетёр	[muʃketɜr]
cardinal	кардинал	[kardinal]
heraldry	геральдика	[geraʎdika]
heraldic	геральдически	[geraʎditʃeski]

189. Leader. Chief. Authorities

king	паччахь	[patʃah]
queen	зуда-паччахь	[zuda patʃah]
royal	паччахьан	[patʃahan]
kingdom	паччахьалла	[patʃahal:a]
prince	принц	[prints]
princess	принцесса	[printses:a]
president	президент	[patʃah]
vice-president	вице-президент	[witse prezident]
senator	сенатхо	[senatho]
monarch	монарх	[mɔnarh]
ruler (sovereign)	урхалча	[urhaltʃa]
dictator	диктатор	[diktatɔr]
tyrant	Iазапхо	[əazapho]
magnate	магнат	[magnat]
director	директор	[direktɔr]
chief	куьйгалхо	[kyjgalho]
manager (director)	урхалхо	[urhalho]
boss	хьаькам	[hækam]
owner	да	[da]
head (~ of delegation)	куьйгалхо	[kyjgalho]
authorities	хьаькамаш	[hækamaʃ]
management (of hotel etc.)	хьаькамаш	[hækamaʃ]
governor	губернатор	[gubernatɔr]
consul	консул	[kɔnsul]
diplomat	дипломат	[diplɔmat]
mayor	мэр	[mɛr]
sheriff	шериф	[ʃərif]
emperor	император	[imperatɔr]
tsar, czar	паччахь	[patʃah]
Pharaoh	пирIон	[pirəon]
khan	хан	[han]

190. Road. Way. Directions

road	некъ	[neqh]
way	некъ	[neqh]
freeway	силам-некъ	[silam neqh]
highway, freeway	автонекъ	[avtɔneqh]
interstate	къаьмнийн некъ	[qhæmni:n neqh]

main road	коьрта некъ	[kørta neqh]
dirt road	ворданан некъ	[vɔrdanan neqh]
pathway	тача	[tatʃa]
footpath	тача	[tatʃa]
Where?	Мичахь?	[mitʃah]
Where (to)?	Мича?	[mitʃa]
Where … from?	Мичара?	[mitʃara]
direction (way)	арло, т!едерзор	[arɔ], [thederzɔr]
to point (e.g., ~ the way)	гайта	[gajta]
to the left	аьрру арлоп	[ær:u aɣɔr]
to the right	аьтту арлоп	[æt:u aɣɔr]
straight ahead	дуьххьал д!а	[dyhal dəa]
back (e.g., to turn ~)	юха	[juha]
turn, curve	гола	[gɔla]
to turn (left, right etc.)	д!адерза	[dəaderza]
to make a U-turn	духадерзар	[duhaderzar]
to be visible	гуш хила	[guʃ hila]
to appear (come into view)	гучудала	[gutʃudala]
stop, halt (in journey)	сацор	[satsɔr]
to rest, to halt (vi)	садала	[sadaəa]
rest (pause)	садалар	[sadaəar]
to lose one's way	тила	[tila]
to lead to … (about road)	дига	[diga]
to reach … (arrive at)	арадала	[aradala]
stretch (of road)	дакъа	[daqha]
asphalt	асфальт	[asfaʌt]
curb	дийна дист	[di:na dist]
ditch	саьнгар	[sæŋar]
manhole	люк	[lyk]
roadside	некъан йист	[neqhan jıst]
pit, pothole	ор	[ɔr]
to go (on foot)	даха	[daha]
to pass (overtake)	хьалхадала	[halhadala]
step (footstep)	г!улч	[ɣultʃ]
on foot	г!аш	[ɣaʃ]
to block (road)	юкъарло ян	[juqharlɔ jan]
boom barrier	шлагбаум	[ʃlagbaum]
dead end	к!ажбухе	[k:aʒbuhe]

191. Breaking the law. Criminals. Part 1

bandit	талорхо	[talɔrhɔ]
crime	зулам	[zulam]
criminal (person)	зуламхо	[zulamho]

| thief | къу | [qhu] |
| stealing, theft | къола | [qhɔla] |

to kidnap (vt)	лачкъо	[latʃqhɔ]
kidnapping	лачкъор	[latʃqhɔr]
kidnapper	лачкъийнарг	[latʃqhi:narg]

| ransom | мах | [mah] |
| to ask for ransom | мехах схьаэцар | [mehah shaetsar] |

to rob (vt)	талор дан	[talɔr dan]
robbery	талор, талор дар	[talɔr], [talɔr dar]
robber	талорхо	[talɔrhɔ]

to extort (vt)	нуьцкъала даккха	[nytsqhala dak:a]
extortionist	даккха гӀертарг	[dak:a ɣertarg]
extortion	нуьцкъала даккхар	[nytsqhala dak:ar]

to murder, to kill	ден	[den]
murder	дер	[der]
murderer	дийнарг	[di:narg]

gunshot	ялар	[jalar]
to fire a shot	кхосса	[qɔs:a]
to shoot down	тоьпаца ден	[tøpatsa den]
to shoot (vi)	кхийса	[qi:sa]
shooting	кхийсар	[qi:sar]

incident (fight etc.)	хилларг	[hil:arg]
fight, brawl	вовшахлатар	[vɔvʃahlatar]
Help!	Ло дан кхайкха! Орца дала!	[ɣɔ dan qajqa ɔrtsa dala]
victim	хӀаллакъхилларг	[hal:aqhil:arg]

to damage (vt)	зен дан	[zen dan]
damage	зен	[zen]
dead body	дакъа	[daqha]
grave (e.g., ~ crime)	доккха	[dɔk:a]

to attack (vi, vt)	тӀелата	[thelata]
to beat (dog, person)	етта	[et:a]
to beat sb up	етта	[et:a]
to take (snatch)	дӀадаккха	[dɛadak:a]
to stab to death	урс хьакха	[urs haqa]
to maim (vt)	заьлап дан	[zæɐap dan]

to wound (vi, vt)	чов ян	[tʃov jan]
blackmail	шантаж	[ʃantaʒ]
to blackmail (vt)	шантаж ян	[ʃantaʒ jan]
blackmailer	шантажхо	[ʃantaʒho]

racketeering	рэкет	[rɛket]
racketeer	рэкитхо	[rɛkitho]
gangster	гангстер	[gaŋster]
mafia, Mob	мафи	[mafi]

pickpocket	кисанан курхалча	[kisanan kurhaltʃa]
burglar	къу	[qhu]
smuggling	контрабанда	[kontrabanda]
smuggler	контрабандхо	[kontrabandho]

forgery	харц хӏума дар	[harts huma dar]
to forge (counterfeit)	тардан	[tardan]
fake, forged (adj)	харц	[harts]

192. Breaking the law. Criminals. Part 2

rape	хьийзор	[hi:zor]
to rape (vt)	хьийзо	[hi:zo]
rapist	ницкъбархо	[nitsqhbarho]
maniac	маньяк	[maɲjak]

prostitute (woman)	кхахьпа	[qahpa]
prostitution	кхахьпалла	[qahpal:a]
pimp	сутенёр	[sutenзr]

| drug addict | наркоман | [narkɔman] |
| drug dealer | наркотикаш йохкархо | [narkotikaʃ johkarho] |

to blow up (bomb)	эккхийта	[ɛk:i:ta]
explosion	эккхар	[ɛk:ar]
to set fire	лато	[latɔ]
incendiary (arsonist)	цӏетасархо	[tshetasarhɔ]

terrorism	терроризм	[ter:ɔrizm]
terrorist	террорхо	[ter:ɔrhɔ]
hostage	закъалт	[zaqhalt]

to swindle (vt)	lехо	[əeho]
swindle	lехор	[əehor]
swindler	хӏилланча	[hil:antʃa]

to bribe (vt)	эца	[ɛtsa]
bribery	эцар	[ɛtsar]
bribe	кхаъ	[qa]
poison	дӏовш	[dəɔvʃ]

| to poison (vt) | дӀовш мало | [dəovʃ malɔ] |
| to poison oneself | дӀовш мала | [dəovʃ mala] |

| suicide (act) | ша-шен дар | [ʃa ʃen dar] |
| suicide (person) | ша-шен дийнарг | [ʃa ʃen di:narg] |

to threaten (vt)	кхерам тийса	[qeram ti:sa]
threat	кхерор	[qerɔr]
to make an attempt	гӀерта	[ɣerta]
attempt (attack)	гӀортар	[ɣɔrtar]

| to steal (a car) | дӀадига | [dəadiga] |
| to hijack (a plane) | дӀадига | [dəadiga] |

| revenge | чӀир | [tʃhir] |
| to avenge (vt) | бекхам бан | [beqam ban] |

to torture (vt)	Ӏазап дан	[əazap dan]
torture	Ӏазап	[əazap]
to abuse (treat cruelly)	Ӏазап далло	[əazap dal:ɔ]

pirate	пират	[pirat]
hooligan	хулиган	[huligan]
armed	герзан	[gerzan]
violence	ницкъ бар	[nitsqh bar]

| spying (noun) | шпионаж | [ʃpiɔnaʒ] |
| to spy (vi) | зен | [zen] |

193. Police. Law. Part 1

| justice | дов хаттар | [dɔv hat:ar] |
| court (court room) | суд | [sud] |

judge	суьдхо	[sydhɔ]
jurors	векалш	[wekalʃ]
jury trial	векалашан суьд	[wekalaʃan syd]
to judge (vt)	суд ян	[sud jan]

lawyer, attorney	хьехамча	[hehamtʃa]
accused	суьдерниг	[sydernig]
dock	суьдерниган гӀант	[sydernigan ɣant]

| charge | бехкедар | [behkedar] |
| accused | бехкевийриг | [behkevi:rig] |

sentence	кхел	[qel]
to sentence (vt)	кхел ян	[qel jan]
guilty (e.g., ~ of murder)	бехкениг	[behkenig]
to punish (vt)	тӀаӀзар дан	[taəzar dan]

punishment	таӏзар	[taezar]
fine (penalty)	гӏуда	[ɣuda]
life imprisonment	валлалц чуволлар	[val:alts tʃu:ɔl:ar]
death penalty	ден суд ян	[den sud jan]
electric chair	электрически гӏант	[ɛlektritʃeski ɣant]
gallows	тангӏалкх	[tanɣalq]

| to execute (vt) | ден | [den] |
| execution | ден суд яр | [den sud jar] |

| prison, jail | набахте | [nabahte] |
| cell | камера | [kamera] |

escort	кано	[kanɔ]
prison guard	тӏехьожург	[thehɔʒurg]
prisoner	лаьцна стаг	[lætsna stag]

| handcuffs | гӏоьмаш | [ɣømaʃ] |
| to handcuff (vt) | гӏоьмаш йохка | [ɣømaʃ johka] |

escape	дадар	[dadar]
to escape (vi, vt)	дада	[dada]
to disappear (vi)	къайладала	[qhajladala]
to release (from prison)	мукъадаккха	[muqhadak:a]
amnesty	амнисти	[amnisti]

police	полици	[politsi]
policeman	полици	[politsi]
police station	полицин дакъа	[politsin daqha]
billy club	резинин чхьонкар	[rezinin tʃhɔnkar]
loudspeaker	рупор	[rupɔr]

patrol car	патрулан машина	[patrulan maʃina]
siren	сирена	[sirena]
to turn on the siren	сирена лато	[sirena latɔ]
siren call	уӏрап	[uɣar]

scene of the crime	хилла меттиг	[hil:a met:ig]
witness	теш	[teʃ]
freedom	паргӏато	[parɣatɔ]
accomplice	декъахо	[deqhaho]
to flee	къайладала	[qhajladala]
footprint	лар	[lar]

194. Police. Law. Part 2

search (for a criminal)	лахар	[lahar]
to look for ...	леха	[leha]
suspicion	шекьхилар	[ʃekʲhilar]
suspicious (suspect)	шеконан	[ʃekɔnan]

to stop (cause to halt)	сацо	[satsɔ]
to detain (keep in custody)	сацо	[satsɔ]
case (trial)	дов	[dɔv]
investigation	таллам	[tal:am]
detective	детектив, лахарча	[detektiv], [lahartʃa]
investigator	талламхо	[tal:amhɔ]
version	верси	[wersi]
motive	бахьана	[bahana]
interrogation	ледар	[ledar]
to interrogate (vt)	ледан	[ledan]
to question (interrogate)	ледан	[ledan]
questioning	ледар	[ledar]
checking (police ~)	хьажар	[haʒar]
round-up	го бар	[gɔ bar]
search (by police)	хьажар	[haʒar]
chase (pursuit)	тӏаьхьадалар	[thæhadalar]
to pursue, to chase	тӏаьхьадаьлла лела	[thæhadæl:a lela]
to track (a criminal)	хьежа	[heʒa]
arrest	лацар	[latsar]
to arrest (sb)	лаца	[latsa]
to catch (thief etc.)	схьалаца	[shalatsa]
document	документ	[dɔkument]
proof (evidence)	тешам	[teʃam]
to prove (vt)	тешо	[teʃɔ]
footprint	лар	[lar]
fingerprints	тӏелгийн таммагӏанаш	[thelgi:n tam:aɣanaʃ]
piece of evidence	бахьана	[bahana]
alibi	алиби	[alibi]
innocent (not guilty)	бехке доцу	[behke dɔtsu]
injustice (unjust act)	нийсо цахилар	[ni:sɔ tsahilar]
unjust, unfair	нийса доцу	[ni:sa dɔtsu]
crime (e.g., ~ reporter)	криминалан	[kriminalan]
to confiscate (vt)	пачхьалкхдаккха	[patʃhalqdak:a]
drug (illegal substance)	наркотик	[narkɔtik]
weapon, gun	герз	[gerz]
to disarm (vt)	герз схьадаккха	[gerz shadak:a]
to order (command)	омра дан	[ɔmra dan]
to disappear (vi)	къайладала	[qhajladala]
law	закон	[zakɔn]
legal	законехь	[zakɔneh]
illegal	законехь доцу	[zakɔneh dɔtsu]
responsibility	жоьпалла	[ʒøpal:a]
responsible	жоьпаллин	[ʒøpal:in]

NATURE

The Earth. Part 1

195. Outer space

cosmos	космос	[kɔsmɔs]
space (e.g., ~ flight)	космосан	[kɔsmɔsan]
outer space	космосан меттиг	[kɔsmɔsan metːig]
world	дуьне	[dyne]
galaxy	галактика	[galaktika]

star	седа	[seda]
constellation	седарчий гулам	[sedartʃiː gulam]
planet	дуьне	[dyne]
satellite	спутник	[sputnik]

meteorite	метеорит	[meteɔrit]
comet	комета	[kɔmeta]
asteroid	астероид	[asterɔid]

orbit	орбита	[ɔrbita]
to rotate (vi)	хьийза	[hiːza]
atmosphere	хӀаваъ	[hava]

the Sun	Малх	[malh]
solar system	Маьлхан система	[mælhan sistema]
solar eclipse	малх лацар	[malh latsar]

the Earth	Латта	[latːa]
the Moon	Бутт	[butː]

Mars	Марс	[mars]
Venus	Венера	[wenera]
Jupiter	Юпитер	[jupiter]
Saturn	Сатурн	[saturn]

Mercury	Меркурий	[merkuriː]
Uranus	Уран	[uran]
Neptune	Нептун	[neptun]
Pluto	Плутон	[pluton]

Milky Way	Ча такхийна Тача	[tʃa taqiːna tatʃa]
Great Bear	Ворхӏ вешин ворхӏ седа	[vɔrh weʃin vɔrh seda]

Pole Star	Къилбаседа	[qhilbaseda]
Martian	марсианин	[marsianin]
extraterrestrial	инопланетянин	[inoplanet'anin]
alien	пришелец	[priʃelets]
flying saucer	хlаваэхула лела тарелка	[havahula lela tarelka]

spaceship	космосан кема	[kɔsmɔsan kema]
space station	орбитин станци	[ɔrbitin stantsi]
blast-off	старт	[start]

engine	двигатель	[dwigateʎ]
nozzle	сопло	[sɔplɔ]
fuel	ягорг	[jagɔrg]

cockpit, flight deck	кабина	[kabina]
antenna	антенна	[anteŋa]
porthole	иллюминатор	[il:yminatɔr]
solar battery	маьлхан батарей	[mælhan batarej]
spacesuit	скафандр	[skafandr]

| weightlessness | йозалла яр | [jozal:a jar] |
| oxygen | кислород | [kislɔrɔd] |

| docking (in space) | вовшахтасар | [vɔvʃahtasar] |
| to dock (vi, vt) | вовшахтасса | [vɔvʃahtas:a] |

observatory	обсерватори	[ɔbservatɔri]
telescope	телескоп	[teleskɔp]
to observe (vt)	тергам бан	[tergam ban]
to explore (vt)	талла	[tal:a]

196. The Earth

the Earth	Латта	[lat:a]
globe	дуьне	[dyne]
planet	дуьне, планета	[dyne], [planeta]

atmosphere	атмосфера	[atmɔsfera]
geography	географи	[geɔgrafi]
nature	lалам	[əalam]

globe (model of Earth)	глобус	[glɔbus]
map	карта	[karta]
atlas	атлас	[atlas]

Europe	Европа	[evrɔpa]
Asia	Ази	[azi]
Africa	Африка	[afrika]
Australia	Австрали	[avstrali]

America	Америка	[amerika]
North America	Къилбаседан Америка	[qhilbasedan amerika]
South America	Къилбера Америка	[qhilbera amerika]

| Antarctica | Антарктида | [antarktida] |
| the Arctic | Арктика | [arktika] |

197. Cardinal directions

north	къилбаседа	[qhilbaseda]
to the north	къилбаседехьа	[qhilbasedeha]
in the north	къилбаседехь	[qhilbasedeh]
northern	къилбаседан	[qhilbasedan]

south	къилбе	[qhilbe]
to the south	къилбехьа	[qhilbeha]
in the south	къилбехь	[qhilbeh]
southern	къилбера	[qhilbera]

west	малхбузе	[malhbuze]
to the west	малхбузехьа	[malhbuzeha]
in the west	малхбузехь	[malhbuzeh]
western	малхбузера	[malhbuzera]

east	малхбале	[malhbale]
to the east	малхбалехьа	[malhbaleha]
in the east	малхбалехь	[malhbaleh]
eastern	малхбалехьара	[malhbalehara]

198. Sea. Ocean

sea	хӀорд	[hɔrd]
ocean	хӀорд, океан	[hɔrd], [ɔkean]
gulf (bay)	айма	[ajma]
straits	хидоькъе	[hidøqhe]

| land | латта | [lat:a] |
| continent (mainland) | материк | [materik] |

island	гӀайре	[ɣajre]
peninsula	ахгӀайре	[ahɣajre]
archipelago	архипелаг	[arhipelag]

bay	бухта	[buhta]
harbor	гавань	[gavaɲ]
lagoon	лагуна	[laguna]
cape	мара	[mara]
atoll	атолл	[atɔl:]

reef	риф	[rif]
coral	маржак	[marʒak]
coral reef	маржанийн риф	[marʒani:n rif]

deep	кӀоарга	[k:ɔarga]
depth (deep water)	кӀоргалла	[k:ɔrgal:a]
abyss	бух боцу Ӏин	[buh bɔtsu ein]
trench (e.g., Mariana ~)	кӀаг	[k:ag]

| current | дӀаэхар | [dəaehar] |
| to surround (vt) | го баьккхина хи хила | [gɔ bæk:ina hi hila] |

| shore | хийист | [hi:ist] |
| coast | йист | [jist] |

high tide	хӀорд тӀекхетар	[hɔrd theqetar]
low tide	хӀорд чубожа боьлла	[hɔrd tʃubɔʒa bøl:a]
sandbank	гомхе	[gɔmhe]
bottom	бух	[buh]

wave	тулгӀе	[tulɣe]
crest (~ of a wave)	тулгӀийн дукъ	[tulɣi:n duqh]
foam	чопа	[tʃɔpa]

hurricane	мох балар	[mɔh balar]
tsunami	цунами	[tsunami]
calm	штиль	[ʃtiʎ]
quiet (e.g., ~ ocean)	тийна	[ti:na]

| pole | полюс | [pɔlys] |
| polar | полюсан | [pɔlysan] |

latitude	шоралла	[ʃɔral:a]
longitude	дохалла	[dɔhal:a]
parallel	параллель	[paral:eʎ]
equator	экватор	[ɛkvatɔr]

sky	дуьне	[dyne]
horizon	ана	[ana]
air	хӀаваъ	[hava]

lighthouse	маяк	[majak]
to dive (vi)	чулелха	[tʃulelha]
to sink (about boat)	бухадаха	[buhadaha]
treasures	хазна	[hazna]

199. Seas' and Oceans' names

| Atlantic Ocean | Атлантически хӀорд | [atlantitʃeski hɔrd] |
| Indian Ocean | Индихойн хӀорд | [indihojn hɔrd] |

| Pacific Ocean | Тийна хӀорд | [ti:na hɔrd] |
| Arctic Ocean | Къилбаседанан Шен хӀорд | [qhilbasedanan ʃen hɔrd] |

Black Sea	Ӏаьржа хӀорд	[əærʒa hɔrd]
Red Sea	ЦӀен хӀорд	[tʃen hɔrd]
Yellow Sea	Можа хӀорд	[mɔʒa hɔrd]
White Sea	КӀайн хӀорд	[k:ajn hɔrd]

Caspian Sea	Каспи хӀорд	[kaspi hɔrd]
Dead Sea	Са доцу хӀорд	[sa dɔtsu hɔrd]
Mediterranean Sea	Средиземни хӀорд	[sredizemni hɔrd]

| Aegean Sea | Эгейски хӀорд | [ɛgejski hɔrd] |
| Adriatic Sea | Адреатически хӀорд | [adreatitʃeski hɔrd] |

Arabian Sea	Аравийски хӀорд	[aravi:ski hɔrd]
Sea of Japan	Японийн хӀорд	[japoni:n hɔrd]
Bering Sea	Бериногово хӀорд	[beriŋɔvɔ hɔrd]
South China Sea	Къилба-Китайн хӀорд	[qhilba kitajn hɔrd]

Coral Sea	Маржанийн хӀорд	[marʒani:n hɔrd]
Tasman Sea	Тасманово хӀорд	[tasmanɔvɔ hɔrd]
Caribbean Sea	Карибски хӀорд	[karibski hɔrd]

Barents Sea	Баренцово хӀорд	[barentsɔvɔ hɔrd]
Kara Sea	Карски хӀорд	[karski hɔrd]
North Sea	Къилбаседан хӀорд	[qhilbasedan hɔrd]
Baltic Sea	Балтийски хӀорд	[balti:ski hɔrd]
Norwegian Sea	Норвержски хӀорд	[nɔrwerʒski hɔrd]

200. Mountains

mountain	лам	[lam]
mountain range	ламнийн морӀа	[lamni:n mɔɣa]
mountain ridge	ламанан дукъ	[lamanan duqh]

| summit, top | бохь | [bɔh] |
| peak | бохь | [bɔh] |

| foot (of mountain, hill) | кӀажа | [k:aʒa] |
| slope (mountainside) | басе | [base] |

volcano	тӀаплам	[thaplam]
active volcano	тӀепинг	[thepiŋ]
dormant volcano	байна тӀаплам	[bajna thaplam]

eruption	хьалатохар	[halatɔhar]
crater	кратер	[krater]
magma	магма	[magma]

| lava | лава | [lava] |
| molten (~ lava) | цӏийдина | [tshi:dina] |

canyon	Ӏин	[əin]
gorge	чӏож	[t͡ʃhɔʒ]
crevice	чӏаж	[t͡ʃhaʒ]

| pass, col | ламанан дукъ | [lamanan duqh] |
| plateau | акъари | [aqhari] |

| cliff | тарх | [tarh] |
| hill | гу | [gu] |

glacier	ша-ор	[ʃa ɔr]
waterfall	чухчари	[t͡ʃuht͡ʃari]
geyser	гейзер	[gejzer]
lake	Ӏам	[əam]

plain	аре	[are]
landscape	пейзаж	[pejzaʒ]
echo	йилбазмохь	[jɪlbazmɔh]

| alpinist | алтпинист | [altpinist] |
| rock climber | тархашхо | [tarhaʃho] |

| conquer (in climbing) | карадало | [karadalɔ] |
| climb (e.g., an easy ~) | тӏедалар | [thedalar] |

201. Mountains names

Alps	Альпаш	[aʎpaʃ]
Mont Blanc	Монблан	[mɔnblan]
Pyrenees	Пиренеи	[pirenei]

| Carpathians | Карпаташ | [karpataʃ] |
| Ural Mountains | Уралан лаьмнаш | [uralan læmnaʃ] |

| Caucasus | Кавказ | [kavkaz] |
| Elbrus | Эльбрус | [ɛʎbrus] |

Altai	Алтай	[altaj]
Tien Shan	Тянь-Шань	[tʲaɲ ʃaɲ]
Pamir Mountains	Памир	[pamir]

| Himalayas | Гималаи | [gimalai] |
| Everest | Эверест | [ɛwerest] |

Andes	Анднаш	[andnaʃ]
Cordilleras	Кордильераш	[kɔrdiʎjeraʃ]
Kilimanjaro	Килиманджаро	[kilimand͡ʒarɔ]

202. Rivers

river	доьду хи	[dødu hi]
spring (natural source)	хьост, шовда	[hɔst], [ʃɔvda]
bed (of the river)	харш	[harʃ]
basin	бассейн	[bas:ejn]
to flow into …	кхета	[qeta]
tributary	га	[ga]
bank (of river)	хийист	[hi:ist]
current, stream	дӀаэхар	[dəaəhar]
downstream	хица охьа	[hitsa ɔha]
upstream	хица хьала	[hitsa hala]
flood	хи тӀедалар	[hi thedalar]
flooding	дестар	[destar]
to overflow (vi)	деста	[desta]
to flood (vt)	дӀахьулдан	[dəahuldan]
shallows (shoal)	гомхалла	[gɔmhal:a]
rapids	тарх	[tarh]
dam	сунт	[sunt]
canal	татол	[tatɔl]
reservoir, artificial lake	латтийла	[lat:i:la]
sluice, lock	шлюз	[ʃlyz]
reservoir (water body)	Ӏам	[əam]
marsh, swamp	уьшал	[yʃal]
bog	уьшал	[yʃal]
whirlpool	айма	[ajma]
stream (brook)	татол	[tatɔl]
drinking (about water)	молу	[mɔlu]
fresh (not salt)	теза	[teza]
ice	ша	[ʃa]
to ice over	ша бан	[ʃa ban]

203. Rivers' names

Seine	Сена	[sena]
Loire	Луара	[luara]
Thames	Темза	[temza]
Rhine	Рейн	[rejn]
Danube	Дунай	[dunaj]
Volga	Волга	[vɔlga]

| Don | Дон | [dɔn] |
| Lena | Лена | [lena] |

Yellow River	Хуанхэ	[huanhɛ]
Yangtze	Янцзы	[jantszɪ]
Mekong	Меконг	[mekɔŋ]
Ganges	Ганг	[gaŋ]

Nile River	Нил	[nil]
Congo	Конго	[kɔŋɔ]
Okavango	Окаванго	[ɔkavaŋɔ]
Zambezi	Замбези	[zambezi]
Limpopo	Лимпопо	[limpɔpɔ]
Mississippi River	Миссисипи	[misːisipi]

204. Forest

| forest | хьун | [hun] |
| forest (attr) | хьунан | [hunan] |

thick forest	варш	[varʃ]
grove	боьлак	[bølak]
clearing	ирзу	[irzu]

| thicket | коьллаш | [kølːaʃ] |
| scrubland | колл | [kɔlː] |

pathway	тача	[tatʃa]
footpath	тача	[tatʃa]
gully	боьра	[børa]

tree	дитт	[ditː]
leaf	рла	[ɣa]
leaves	рлаш	[ɣaʃ]

falling leaves	рла дожар	[ɣa dɔʒar]
to fall (about leaves)	охьа дожа	[ɔha dɔʒa]
top (of the tree)	бохь	[bɔh]

branch	га	[ga]
bough	га	[ga]
bud (on shrub, tree)	патар	[patar]
needle (of pine tree)	кӏохцалг	[kːɔhtsalg]
cone (of pine, fir)	бӏар	[bəar]

hollow (in a tree)	хара	[hara]
nest	бен	[ben]
burrow, animal hole	ӏуьрг	[əyrg]
trunk (of a tree)	рлад	[ɣad]
root	орам	[ɔram]

bark (of a tree)	кевстиг	[kevstig]
moss	корсам	[kɔrsɑm]
to uproot (vt)	бухдаккха	[buhdɑk:ɑ]
to chop down	хьакха	[hɑqɑ]
to deforest (vt)	хьакха	[hɑqɑ]
tree stump	юьхк	[juhk]
campfire	цӀе	[ʦhe]
forest fire	цӀе	[ʦhe]
to extinguish (vt)	дӀадайа	[dədɑjɑ]
forest ranger	хьуьнхо	[hynhɔ]
protection	лардар	[lɑrdɑr]
to protect (e.g., ~ nature)	лардан	[lɑrdɑn]
poacher	браконьер	[brɑkɔɲjer]
trap (e.g., bear ~)	гура	[gurɑ]
to gather, to pick (vt)	лахьо	[lɑhɔ]
to lose one's way	тила	[tilɑ]

205. Natural resources

natural resources	Ӏаламан тӀаьхьалонаш	[əɑlɑmɑn thæhɑlɔnɑʃ]
minerals	пайде маьйданаш	[pɑjde mæədɑnɑʃ]
deposit (e.g., coal ~)	маьйданаш	[mæədɑnɑʃ]
field (e.g., oilfield)	маьйданаш дохку	[mæədɑnɑʃ dɔhku]
to mine (extract)	даккха	[dɑk:ɑ]
mining (extraction)	даккхар	[dɑk:ɑr]
ore	маьйда	[mæədɑ]
mine (e.g., for coal)	маьйда доккхийла, шахта	[mæədɑ dɔk:i:lɑ, ʃɑhtɑ]
mine shaft, pit	шахта	[ʃɑhtɑ]
miner	кӀорабаккхархо	[k:ɔrɑbɑk:ɑrhɔ]
gas	газ	[gɑz]
gas pipeline	газъюьргург	[gɑzʰjugurg]
oil (petroleum)	нефть	[neftʲ]
oil pipeline	нефтьузург	[neftʲuzurg]
oil rig	нефтан чардакх	[neftɑn ʧɑrdɑq]
derrick	буру туху вышка	[buru tuhu vɪʃkɑ]
tanker	танкер	[tɑŋker]
sand	гӀум	[ɣum]
limestone	кир-маьйда	[kir mæədɑ]
gravel	жарла	[ʒɑɣɑ]
peat	Ӏеха	[əehɑ]
clay	поппар	[pɔp:ɑr]

coal	кӏора	[kːɔra]
iron	эчиг	[ɛtʃig]
gold	деши	[deʃi]
silver	дети	[deti]
nickel	никель	[nikeʎ]
copper	цӏаста	[tʃhasta]
zinc	цинк	[tʃsiŋk]
manganese	марганец	[marganets]
mercury	гинсу	[ginsu]
lead	даш	[daʃ]
mineral	минерал	[mineral]
crystal	кристалл	[kristalː]
marble	шагатӏулг	[ʃagathulg]
uranium	уран	[uran]
diamond (stone)	алмаз	[almaz]

The Earth. Part 2

206. Weather

weather	хенан хӀоттам	[henan hot:am]
weather forecast	хенан хӀоттаман прогноз	[henan hot:aman prognɔz]
temperature	температура	[temperatura]
thermometer	термометр	[termɔmetr]
barometer	барометр	[barɔmetr]
humidity	тӀуьнан	[thynan]
heat (of summer)	йовхо	[jovho]
hot (torrid)	довха	[dovha]
it's hot	йовха	[jovha]
it's warm	йовха	[jovha]
warm (moderately hot)	довха	[dovha]
it's cold	шийла	[ʃiːla]
cold	шийла	[ʃiːla]
sun	малх	[malh]
to shine	кхета	[qeta]
sunny (day)	маьлхан	[mælhan]
to come up (vi)	схьакхета	[shaqeta]
to set (vi)	чубуза	[ʧubuza]
cloud	марха	[marha]
cloudy	мархаш йолу	[marhaʃ jolu]
rain cloud	марха	[marha]
somber (gloomy)	кхоьлина	[qølina]
rain	доꙇла	[dɔɣa]
it's raining	доꙇла доꙇлу	[dɔɣa dɔɣu]
rainy (day)	доꙇлане	[dɔɣane]
to drizzle (vi)	серса	[sersa]
pouring rain	кхевсина доꙇла	[qevsina dɔɣa]
downpour	доꙇла	[dɔɣa]
heavy (e.g., ~ rain)	чӀоꙇла	[ʧhɔɣa]
puddle	Ӏам	[eam]
to get wet (in rain)	тӀадо	[thadɔ]
mist (fog)	дохк	[dɔhk]
misty	дохк долу	[dɔhk dɔlu]

snow	ло	[lɔ]
it's snowing	ло догɩу	[lɔ dɔɣu]

207. Severe weather. Natural disasters

thunderstorm	йочана	[joʧana]
lightning (~ strike)	ткъес	[tqhes]
to flash (vi)	стега	[stega]
thunder	стигал къовкъар	[stigal qhɔvqhar]
to thunder (vi)	къекъа	[qheqha]
it's thundering	стигал къекъа	[stigal qheqha]
hail	къора	[qhɔra]
it's hailing	къора йогɩу	[qhɔra joɣu]
to flood (vt)	дɩахьулдан	[dəahuldan]
flood	хи тɩедалар	[hi thedalar]
earthquake	мохк бегор	[mɔhk begɔr]
tremor, quake	дегар	[degar]
epicenter	эпицентр	[ɛpiʦentr]
eruption	хьалатохар	[halatɔhar]
lava	лава	[lava]
tornado	торнадо	[tɔrnadɔ]
typhoon	тайфун	[tajfun]
hurricane	мох балар	[mɔh balar]
storm	дарц	[darʦ]
tsunami	цунами	[ʦunami]
cyclone (e.g., tropical ~)	дарц	[darʦ]
bad weather	йочана	[joʧana]
fire (e.g., house on ~)	цɩе	[ʦhe]
disaster	катастрофа	[katastrɔfa]
meteorite	метеорит	[meteɔrit]
avalanche	хьаьтт	[hæt:]
snowslide	чухарцар	[ʧuharʦar]
blizzard	дарц	[darʦ]
snowstorm	дарц	[darʦ]

208. Noises. Sounds

quiet, silence	тийналла	[tajnal:a]
sound	аз	[az]

noise	**гӀовгӀа**	[ɣɔvɣɑ]
to make noise	**гӀовгӀа ян**	[ɣɔvɣɑ jan]
noisy	**гӀовгӀа йолу**	[ɣɔvɣɑ jolu]
loudly (to speak etc.)	**чӀорла**	[tʃhɔɣa]
loud (voice etc.)	**чӀорла**	[tʃhɔɣa]
constant (continuous)	**хаддаза**	[had:aza]
shout (noun)	**мохь**	[mɔh]
to shout (vi)	**мохь бетта**	[mɔh bet:a]
whisper	**шабар-шибар**	[ʃabar ʃibar]
to whisper (vi, vt)	**шабар-шибар дан**	[ʃabar ʃibar dan]
barking (of dog)	**гӀалх**	[ɣalh]
to bark (vi)	**гӀалх дан**	[ɣalh dan]
groan (of pain)	**узар**	[uzar]
to groan (vi)	**узарш дан**	[uzarʃ dan]
cough	**йовхарш**	[jovharʃ]
to cough (vi)	**йовхарш етта**	[jovharʃ et:a]
whistle	**шок**	[ʃɔk]
to whistle (vi)	**шок етта**	[ʃɔk et:a]
knock (at the door)	**тӀак**	[thak]
to knock (vi)	**детта**	[det:a]
to crackle (vi)	**лелха**	[lelha]
crackle	**къарс**	[qhars]
siren	**сирена**	[sirena]
whistle (factory's ~)	**мохь**	[mɔh]
to whistle (ship, train)	**дека**	[deka]
honk (signal)	**сигнал**	[signal]
to honk (about car)	**сигнал етта**	[signal et:a]

209. Winter

winter (noun)	**Ӏа**	[əa]
winter (attr)	**Ӏаьнан**	[əænan]
in the winter	**Ӏай**	[əaj]
snow	**ло**	[lo]
it's snowing	**ло догӀу**	[lo dɔɣu]
snowfall	**ло диллар**	[lo dil:ar]
snowdrift	**оьла**	[øla]
snowflake	**лайн чим**	[lajn tʃim]
snowball	**ло**	[lo]
snowman	**снеговик**	[snegɔwik]
icicle	**кхазарг**	[qazarg]

December	**декабрь**	[dekabrʲ]
January	**январь**	[janvarʲ]
February	**февраль**	[fevraʎ]
New Year	**Керла шо**	[kerla ʃɔ]
Christmas tree	**Ёлка**	[ɜlka]
Christmas	**Рождество**	[rɔʒdestvɔ]
heavy frost	**шело**	[ʃelɔ]
frosty (weather, air)	**шийла**	[ʃiːla]
below zero	**нолал лохаха**	[nɔlal lɔhaha]
light frost	**йис**	[jɪs]
hoarfrost	**йис**	[jɪs]
cold (cold weather)	**шело**	[ʃelɔ]
it's cold	**шийла**	[ʃiːla]
fur coat	**кетар**	[ketar]
mittens	**каранаш**	[karanaʃ]
to get sick	**цамгар кхета**	[tsamgar qeta]
cold (illness)	**шелдалар**	[ʃeldalar]
to catch a cold	**шелдала**	[ʃeldala]
ice	**ша**	[ʃa]
black ice	**ша**	[ʃa]
to ice over	**ша бан**	[ʃa ban]
ice floe	**окъам**	[ɔqham]
skis	**когсалазаш**	[kɔgsalazaʃ]
skier	**лыжашхо**	[lɪʒaʃhɔ]
to ski (vi)	**когсалазаш хехка**	[kɔgsalazaʃ hehka]
to skate (vi)	**конькаш хехка**	[kɔɲkaʃ hehka]

Fauna

210. Mammals. Predators

predator	гӀира экха	[ɣira ɛqa]
tiger	цӀоькъалом	[tsʰøqhalɔm]
lion	лом	[lɔm]
wolf	борз	[bɔrz]
fox	цхьогал	[tshɔgal]
jaguar	ягуар	[jaguar]
leopard	леопард	[leɔpard]
cheetah	гепард	[gepard]
black panther	пантера	[pantera]
puma	пума	[puma]
snow leopard	лайн цӀокъ	[lajn tshɔqh]
lynx	акха цициг	[aqa tsitsig]
coyote	койот	[kɔjot]
jackal	чагӀалкх	[ʧaɣalq]
hyena	чагӀалкх	[ʧaɣalq]

211. Wild animals

animal	дийнат	[di:nat]
beast (animal)	экха	[ɛqa]
squirrel	тарсал	[tarsal]
hedgehog	зу	[zu]
hare	пхьагал	[phagal]
rabbit	кролик	[krɔlik]
badger	даӀам	[daəam]
raccoon	акха жӀаьла	[aqa ʒæəla]
hamster	оьпа	[øpa]
marmot	дӀам	[dəam]
mole	боьлкъазар	[bølqhazar]
mouse	дахка	[dahka]
rat	мукадахка	[mukadahka]
bat	бирдолаг	[birdɔlag]
ermine	горностай	[gɔrnɔstaj]
sable	салор	[salɔr]

marten	салор	[salɔr]
weasel	дингад	[diŋad]
mink	норка	[nɔrka]
beaver	бобр	[bɔbr]
otter	хешт	[heʃt]
horse	говр	[gɔvr]
moose	боккха сай	[bɔqa saj]
deer	сай	[saj]
camel	эмкал	[ɛmkal]
bison	бизон	[bizɔn]
aurochs	була	[bula]
buffalo	гомаш-буга	[gɔmaʃ buga]
zebra	зебр	[zebra]
antelope	антилопа	[antilɔpa]
roe deer	лу	[lu]
fallow deer	шоьккари	[ʃøk:ari]
chamois	масар	[masar]
wild boar	нал	[nal]
whale	кит	[kit]
seal	тюлень	[tyleɲ]
walrus	морж	[mɔrʒ]
fur seal	котик	[kɔtik]
dolphin	дельфин	[deʎfin]
bear	ча	[t͡ʃa]
polar bear	кӏайн ча	[k:ajn t͡ʃa]
panda	панда	[panda]
monkey	маймал	[majmal]
chimpanzee	шимпанзе	[ʃimpanze]
orangutan	орангутанг	[ɔraŋutaŋ]
gorilla	горилла	[gɔril:a]
macaque	макака	[makaka]
gibbon	гиббон	[gib:ɔn]
elephant	пийл	[pi:l]
rhinoceros	мермалa	[mermaəa]
giraffe	жираф	[ʒiraf]
hippopotamus	бегемот	[begemɔt]
kangaroo	кенгуру	[keŋuru]
koala (bear)	коала	[kɔala]
mongoose	мангуст	[maŋust]
chinchilla	шиншилла	[ʃinʃil:a]
skunk	скунс	[skuns]
porcupine	дикобраз	[dikɔbraz]

212. Domestic animals

| cat | цициг | [ʦiʦig] |
| tomcat | цициг | [ʦiʦig] |

horse	говр	[gɔvr]
stallion	айгӀар	[ajɣar]
mare	кхела	[qela]

cow	етта	[et:a]
bull	сту	[stu]
ox	сту	[stu]

sheep	жий	[ʒi:]
ram	уьстагӀ	[ystaɣ]
goat	газа	[gaza]
billy goat, he-goat	бож	[bɔʒ]

| donkey | вир | [wir] |
| mule | бӀарза | [bəarza] |

pig	хьакха	[haqa]
piglet	хуьрсик	[hyrsik]
rabbit	кролик	[krɔlik]

| hen (chicken) | котам | [kɔtam] |
| rooster | боргӀал | [bɔrɣal] |

duck	бад	[bad]
drake	нӀаьна-бад	[nəæna bad]
goose	гӀаз	[ɣaz]

| turkey cock | москал-нӀаьна | [mɔskal nəæna] |
| turkey (hen) | москал-котам | [mɔskal kɔtam] |

domestic animals	цӀера дийнаташ	[ʦhera di:nataʃ]
tame (e.g., ~ hamster)	караламийна	[karaəami:na]
to tame (vt)	караламо	[karaəamɔ]
to breed (vt)	лело	[lelɔ]

| farm | ферма | [ferma] |
| poultry | зӀакардаьхний | [zəakardæhni:] |

| cattle | хьайбанаш | [hajbanaʃ] |
| herd (of cattle, goats) | бажа | [baʒa] |

stable	божал	[bɔʒal]
pigpen	хьакхарчийн божал	[haqarʧi:n bɔʒal]
cowshed	божал	[bɔʒal]
rabbit hutch	кроликийн бун	[krɔliki:n bun]
hen house	котаман бун	[kɔtaman bun]

213. Dogs. Dog breeds

dog	жIаьла	[ʒəælɑ]
sheepdog	жен жIаьла	[ʒen ʒəælɑ]
poodle	пудель	[pudeʎ]
dachshund	такса	[tɑksɑ]
bulldog	бульдог	[buʎdɔg]
boxer	боксёр	[bɔksɜr]
mastiff	мастиф	[mɑstif]
rottweiler	ротвейлер	[rɔtwejler]
Doberman	доберман	[dɔbermɑn]
basset	бассет	[bɑs:et]
bobtail	бобтейл	[bɔbtejl]
Dalmatian	далматинец	[dɑlmɑtinets]
cocker spaniel	кокер-спаниель	[kɔker spɑnieʎ]
Newfoundland	ньюфаундленд	[njyfɑundlend]
Saint Bernard	сенбернар	[senbernɑr]
husky	хаски	[hɑski]
chow-chow	чау-чау	[ʧɑu ʧɑu]
spitz	кIезалг	[k:ezɑlg]
pug	мопс	[mɔps]

214. Sounds made by animals

barking (noun)	гIалх	[ɣɑlh]
to bark (vi)	гIалх дан	[ɣɑlh dɑn]
to meow (vi)	Iаха	[əɑhɑ]
to purr (vi)	мур дан	[mur dɑn]
to moo (vi)	Iеха	[əehɑ]
to bellow (bull)	Iеха	[əehɑ]
to growl (vi)	гIигI дан	[ɣiɣ dɑn]
howl (noun)	угIар	[uɣɑr]
to howl (vi)	угIа	[uɣɑ]
to whine (vi)	цIовза	[tshɔvzɑ]
to bleat (sheep)	Iеха	[əehɑ]
to oink, to grunt (pig)	хур-хур дан	[hur hur dɑn]
to squeal (vi)	цIовза	[tshɔvzɑ]
to croak (frog)	вакъ-вакъ баха	[vɑqh vɑqh bɑhɑ]
to buzz (insect)	зуз дан	[zuz dɑn]
to stridulate (vi)	чIа-чIа дан	[ʧhɑ ʧhɑ dɑn]

215. Young animals

cub	кӀорни	[k:ɔrni]
kitten	цициган кӀорни	[tsitsigan k:ɔrni]
baby mouse	дехкан кӀорни	[dehkan k:ɔrni]
pup, puppy	кӀеза	[k:eza]
leveret	пхьагалан кӀорни	[phagalan k:ɔrni]
baby rabbit	кроликан кӀорни	[krɔlikan k:ɔrni]
wolf cub	берзан кӀеза	[berzan k:eza]
fox cub	цхьогалан кӀорни	[tshɔgalan k:ɔrni]
bear cub	чайтӀа	[tʃajtaə]
lion cub	лоьман кӀорни	[løman k:ɔrni]
tiger cub	цӀоькъалоьман кӀорни	[tshøqhaløman k:ɔrni]
elephant calf	пийлан кӀорни	[pi:lan k:ɔrni]
piglet	хуьрсик	[hyrsik]
calf (young cow, bull)	эса	[ɛsa]
kid (young goat)	буьхьиг	[byhig]
lamb	лахар	[əahar]
fawn (deer)	сен бекъа	[sen beqha]
young camel	эмкалан бекъа	[ɛmkalan beqha]
baby snake	лаьхьанан кӀорни	[læhanan k:ɔrni]
baby frog	пхьидан кӀорни	[phidan k:ɔrni]
nestling	чантал	[tʃantal]
chick (of chicken)	кӀорни	[k:ɔrni]
duckling	бедан кӀорни	[bedan k:ɔrni]

216. Birds

bird	олхазар	[ɔlhazar]
pigeon	кхокха	[qɔqa]
sparrow	хьоза	[hɔza]
tit	цӀирцӀирхьоза	[tshirtshirhɔza]
magpie	къорза къиг	[qhɔrza qhig]
raven	хьапрӀа	[harɣa]
hooded crow	къиг	[qhig]
jackdaw	жагӀжагӀа	[ʒaɣʒaɣa]
rook	човка	[tʃɔvka]
duck	бад	[bad]
goose	гӀаз	[ɣaz]
pheasant	акха котам	[aqa kɔtam]
eagle	аьрзу	[ærzu]
hawk	куьйра	[kyjra]

falcon	леча	[letʃa]
vulture	ломъаьрзу	[lɔmʰærzu]
condor	кондор	[kɔndɔr]

swan	гӏургӏаз	[ɣurɣaz]
crane	гӏаргӏули	[ɣarɣuli]
stork	чӏерийдохург	[tʃheri:dɔhurg]

parrot	тоти	[tɔti]
hummingbird	колибри	[kɔlibri]
peacock	тӏаус	[thaus]

ostrich	страус	[straus]
heron	чӏерийлоьцург	[tʃheri:løtsurg]
flamingo	фламинго	[flamiɲɔ]
pelican	пеликан	[pelikan]

| nightingale | зарзар | [zarzar] |
| swallow | чӏерлардиг | [tʃheɣardig] |

fieldfare	шоршал	[ʃɔrʃal]
song thrush	дека шоршал	[deka ʃɔrʃal]
blackbird	Iаьржа шоршал	[əærʒa ʃɔrʃal]

swift	мерцхалдиг	[mertshaldig]
lark	нӏаьвла	[nəævla]
quail	лекъ	[leqh]

woodpecker	хенакӏур	[henak:ur]
cuckoo	хӏуттут	[hut:ut]
owl	бухӏа	[buha]
eagle owl	соька	[søka]
wood grouse	къоракуота	[qhɔrakuɔta]
black grouse	акха котам	[aqa kɔtam]
partridge	моша	[mɔʃa]

starling	алкханч	[alqantʃ]
canary	можа хьоза	[mɔʒa hɔza]
hazel grouse	акха котам	[aqa kɔtam]
chaffinch	хьуьнан хьоза	[hynan hɔza]
bullfinch	лайн хьоза	[lajn hɔza]

gull (seagull)	чайка	[tʃajka]
albatross	альбатрос	[aʎbatrɔs]
penguin	пингвин	[piɲwin]

217. Birds. Singing and sounds

| to sing (vi) | дека | [deka] |
| to call (shout) | мохь бетта | [mɔh bet:a] |

| to crow (rooster) | кхайкха | [qɑjqɑ] |
| cock-a-doodle-doo | Iуы́ Iаре-Iуь | [əyə əare əy] |

to cluck (hen)	кIа-кIа дан	[k:a k:a dan]
to caw (vi)	къа-къа дан	[qha qha dan]
to quack (duck)	вакъ-вакъ баха	[vaqh vaqh baha]
to cheep (vi)	цIийза	[ʦhi:za]
to chirp, to twitter	гIир-гIир дан	[ɣir ɣir dan]

218. Fish. Marine animals

bream	чабакх-чIара	[ʧabaq ʧhara]
carp	карп	[karp]
perch	окунь	[ɔkuɲ]
catfish	яй	[jaj]
pike	гIазкхийн чIара	[ɣazqi:n ʧhara]

| salmon | лосось | [lɔsɔsʲ] |
| sturgeon | цIен чIара | [ʦhen ʧhara] |

herring	сельдь	[seʎdʲ]
Atlantic salmon	сёмга	[sɜmga]
mackerel	скумбри	[skumbri]
flatfish	камбала	[kambala]

zander, pike perch	судак	[sudak]
cod	треска	[treska]
tuna	тунец	[tuneʦ]
trout	бакъ чIара	[baqh ʧhara]
eel	жIаьлин чIара	[ʒæælin ʧhara]
electric ray	электрически скат	[ɛlektriʧeski skat]
moray eel	мурена	[murena]
piranha	пиранья	[piraɲja]

shark	гIоркхма	[ɣɔrqma]
dolphin	дельфин	[deʎfin]
whale	кит	[kit]

crab	краб	[krab]
jellyfish	медуза	[meduza]
octopus	бархIкогберг	[barhkɔgberg]

starfish	хIордан седа	[hɔrdan seda]
sea urchin	хIордан зу	[hɔrdan zu]
seahorse	хIордан говр	[hɔrdan gɔvr]

oyster	устрица	[ustriʦa]
shrimp	креветка	[krewetka]
lobster	омар	[ɔmar]
spiny lobster	лангуст	[laŋust]

219. Amphibians. Reptiles

snake	лаьхьа	[læha]
poisonous	дӏаьвше	[dəævʃə]
viper	лаьхьа	[læha]
cobra	кобра	[kɔbra]
python	питон	[pitɔn]
boa	саьрмикъ	[særmiqh]
grass snake	вотангар	[vɔtaŋar]
rattle snake	шов ден лаьхьа	[ʃɔv den læha]
anaconda	анаконда	[anakɔnda]
lizard	моьлкъа	[mølqha]
iguana	игуана	[iguana]
monitor lizard	варан	[varan]
salamander	саламандра	[salamandra]
chameleon	хамелион	[hameliɔn]
scorpion	скорпион	[skɔrpiɔn]
turtle	уьнтӏапхьид	[ynthaphid]
frog	пхьид	[phid]
toad	бецан пхьид	[betsan phid]
crocodile	саьрмикъ	[særmiqh]

220. Insects

insect, bug	сагалмат	[sagalmat]
butterfly	полла	[pɔl:a]
ant	зингат	[ziŋat]
fly	моза	[mɔza]
mosquito	чуьрк	[tʃyrk]
beetle	чхьаьвриг	[tʃhævrig]
wasp	зӏуга	[zəuga]
bee	накхармоза	[naqarmɔza]
bumblebee	бумбари	[bumbari]
gadfly	тӏод	[thɔd]
spider	гезг	[gezg]
spider's web	гезгмаша	[gezgmaʃa]
dragonfly	шайтӏанан дин	[ʃajthanan din]
grasshopper	цӏаьпцалг	[tshæptsalg]
moth (night butterfly)	полла	[pɔl:a]
cockroach	чхьаьвриг	[tʃhævrig]
tick	веччалг	[wetʃalg]

| flea | сагал | [sagal] |
| midge | пхьажбуург | [phaӡbu:rg] |

locust	цӏоз	[tshɔz]
snail	этмаьиг	[ɛtmæəig]
cricket	цаьпцалг	[tsæptsalg]

lightning bug	бумбари	[bumbari]
ladybug	дедо	[dedɔ]
cockchafer	бумбари	[bumbari]

leech	цӏубдар	[tshubdar]
caterpillar	нӏаьвцициг	[nəævtsitsig]
worm	нӏаьна	[nəæna]
larva	нӏаьна	[nəæna]

221. Animals. Body parts

beak	зӏок	[zəɔk]
wings	тӏемаш	[themaʃ]
foot (of bird)	ког	[kɔg]
feathering	мас ялар	[mas jalar]

| feather | пелаг | [pelag] |
| crest | жима кӏужал | [ӡima k:uӡal] |

gill	жӏараш	[ӡəaraʃ]
spawn	зирх	[zirh]
larva	нӏаьвцициг	[nəævtsitsig]

| fin | пелаг | [pelag] |
| scales (of fish, reptile) | пелаг | [pelag] |

fang (of wolf etc.)	пхьарцерг	[phartserg]
paw (e.g., cat's ~)	тӏод	[thɔd]
muzzle	муцӏар	[mutshar]
mouth (of cat, dog)	бага	[baga]

| tail | цӏога | [tshɔga] |
| whiskers | мекхаш | [meqaʃ] |

| hoof | берг | [berg] |
| horn | мӏаӏ | [maəa] |

carapace	у	[u]
shell (of mollusk)	лахьорч	[lahɔrtʃ]
shell (of egg)	чкъуьйриг	[tʃqhyjrig]

| hair (e.g., dog's ~) | тӏапрӏа | [tharɣa] |
| skin (of animal) | цӏока | [tshɔka] |

222. Actions of animals

to fly (bird, insect)	лела	[lela]
to make circles	хьийза	[hi:za]
to fly away	дӀадаха	[dəadaha]
to flap (~ the wings)	лесто	[lestɔ]
to peck (vi)	зӀок етта	[zɔk et:a]
to incubate (vt)	тевна даккха	[tevna dak:a]
to hatch out (vi)	даха	[daha]
to build (nest)	дала	[daəa]
to slither, to crawl	текха	[teqa]
to sting, to bite (insect)	ю тоха	[ju tɔha]
to bite (about animal)	леца	[letsa]
to sniff (vt)	хьожа яха	[hɔʒa jaha]
to bark (vi)	гӀаӀх дан	[ɣalh dan]
to hiss (snake)	хиш-ш дан	[hiʃʃ dan]
to scare (vt)	кхеро	[qerɔ]
to attack (vt)	тӀелата	[thelata]
to gnaw (bone etc.)	Ӏийша	[əi:ʃa]
to scratch (with claws)	сизаш дан	[sizaʃ dan]
to hide (vi)	дӀалечкъа	[dəaletʃqha]
to play (kittens etc.)	ловза	[lovza]
to hunt (vi, vt)	талла эха	[tal:a ɛha]
to hibernate (vi)	дӀадижан хила	[dəadiʒan hila]
to become extinct	хӀу дан	[hu dan]

223. Animals. Habitats

habitat	дахаран хьал	[daharan hal]
migration	миграци	[migratsi]
mountain	лам	[lam]
reef	риф	[rif]
cliff	тарх	[tarh]
forest	хьун	[hun]
jungle	джунглеш	[dʒuŋleʃ]
savanna	саванна	[savaŋa]
tundra	тундра	[tundra]
steppe	аре	[are]
desert	гӀум-аре	[ɣum are]
oasis	оазис	[ɔazis]
sea	хӀорд	[hɔrd]

lake	**Iам**	[əam]
ocean	**хIорд, океан**	[hɔrd], [ɔkean]
wetland	**уьшал**	[yʃal]
freshwater	**тезачу хин**	[tezaʧu hin]
pond	**Iам**	[əam]
river	**доьду хи**	[dødu hi]
den	**чен бен**	[ʧen ben]
nest	**бен**	[ben]
hollow (in tree)	**хара**	[hara]
burrow (animal hole)	**Iуьрг**	[əyrg]
anthill	**туьйлиг**	[tyjlig]

224. Animal care

zoo	**дийнатийн парк**	[di:nati:n park]
nature preserve	**заповедник**	[zapɔwednik]
breeder, breed club	**питомник**	[pitɔmnik]
open-air cage	**вольер**	[vɔʎjer]
cage	**ога**	[ɔga]
doghouse	**перги**	[pergi]
dovecot	**кхокхийн бун**	[qɔqi:n bun]
aquarium	**аквариум**	[akvarium]
dolphinarium	**дельфинари**	[deʎfinari]
to breed (animals)	**доло**	[dɔlɔ]
brood, litter	**тIаьхье**	[thæhe]
to tame (vt)	**караламо**	[karaəamɔ]
feed (for animal)	**докъар**	[dɔqhar]
to feed (vt)	**хIума яла**	[huma jala]
to train (animals)	**караламо**	[karaəamɔ]
pet store	**зоотуька**	[zo:tyka]
muzzle (for dog)	**бетахъюллург**	[betahʰjul:urg]
collar (for animal)	**кочатосург**	[kɔʧatɔsurg]
name (of animal)	**яхна цIе**	[jahna ʦhe]
pedigree (of dog)	**тайпа**	[tajpa]

225. Animals. Miscellaneous

pack (wolves)	**арданг**	[ardaŋ]
flock (birds)	**жIуга**	[ʒəuga]
shoal (fish)	**жIуга**	[ʒəuga]
herd	**рема**	[rema]
male (noun)	**боьрша хIума**	[børʃa huma]

female (noun)	стен хІума	[sten huma]
hungry	меца	[metsa]
wild	акха	[aqa]
dangerous	кхераме	[qerame]

226. Horses

breed (race)	тайпа	[tajpa]
foal (of horse)	бекъа	[beqha]
mare	кхела	[qela]
mustang	мустанг	[mustaŋ]
pony (small horse)	пони	[poni]
draft horse	дезчу киранийн говр	[deztʃu kirani:n gɔvr]
mane	кхес	[qes]
tail	цІога	[tshɔga]
hoof	берг	[berg]
horseshoe	лан	[lan]
to shoe (vt)	лан тоха	[lan tɔha]
blacksmith	аьчкан пхьар	[ætʃkan phar]
saddle	нуьйр	[nyjr]
stirrup	луьйта	[lyjta]
bridle	дирста	[dirsta]
reins	архаш	[arhaʃ]
whip (for riding)	шед	[ʃed]
rider	бере	[bere]
to break in (horse)	дин Іамор	[din eamɔr]
to saddle (vt)	нуьйр тилла	[nyjr til:a]
to mount (a horse)	нуьйра хаа	[nyjra ha:]
gallop	юм	[jum]
to gallop (vi)	кхийсалуш ядар	[qi:saluʃ jadar]
trot (noun)	чабол	[tʃabɔl]
at a trot	чаболехь	[tʃabɔleh]
racehorse	хохку говр	[hohku gɔvr]
races	хахкар	[hahkar]
stable	божал	[bɔʒal]
to feed (vt)	хІума яла	[huma jala]
hay	йол	[jol]
to water (animals)	мийло	[mi:lɔ]
to wash (horse)	цІандан	[tshandan]
to hobble (vt)	баргол тоха	[bargɔl tɔha]
horse-drawn cart	ворда	[vɔrda]
to graze (vi)	дажа	[daʒa]

to neigh (vi)	**терса**	[tersɑ]
to kick (horse)	**мийра тоха**	[miːrɑ tɔha]

Flora

227. Trees

tree	дитт	[dit:]
deciduous	гӀаш долу	[ɣaʃ dɔlu]
coniferous	баганан	[baɡanan]
evergreen	гуттар сийна	[ɡut:ar si:na]

apple tree	Ӏаж	[əaʒ]
pear tree	кхор	[qɔr]
cherry tree	балл	[bal:]
plum tree	хьач	[hatʃ]

birch	дакх	[daq]
oak	наж	[naʒ]
linden tree	хьех	[heh]
aspen	мах	[mah]
maple	къахк	[qhahk]

fir tree	база	[baza]
pine	зез	[zez]
larch	бага	[baɡa]
silver fir	пихта	[pihta]
cedar	кедр	[kedr]

| poplar | талл | [tal:] |
| rowan | датта | [dat:a] |

| willow | дак | [dak] |
| alder | маъ | [ma] |

| beech | поп | [pɔp] |
| elm | муьшдечиг | [myʃdetʃiɡ] |

| ash (tree) | къахьашту | [qhahaʃtu] |
| chestnut | каштан | [kaʃtan] |

magnolia	магноли	[maɡnɔli]
palm tree	пальма	[paʎma]
cypress	кипарис	[kiparis]

mangrove	мангрови дитт	[maŋrɔwi dit:]
baobab	баобаб	[baobab]
eucalyptus	эквалипт	[ɛkvalipt]
redwood	секвойя	[sekvɔja]

228. Shrubs

| bush | колл | [kɔl:] |
| shrub | колл | [kɔl:] |

| grapevine | кемсаш | [kemsaʃ] |
| vineyard | кемсийн беш | [kemsi:n beʃ] |

raspberry bush	цlен комар	[tshen kɔmar]
redcurrant bush	цlен кхезарш	[tshen qezarʃ]
gooseberry bush	кlудалгаш	[k:udalgaʃ]

acacia	акаци	[akatsi]
barberry	муьстарг	[mystarg]
jasmine	жасмин	[ʒasmin]

juniper	жlолам	[ʒəolam]
rosebush	розанийн кол	[rɔzani:n kɔl]
dog rose	хьармак	[harmak]

229. Mushrooms

| mushroom | жlаьлин нускал | [ʒəælin nuskal] |
| edible mushroom | даа мегаш долу жlаьлин нускал | [da: megaʃ dɔlu ʒəælin nuskal] |

toadstool	дlовше жlаьлин нускал	[dəovʃə ʒəælin nuskal]
cap (of mushroom)	жlаьлин нускалан корта	[ʒəælin nuskalan kɔrta]
foot (of mushroom)	жlаьлин нускалан кога	[ʒəælin nuskalan kɔga]

boletus	кlайн жlаьлин нускал	[k:ajn ʒəælin nuskal]
orange-cap boletus	подосиновик	[pɔdɔsinɔwik]
brown-cap boletus	подберёзовик	[pɔdberзɔwik]
chanterelle	лисичка	[lisitʃka]
russula	буьйдалг	[byjdalg]

morel	сморчок	[smɔrtʃɔk]
fly agaric	мухомор	[muhomɔr]
death cap	поганка	[pɔgaŋka]

230. Fruits. Berries

| fruit | стом | [stɔm] |
| fruits | стоьмаш | [stømaʃ] |

apple	lаж	[əaʒ]
pear	кхор	[qɔr]
plum	хьач	[hatʃ]

225

strawberry	цlазам	[ʦhazam]
cherry	балл	[bal:]
grapes	кемсаш	[kemsaʃ]

raspberry	цlен комар	[ʦhen kɔmar]
blackcurrant	lаьржа кхезарш	[əærʒa qezarʃ]
redcurrant	цlен кхезарш	[ʦhen qezarʃ]
gooseberry	кlудалгаш	[k:udalgaʃ]
cranberry	клюква	[klykva]

orange	апельсин	[apeʎsin]
mandarin	мандарин	[mandarin]
pineapple	ананас	[ananas]
banana	банан	[banan]
date	хурма	[hurma]

lemon	лимон	[limɔn]
apricot	туьрк	[tyrk]
peach	гlаммагlа	[ɣam:aɣa]
kiwi	киви	[kiwi]
grapefruit	грейпфрут	[grejpfrut]

berry	цlазам	[ʦhazam]
berries	цlазамаш	[ʦhazamaʃ]
cowberry	брусника	[brusnika]
field strawberry	пхьагал-цlазам	[phagal ʦhazam]
bilberry	lаьржа балл	[əærʒa bal:]

231. Flowers. Plants

| flower | зезеаг | [zezeag] |
| bouquet (of flowers) | курс | [kurs] |

rose (flower)	роза	[rɔza]
tulip	алцlензlам	[alʦhenzeam]
carnation	гвоздика	[gvɔzdika]
gladiolus	гладиолус	[gladiɔlus]

cornflower	сендарг	[sendarg]
bluebell	тухтати	[tuhtati]
dandelion	баппа	[bap:a]
camomile	кlайдарг	[k:ajdarg]

aloe	алоэ	[alɔɛ]
cactus	кактус	[kaktus]
rubber plant	фикус	[fikus]

lily	лили	[lili]
geranium	герань	[geraɲ]
hyacinth	гиацинт	[giaʦint]

mimosa	мимоза	[mimɔza]
narcissus	нарцисс	[nartsis:]
nasturtium	настурция	[nasturtsi]

orchid	орхидей	[ɔrhidej]
peony	цӏен лерг	[tshen lerg]
violet	тобалкх	[tɔbalq]

pansy	анютийн бӏаьргаш	[anyti:n bæærgaʃ]
forget-me-not	незабудка	[nezabudka]
daisy	маргаритка	[margaritka]

poppy	петӏамат	[pethamat]
hemp	кӏомал	[k:ɔmal]
mint	Ӏаждарбуц	[ɑaʒdarbuts]
lily of the valley	чӏерӏардиган кӏа	[tʃheɣardigan k:a]
snowdrop	лайн зезаг	[lajn zezag]

nettle	нитташ	[nit:aʃ]
sorrel	муьстарг	[mystarg]
water lily	кувшинка	[ku:ʃiŋka]
fern	чураш	[tʃuraʃ]
lichen	корсам	[kɔrsam]

greenhouse (tropical ~)	оранжерей	[ɔranʒerej]
lawn	бешмайда	[beʃmajda]
flowerbed	хас	[has]

plant	орамат	[ɔramat]
grass	буц	[buts]
blade (of grass)	бецан хелиг	[betsan helig]

leaf	гӏа	[ɣa]
petal (of flower)	жаз	[ʒaz]
stem (of plant)	гӏодам	[ɣɔdam]
tuber	орамстом	[ɔramstɔm]

| young plant (shoot) | зӏийдиг | [zəi:dig] |
| thorn | кӏохцал | [k:ɔhtsal] |

to blossom (vi)	заза даккха	[zaza dak:a]
to fade, to wither	маргӏалдола	[marɣaldɔla]
smell (odor)	хьожа	[hɔʒa]
to cut (flowers)	дӏахадо	[deahadɔ]
to pick (a flower)	схьадаккха	[shadak:a]

232. Cereals, grains

| grain | буьртиг | [byrtig] |
| cereals | буьртиган ораматаш | [byrtigan ɔramataʃ] |

ear (of grain)	кан	[kan]
wheat	кӀа	[k:a]
rye	божан	[bɔʒan]
oats	сула	[sula]
millet	борц	[bɔrts]
barley	мукх	[muq]

corn	хьаьжкӀа	[hæʒk:a]
rice	дуга	[duga]
buckwheat	цӀен дуга	[tshen duga]

pea	кхоьш	[qøʃ]
kidney beans	кхоь	[qø]
soy beans	кхоь	[qø]
lentil	хьоьзийн кхоьш	[høzi:n qøʃ]
beans	кхоьш	[qøʃ]

233. Vegetables. Greens

| vegetables | хасстоьмаш | [has:tømaʃ] |
| greens | гӀабуц | [ɣabuts] |

tomato	помидор	[pɔmidɔr]
cucumber	наьрс	[nærs]
carrot	жӀонка	[ʒəɔŋka]
potato	картол	[kartɔl]
onion	хох	[hoh]
garlic	саьрмасекх	[særmaseq]

cabbage	копаста	[kɔpasta]
cauliflower	къорза копаста	[qhɔrza kɔpasta]
Brussels sprouts	брюссельски копаста	[brys:eʎski kɔpasta]

beetroot	бурак	[burak]
eggplant	баклажан	[baklaʒan]
zucchini	кабачок	[kabatʃok]
pumpkin	гӀабакх	[ɣabaq]
turnip	хорсам	[horsam]

parsley	чам-буц	[tʃam buts]
dill	оччам	[otʃam]
lettuce	салат	[salat]
celery	сельдерей	[seʎderej]
asparagus	спаржа	[sparʒa]
spinach	шпинат	[ʃpinat]

pea	кхоьш	[qøʃ]
beans	кхоьш	[qøʃ]
corn (maize)	хьаьжкӀа	[hæʒk:a]
kidney beans	кхоь	[qø]

bell pepper	бурч	[burtʃ]
radish	цӏен хорсам	[tshen horsam]
artichoke	артишок	[artiʃok]

REGIONAL GEOGRAPHY

Countries. Nationalities

234. Western Europe

Europe	Европа	[evrɔpɑ]
European Union	Европин Союз	[evrɔpin sɔjuz]
European (noun)	европахо	[evrɔpɑho]
European (adj)	европин	[evrɔpin]
Austria	Австри	[ɑvstri]
Austrian (man)	австрихо	[ɑvstriho]
Austrian (woman)	австрихо	[ɑvstriho]
Austrian (adj)	австрихойн	[ɑvstrihojn]
Great Britain	Великобритани	[welikɔbritɑni]
England	Ингалс	[iŋɑls]
British (man)	ингалсхо	[iŋɑlsho]
British (woman)	ингалсхо	[iŋɑlsho]
English, British (adj)	ингалсан	[iŋɑlsɑn]
Belgium	Бельги	[beʌgi]
Belgian (man)	бельгихо	[beʌgiho]
Belgian (woman)	бельгихо	[beʌgiho]
Belgian (adj)	бельгин	[beʌgin]
Germany	Германи	[germɑni]
German (man)	немцой	[nemtsɔj]
German (woman)	немцой	[nemtsɔj]
German (adj)	немцойн	[nemtsɔjn]
Netherlands	Нидерланды	[niderlɑndɪ]
Holland	Голланди	[gɔl:ɑndi]
Dutchman	голландхо	[gɔl:ɑndho]
Dutchwoman	голландхо	[gɔl:ɑndho]
Dutch (adj)	голландхойн	[gɔl:ɑndhojn]
Greece	Греци	[gretsi]
Greek (man)	грек	[grek]
Greek (woman)	грек	[grek]
Greek (adj)	грекийн	[greki:n]
Denmark	Дани	[dɑni]
Dane (man)	датхо	[dɑtho]

| Dane (woman) | датхо | [dɑtho] |
| Danish (adj) | датхойн | [dɑthojn] |

Ireland	Ирланди	[irlɑndi]
Irishman	ирландхо	[irlɑndho]
Irishwoman	ирландхо	[irlɑndho]
Irish (adj)	ирландхойн	[irlɑndhojn]

Iceland	Исланди	[islɑndi]
Icelander (man)	исландхо	[islɑndho]
Icelander (woman)	исландхо	[islɑndho]
Icelandic (adj)	исландхойн	[islɑndhojn]

Spain	Испани	[ispɑni]
Spaniard (man)	испанхо	[ispɑnho]
Spaniard (woman)	испанхо	[ispɑnho]
Spanish (adj)	испанхойн	[ispɑnhojn]

Italy	Итали	[itɑli]
Italian (man)	итальян	[itɑʎjɑn]
Italian (woman)	итальян	[itɑʎjɑn]
Italian (adj)	итальянийн	[itɑʎjɑni:n]

Cyprus	Кипр	[kipr]
Cypriot (man)	кипрхо	[kiprɔ]
Cypriot (woman)	кипрхо	[kiprɔ]
Cypriot (adj)	кипрхойн	[kiprɔjn]

Malta	Мальта	[mɑʎtɑ]
Maltese (man)	мальтахо	[mɑʎtɑho]
Maltese (woman)	мальтахо	[mɑʎtɑho]
Maltese (adj)	мальтахойн	[mɑʎtɑhojn]

Norway	Норвеги	[nɔrwegi]
Norwegian (man)	норвег	[nɔrweg]
Norwegian (woman)	норвег	[nɔrweg]
Norwegian (adj)	норвегийн	[nɔrwegi:n]

Portugal	Португали	[portugɑli]
Portuguese (man)	португалихо	[portugɑliho]
Portuguese (woman)	португалихо	[portugɑliho]
Portuguese (adj)	португалихойн	[portugɑlihojn]

Finland	Финлянди	[finʎɑndi]
Finn (man)	финн	[fiŋ]
Finn (woman)	финн	[fiŋ]
Finnish (adj)	финнийн	[fiŋi:n]

France	Франци	[frɑnʦi]
Frenchman	француз	[frɑnʦuz]
Frenchwoman	француз	[frɑnʦuz]
French (adj)	французийн	[frɑnʦuzi:n]

Sweden	Швеци	[ʃwetsi]
Swede (man)	швед	[ʃwed]
Swede (woman)	швед	[ʃwed]
Swedish (adj)	шведийн	[ʃwedi:n]

Switzerland	Швейцари	[ʃwejtsari]
Swiss (man)	швейцар	[ʃwejtsar]
Swiss (woman)	швейцар	[ʃwejtsar]
Swiss (adj)	швейцарин	[ʃwejtsarin]

Scotland	Шотланди	[ʃotlandi]
Scottish (man)	шотланди	[ʃotlandi]
Scottish (woman)	шотланди	[ʃotlandi]
Scottish (adj)	шотландийн	[ʃotlandi:n]

Vatican	Ватикан	[vatikan]
Liechtenstein	Лихтенштейн	[lihtenʃtejn]
Luxembourg	Люксембург	[lyksemburg]
Monaco	Монако	[monakɔ]

235. Central and Eastern Europe

Albania	Албани	[albani]
Albanian (man)	албанихо	[albaniho]
Albanian (woman)	албанихо	[albaniho]
Albanian (adj)	албанихойн	[albanihojn]

Bulgaria	Болгари	[bɔlgari]
Bulgarian (man)	болгар	[bɔlgar]
Bulgarian (woman)	болгар	[bɔlgar]
Bulgarian (adj)	болгарийн	[bɔlgari:n]

Hungary	Венгри	[weŋri]
Hungarian (man)	венгр	[weŋr]
Hungarian (woman)	венгр	[weŋr]
Hungarian (adj)	венгрийн	[weŋri:n]

Latvia	Латви	[latwi]
Latvian (man)	латыш	[latıʃ]
Latvian (woman)	латыш	[latıʃ]
Latvian (adj)	латвийн	[latvi:n]

Lithuania	Литва	[litva]
Lithuanian (man)	литвахо	[litvaho]
Lithuanian (woman)	литвахо	[litvaho]
Lithuanian (adj)	литвахойн	[litvahojn]

Poland	Польша	[pɔʎʃa]
Pole (man)	поляк	[pɔʎak]
Pole (woman)	поляк	[pɔʎak]

Polish (adj)	полякийн	[poˈʎakiːn]
Romania	Румыни	[rumɪni]
Romanian (man)	румын	[rumɪn]
Romanian (woman)	румын	[rumɪn]
Romanian (adj)	румынийн	[rumɪniːn]

Serbia	Серби	[serbi]
Serbian (man)	серб	[serb]
Serbian (woman)	серб	[serb]
Serbian (adj)	сербийн	[serbiːn]

Slovakia	Словаки	[slɔvaki]
Slovak (man)	словак	[slɔvak]
Slovak (woman)	словак	[slɔvak]
Slovak (adj)	словакийн	[slɔvakiːn]

Croatia	Хорвати	[horvati]
Croatian (man)	хорват	[horvat]
Croatian (woman)	хорват	[horvat]
Croatian (adj)	хорватийн	[horvatiːn]

The Czech Republic	Чехи	[ʧehi]
Czech (man)	чех	[ʧeh]
Czech (woman)	чех	[ʧeh]
Czech (adj)	чехийн	[ʧehiːn]

Estonia	Эстони	[ɛstɔni]
Estonian (man)	эстон	[ɛstɔn]
Estonian (woman)	эстон	[ɛstɔn]
Estonian (adj)	эсонийн	[ɛsɔniːn]

Bosnia-Herzegovina	Босни е Герцоговина е	[bɔsni e gerʦɔgɔwina e]
Macedonia	Македони	[makedɔni]
Slovenia	Словени	[slɔweni]
Montenegro	Черногори	[ʧernɔgɔri]

236. Former USSR countries

Azerbaijan	Азербайджан	[azerbajʤan]
Azerbaijani (man)	азербайджанхо	[azerbajʤanhɔ]
Azerbaijani (woman)	азербайджанхо	[azerbajʤanhɔ]
Azerbaijani (adj)	азербайджанхойн	[azerbajʤanhɔjn]

Armenia	Армени	[armeni]
Armenian (man)	эрмало	[ɛrmalɔ]
Armenian (woman)	эрмало	[ɛrmalɔ]
Armenian (adj)	эрмалойн	[ɛrmalɔjn]

Belarus	Беларусь	[belarusʲ]
Belarusian (man)	белорусхо	[belɔrushɔ]

Belarusian (woman)	**белорусхо**	[belɔrusho]
Belarusian (adj)	**белорусхойн**	[belɔrushojn]
Georgia	**Грузи**	[gruzi]
Georgian (man)	**гуьржи**	[gyrʒi]
Georgian (woman)	**гуьржи**	[gyrʒi]
Georgian (adj)	**гуьржийн**	[gyrʒi:n]
Kazakhstan	**Казахстан**	[kazahstan]
Kazakh (man)	**казах**	[kazah]
Kazakh (woman)	**казах**	[kazah]
Kazakh (adj)	**казахийн**	[kazahi:n]
Kirghizia	**Кыргызстан**	[kɪrgɪzstan]
Kirghiz (man)	**киргиз**	[kirgiz]
Kirghiz (woman)	**киргиз**	[kirgiz]
Kirghiz (adj)	**киргизийн**	[kirgizi:n]
Moldavia	**Молдова**	[mɔldɔva]
Moldavian (man)	**молдован**	[mɔldɔvan]
Moldavian (woman)	**молдован**	[mɔldɔvan]
Moldavian (adj)	**молдованийн**	[mɔldɔvani:n]
Russia	**Росси**	[rɔs:i]
Russian (man)	**оьрси**	[ørsi]
Russian (woman)	**оьрси**	[ørsi]
Russian (adj)	**оьрсийн**	[ørsi:n]
Tajikistan	**Таджикистан**	[tadʒikistan]
Tajik (man)	**таджик**	[tadʒik]
Tajik (woman)	**таджик**	[tadʒik]
Tajik (adj)	**таджикийн**	[tadʒiki:n]
Turkmenistan	**Туркменистан**	[turkmenistan]
Turkmen (man)	**туркмен**	[turkmen]
Turkmen (woman)	**туркмен**	[turkmen]
Turkmenian (adj)	**туркменийн**	[turkmeni:n]
Uzbekistan	**Узбекистан**	[uzbekistan]
Uzbek (man)	**узбек**	[uzbek]
Uzbek (woman)	**узбек**	[uzbek]
Uzbek (adj)	**узбекийн**	[uzbeki:n]
Ukraine	**Украина**	[ukraina]
Ukrainian (man)	**украин**	[ukrain]
Ukrainian (woman)	**украин**	[ukrain]
Ukrainian (adj)	**украинийн**	[ukraini:n]

237. Asia

Asia	**Ази**	[azi]
Asian	**азиатский**	[aziatski:]

Vietnam	Вьетнам	[vjetnam]
Vietnamese (man)	вьетнамхо	[vjetnamho]
Vietnamese (woman)	вьетнамхо	[vjetnamho]
Vietnamese (adj)	вьетнамхойн	[vjetnamhojn]

India	Инди	[indi]
Indian (man)	индус	[indus]
Indian (woman)	индус	[indus]
Indian (adj)	индихойн	[indihojn]

Israel	Израиль	[izraiʎ]
Israeli (man)	израильхо	[izraiʎho]
Israeli (woman)	израильхо	[izraiʎho]
Israeli (adj)	израильхойн	[izraiʎhojn]

Jew (noun)	жуьгти	[ʒygti]
Jewess (noun)	жуьгти	[ʒygti]
Jewish (adj)	жуьгтийн	[ʒygti:n]

China	Китай	[kitaj]
Chinese (man)	китай	[kitaj]
Chinese (woman)	китай	[kitaj]
Chinese (adj)	китайн	[kitajn]

Korean (man)	корей	[kɔrej]
Korean (woman)	корей	[kɔrej]
Korean (adj)	корейн	[kɔrejn]

Lebanon	Ливан	[livan]
Lebanese (man)	ливан	[livan]
Lebanese (woman)	ливан	[livan]
Lebanese (adj)	ливанийн	[livani:n]

Mongolia	Монголи	[mɔŋɔli]
Mongolian (man)	монгол	[mɔŋɔl]
Mongolian (woman)	монгол	[mɔŋɔl]
Mongolian (adj)	монголийн	[mɔŋɔli:n]

Malaysia	Малази	[malazi]
Malaysian (man)	малаец	[malaets]
Malaysian (woman)	малаец	[malaets]
Malaysian (adj)	малаецан	[malaetsan]

Pakistan	Пакистан	[pakistan]
Pakistani (man)	пакистанхо	[pakistanho]
Pakistani (woman)	пакистанхо	[pakistanho]
Pakistani (adj)	пакистанхойн	[pakistanhojn]

Saudi Arabia	Саудовски Арави	[saudɔvski arawi]
Arab (man)	Iаьрби	[əærbi]
Arab (woman)	Iаьрби	[əærbi]
Arabian (adj)	Iаьрбийн	[əærbi:n]

Thailand	**Таиланд**	[tailand]
Thai (man)	**тайландхо**	[tajlandho]
Thai (woman)	**тайландхо**	[tajlandho]
Thai (adj)	**тайландхойн**	[tajlandhojn]

Taiwan	**Тайвань**	[tajvaɲ]
Taiwanese (man)	**тайваньхо**	[tajvaɲho]
Taiwanese (woman)	**тайваньхо**	[tajvaɲho]
Taiwanese (adj)	**тайваньхойн**	[tajvaɲhojn]

Turkey	**Турци**	[turtsi]
Turk (man)	**турко**	[turkɔ]
Turk (woman)	**турко**	[turkɔ]
Turkish (adj)	**туркойн**	[turkɔjn]

Japan	**Япони**	[japɔni]
Japanese (man)	**япон**	[japɔn]
Japanese (woman)	**япон**	[japɔn]
Japanese (adj)	**японийн**	[japɔni:n]

Afghanistan	**Афганистан**	[afganistan]
Bangladesh	**Бангладеш**	[baŋladeʃ]
Indonesia	**Индонези**	[indɔnezi]
Jordan	**Иордани**	[iɔrdani]

Iraq	**Ирак**	[irak]
Iran	**Иран**	[iran]
Cambodia	**Камбоджа**	[kambɔdʒa]
Kuwait	**Кувейт**	[ku:ejt]

Laos	**Лаос**	[laɔs]
Myanmar	**Мьянма**	[mjanma]
Nepal	**Непал**	[nepal]
United Arab Emirates	**Цхьаьнакхеттачу** **Iаьрбийн Эмираташ**	[tshænaqet:atʃu æærbi:n ɛmirataʃ]

Syria	**Сири**	[siri]
Palestine	**Палестина**	[palestina]
South Korea	**Къилбера Корея**	[qhilbera kɔreja]
North Korea	**Къилбаседера Корея**	[qhilbasedera kɔreja]

238. North America

United States of America	**Америкин** **Цхьаьнакхетта Штаташ**	[amerikin tshænaqet:a ʃtataʃ]
American (man)	**америкахо**	[amerikaho]
American (woman)	**америкахо**	[amerikaho]
American (adj)	**америкин**	[amerikin]
Canada	**Канада**	[kanada]
Canadian (man)	**канадхо**	[kanadho]

| Canadian (woman) | канадхо | [kanadho] |
| Canadian (adj) | канадин | [kanadin] |

Mexico	Мексика	[meksika]
Mexican (man)	мексикахо	[meksikaho]
Mexican (woman)	мексикахо	[meksikaho]
Mexican (adj)	мексикахойн	[meksikahojn]

239. Central and South America

Argentina	Аргентина	[argentina]
Argentinian (man)	аргентинахо	[argentinaho]
Argentinian (woman)	аргентинахо	[argentinaho]
Argentinian (adj)	аргентинахойн	[argentinahojn]

Brazil	Бразили	[brazili]
Brazilian (man)	бразилихо	[braziliho]
Brazilian (woman)	бразилихо	[braziliho]
Brazilian (adj)	бразилихойн	[brazilihojn]

Colombia	Колумби	[kɔlumbi]
Colombian (man)	колумбихо	[kɔlumbiho]
Colombian (woman)	колумбихо	[kɔlumbiho]
Colombian (adj)	колумбихойн	[kɔlumbihojn]

Cuba	Куба	[kuba]
Cuban (man)	кубахо	[kubaho]
Cuban (woman)	кубахо	[kubaho]
Cuban (adj)	кубахойн	[kubahojn]

Chile	Чили	[ʧili]
Chilean (man)	чилихо	[ʧiliho]
Chilean (woman)	чилихо	[ʧiliho]
Chilean (adj)	чилихойн	[ʧilihojn]

Bolivia	Боливи	[bɔliwi]
Venezuela	Венесуэла	[wenesuɛla]
Paraguay	Парагвай	[paragvaj]
Peru	Перу	[peru]

Surinam	Суринам	[surinam]
Uruguay	Уругвай	[urugvaj]
Ecuador	Эквадор	[ɛkvadɔr]

Bahamas	Багамахойн гӀайренаш	[bagamahojn ɣajrenaʃ]
Haiti	Гаити	[gaiti]
Dominican Republic	Доминиканхойн республика	[dɔminikanhojn respublika]

| Panama | Панама | [panama] |
| Jamaica | Ямайка | [jamajka] |

237

240. Africa

Egypt	Мисар	[misar]
Egyptian (man)	мисархо	[misarhɔ]
Egyptian (woman)	мисархо	[misarhɔ]
Egyptian (adj)	мисаран	[misaran]

Morocco	Марокко	[marɔk:ɔ]
Moroccan (man)	мароккохо	[marɔk:ɔho]
Moroccan (woman)	мароккохо	[marɔk:ɔho]
Moroccan (adj)	мароккохойн	[marɔk:ɔhojn]

Tunisia	Тунис	[tunis]
Tunisian (man)	тунисахо	[tunisaho]
Tunisian (woman)	тунисахо	[tunisaho]
Tunisian (adj)	тунисахойн	[tunisahojn]

| Ghana | Гана | [gana] |
| Zanzibar | Занзибар | [zanzibar] |

Kenya	Кени	[keni]
Libya	Ливи	[liwi]
Madagascar	Мадагаскар	[madagaskar]

Namibia	Намиби	[namibi]
Senegal	Сенегал	[senegal]
Tanzania	Танзани	[tanzani]
South Africa	ЮАР	[juar]

African (man)	африкахо	[afrikaho]
African (woman)	африкахо	[afrikaho]
African (adj)	африкахойн	[afrikahojn]

241. Australia. Oceania

| Australia | Австрали | [avstrali] |
| Australian (man) | австралихо | [avstraliho] |

| Australian (woman) | австралихо | [avstraliho] |
| Australian (adj) | австралихойн | [avstralihojn] |

| New Zealand | Керла Зеланди | [kerla zelandi] |
| New Zealander (man) | керлазеландихо | [kerlazelandiho] |

| New Zealander (woman) | керлазеландихо | [kerlazelandiho] |
| New Zealand (attr) | керлазеландихойн | [kerlazelandihojn] |

| Tasmania | Тасмани | [tasmani] |
| French Polynesia | Французийн Полинези | [frantsuzi:n pɔlinezi] |

242. Cities

Amsterdam	**Амстердам**	[amsterdam]
Ankara	**Анкара**	[aŋkara]
Athens	**Афинаш**	[afinaʃ]
Baghdad	**Багдад**	[bagdad]
Bangkok	**Бангкок**	[baŋkɔk]
Barcelona	**Барселона**	[barselɔna]
Beijing	**Пекин**	[pekin]
Beirut	**Бейрут**	[bejrut]
Berlin	**Берлин**	[berlin]
Bombay	**Бомбей**	[bɔmbej]
Bonn	**Бонн**	[bɔŋ]
Bordeaux	**Бордо**	[bɔrdɔ]
Bratislava	**Братислава**	[bratislava]
Brussels	**Брюссель**	[brys:eʎ]
Bucharest	**Бухарест**	[buharest]
Budapest	**Будапешт**	[budapeʃt]
Cairo	**Каир**	[kair]
Calcutta	**Калькутта**	[kaʎkut:a]
Chicago	**Чикаго**	[ʧikagɔ]
Copenhagen	**Копенгаген**	[kɔpeŋagen]
Dar-es-Salaam	**Дар-эс-Салам**	[dar ɛs salam]
Delhi	**Дели**	[deli]
Dubai	**Дубай**	[dubaj]
Dublin	**Дублин**	[dublin]
Düsseldorf	**Дюссельдорф**	[dys:eʎdɔrf]
Florence	**Флоренци**	[flɔrenʦi]
Frankfurt	**Франкфурт**	[fraŋkfurt]
Geneva	**Женева**	[ʒeneva]
Hamburg	**Гамбург**	[gamburg]
Hanoi	**Ханой**	[hanɔj]
Havana	**Гавана**	[gavana]
Helsinki	**Хельсинки**	[heʎsiŋki]
Hiroshima	**Хиросима**	[hirɔsima]
Hong Kong	**Гонконг**	[gɔŋkɔŋ]
Istanbul	**Стамбул**	[stambul]
Jerusalem	**Иерусалим**	[ierusalim]
Kiev	**Киев**	[kiev]
Kuala Lumpur	**Куала-Лумпур**	[kuala lumpur]
Lisbon	**Лиссабон**	[lis:abɔn]
London	**Лондон**	[lɔndɔn]
Los Angeles	**Лос-Анджелес**	[lɔs andʒeles]
Lyons	**Лион**	[liɔn]

Madrid	**Мадрид**	[madrid]
Marseille	**Марсель**	[marseʎ]
Mexico	**Мехико**	[mehikɔ]
Miami	**Майями**	[majami]
Montréal	**Монреаль**	[mɔnreaʎ]
Moscow	**Москва**	[mɔskva]
Munich	**Мюнхен**	[mynhen]
Nairobi	**Найроби**	[najrɔbi]
Naples	**Неаполь**	[neapɔʎ]
New York	**Нью-Йорк**	[ɲjy jork]
Nice	**Ницца**	[nitsa]
Oslo	**Осло**	[ɔslɔ]
Ottawa	**Оттава**	[ɔt:ava]
Paris	**Париж**	[pariʒ]
Prague	**Прага**	[praga]
Rio de Janeiro	**Рио-де-Жанейро**	[riɔ de ʒanejrɔ]
Rome	**Рим**	[rim]
Saint Petersburg	**Санкт-Петербург**	[saŋkt peterburg]
Seoul	**Сеул**	[seul]
Shanghai	**Шанхай**	[ʃanhaj]
Singapore	**Сингапур**	[siŋapur]
Stockholm	**Стокгольм**	[stɔkgɔʎm]
Sydney	**Сидней**	[sidnej]
Taipei	**Тайпей**	[tajpej]
The Hague	**Гаага**	[gɑ:ga]
Tokyo	**Токио**	[tɔkiɔ]
Toronto	**Торонто**	[tɔrɔntɔ]
Venice	**Венеция**	[wenetsi]
Vienna	**Вена**	[wena]
Warsaw	**Варшава**	[varʃava]
Washington	**Вашингтон**	[vaʃiŋtɔn]

243. Politics. Government. Part 1

politics	**политика**	[pɔlitika]
political	**политически**	[pɔlititʃeski]
politician	**политик**	[pɔlitik]
state (country)	**пачхьалкх**	[patʃhalq]
citizen	**гражданин**	[graʒdanin]
citizenship	**гражданалла**	[graʒdanal:a]
national emblem	**къаьмнийн герб**	[qhæmni:n gerb]
national anthem	**пачхьалкхан гимн**	[patʃhalqan gimn]
government	**правительство**	[prawiteʎstvɔ]

head of state	мехкан куьйгалхо	[mehkan kyjgalho]
parliament	парламент	[parlament]
party	парти	[parti]

| capitalism | капитализм | [kapitalizm] |
| capitalist (adj) | капиталистийн | [kapitalisti:n] |

| socialism | социализм | [sɔtsializm] |
| socialist (adj) | социалистийн | [sɔtsialisti:n] |

communism	коммунизм	[kɔm:unizm]
communist (adj)	коммунистически	[kɔm:unistitʃeski]
communist (noun)	коммунист	[kɔm:unist]

democracy	демократи	[demɔkrati]
democrat	демократ	[demɔkrat]
democratic (adj)	демократийн	[demɔkrati:n]
Democratic party	демократийн парти	[demɔkrati:n parti]

| liberal (noun) | либерал | [liberal] |
| liberal (adj) | либералийн | [liberali:n] |

| conservative (noun) | консерватор | [kɔnservatɔr] |
| conservative (adj) | консервативни | [kɔnservativni] |

republic (noun)	республика	[respublika]
republican (noun)	республикахо	[respublikaho]
Republican party	республикански парти	[respublikanski parti]

| poll, elections | харжамаш | [harʒamaʃ] |
| to elect (vt) | харжа | [harʒa] |

| elector, voter | харжамхо | [harʒamho] |
| election campaign | харжамийн компани | [harʒami:n kɔmpani] |

voting (noun)	кхаж тасар	[qaʒ tasar]
to vote (vi, vt)	кхаж таса	[qaʒ tasa]
suffrage, right to vote	бакъо	[baqhɔ]

candidate	кандидат	[kandidat]
to be a candidate	хоржуш хила	[hɔrʒuʃ hila]
campaign	компани	[kɔmpani]

| opposition (attr) | оппозиционни | [ɔp:ɔzitsiɔɲi] |
| opposition (noun) | оппозици | [ɔp:ɔzitsi] |

visit	визит	[wizit]
official visit	лоррина визит	[ler:ina wizit]
international	гӀаланашна юккъера	[ɣalanaʃna jukqhera]

| negotiations | дагадовлар | [dagadɔvlar] |
| to negotiate (vi) | дагабовла | [dagabɔvla] |

244. Politics. Government. Part 2

society	юкъаралла	[juqharal:a]
constitution	конституци	[kɔnstitutsi]
power (political control)	Іедал	[æedal]
corruption	коррупци	[kɔr:uptsi]
law (justice)	закон	[zakɔn]
legal (legitimate)	законехь	[zakɔneh]
justice (fairness)	нийсо	[ni:sɔ]
just (fair)	нийса	[ni:sa]
committee	комитет	[kɔmitet]
bill (draft of law)	законопроект	[zakɔnɔprɔekt]
budget	бюджет	[bydʒet]
policy	политика	[pɔlitika]
reform	хийцар	[hi:tsar]
radical (adj)	кІоргіера	[k:ɔrg:era]
power (strength, force)	ницкъ	[nitsqh]
powerful	чІогІа	[tʃhɔɣa]
supporter (follower)	агІонча	[aɣɔntʃa]
influence	Іаткъар	[æatqhar]
regime (e.g., military ~)	дІахІоттам	[dæahɔt:am]
conflict	конфликт	[kɔnflikt]
conspiracy (plot)	къайлаха барт	[qhajlaha bart]
provocation	питана	[pitana]
to overthrow (regime etc.)	дІадаккха	[dæadak:a]
overthrow (of government)	дІадаккхар	[dæadak:ar]
revolution	революци	[revɔlytsi]
coup d'état	хийцам бар	[hi:tsam bar]
military coup	тІеман хийцам бар	[theman hi:tsam bar]
crisis	кризис	[krizis]
economic recession	экономикин лахдалар	[ɛkɔnɔmikin lahdalar]
demonstrator (protester)	демонстрант	[demɔnstrant]
demonstration	демонстраци	[demɔnstratsi]
martial law	тІеман хьал	[theman hal]
military base	база	[baza]
stability	чІоарла хилар	[tʃhɔaɣa hilar]
stable	чІоарІделла	[tʃhɔaɣdel:a]
exploitation	эксплуатаци	[ɛkspluatatsi]
to exploit (workers)	дацо	[datsɔ]
racism	расизм	[rasizm]
racist	расизмхо	[rasizmhɔ]

| fascism | фашизм | [faʃizm] |
| fascist | фашизмхо | [faʃizmho] |

245. Countries. Miscellaneous

foreigner	арахьарниг	[araharnig]
foreign (adj)	кхечу мехкан	[qetʃu mehkan]
abroad (overseas)	дозанал дехьа	[dɔzanal deha]

emigrant	эмигрант	[ɛmigrant]
emigration	эмиграци	[ɛmigratsi]
to emigrate (vi)	эмиграци ян	[ɛmigratsi jan]

the West	Малхбузе	[malhbuze]
the East	Малхбале	[malhbale]
the Far East	Гена-Малхбале	[gena malhbale]

civilization	цивилизаци	[tsiwilizatsi]
humanity (mankind)	адамалла	[adamal:a]
world (earth)	lалам	[əalam]
peace	машар	[maʃar]
worldwide (adj)	дуьненан	[dynenan]

homeland (native country)	даймохк	[dajmɔhk]
people	халкъ	[halqh]
population	бахархой	[baharhɔj]
people (e.g., a lot of ~)	нах	[nah]

| nation (people) | къам | [qham] |
| generation | тlаьхье | [thæhe] |

territory (area)	латта	[lat:a]
region	регион	[regiɔn]
state (part of a country)	штат	[ʃtat]

tradition	ламаст	[lamast]
custom (tradition)	lадат	[əadat]
ecology	экологи	[ɛkɔlɔgi]

| Indian (Native American) | индей | [indej] |
| Gipsy (man) | цигон | [tsigɔn] |

| Gipsy (woman) | цигон | [tsigɔn] |
| Gipsy (adj) | цигонийн | [tsigɔni:n] |

empire	импери	[imperi]
colony	колони	[kɔlɔni]
slavery	лолла	[lɔl:a]
invasion	тlелатар	[thelatar]
famine	мацалла	[matsal:a]

246. Major religious groups. Confessions

religion	дин	[din]
religious	динан	[dinan]
belief (in God)	динах тешар	[dinah teʃar]
to believe (vi)	теша	[teʃa]
believer	делах тешарг	[delah teʃarg]
atheism	атеизм	[ateizm]
atheist	атеист	[ateist]
Christianity	керсталла	[kerstal:a]
Christian (noun)	керста	[kersta]
Christian (adj)	керстанан	[kerstanan]
Catholicism	Католизм	[katɔlizm]
Catholic (noun)	католик	[katɔlik]
Catholic (adj)	католикийн	[katɔliki:n]
Protestantism	Протестанство	[prɔtestanstvɔ]
Protestant Church	Протестантийн килс	[protestanti:n kils]
Protestant	протестант	[prɔtestant]
Orthodoxy	Керста дин	[kersta din]
Orthodox Church	Керста килс	[kersta kils]
Orthodox	керстанан	[kerstanan]
Presbyterianism	Пресвитерианство	[preswiterianstvɔ]
Presbyterian Church	Пресвитерианийн килс	[preswiteriani:n kils]
Presbyterian (noun)	пресвитерианин	[preswiterianin]
Lutheranism	Лютерианийн килс	[lyteriani:n kils]
Lutheran	лютерианин	[lyterianin]
Baptist Church	Баптизм	[baptizm]
Baptist	баптист	[baptist]
Anglican Church	Ингалсан килс	[iŋalsan kils]
Anglican	англиканин	[aŋlikanin]
Mormonism	Мормонство	[mɔrmɔnstvɔ]
Mormon	мормон	[mɔrmɔn]
Judaism	Иудаизм	[iudaizm]
Jew	жугти	[ʒugti]
Buddhism	Буддизм	[bud:izm]
Buddhist	буддист	[bud:ist]
Hinduism	Индуизм	[induizm]
Hindu	индуист	[induist]

Islam	Ислам	[islam]
Muslim (noun)	бусалба	[busalba]
Muslim (adj)	бусалбанийн	[busalbani:n]

Shiism	Шиизм	[ʃi:zm]
Shiite (noun)	шиизмхо	[ʃi:zmho]
Sunni (religion)	Суннаталла	[suŋatal:a]
Sunnite (noun)	суннатхо	[suŋatho]

247. Religions. Priests

| priest | мозгlап | [mɔzɣar] |
| the Pope | Римера папа | [rimera papa] |

monk, friar	монах	[mɔnah]
nun	монах	[mɔnah]
pastor	пастор	[pastɔr]

abbot	аббат	[ab:at]
vicar	викари	[wikari]
bishop	епископ	[episkɔp]
cardinal	кардинал	[kardinal]
pope (orthodox priest)	мозгlап	[mɔzɣar]

preacher	кхайкхорхо	[qajqɔrhɔ]
preaching	кхайкхор	[qajqɔr]
parishioners	килсе оьхурш	[kilse øhurʃ]

| believer | делах тешарг | [delah teʃarg] |
| atheist | атеист | [ateist] |

248. Faith. Christianity. Islam

| Adam | Адам | [adam] |
| Eve | Хьава | [hava] |

God	Дела	[dela]
the Lord	Аллахl	[al:ah]
the Almighty	Дела	[dela]

sin	къа	[qha]
to sin (vi)	къинош лето	[qhinoʃ letɔ]
sinner (man)	къинош дерг	[qhinoʃ derg]
sinner (woman)	къинош дерг	[qhinoʃ derg]

hell	жоьжахати	[ʒøʒahati]
paradise	ялсамани	[jalsamani]
Jesus	Иисус	[i:sus]

Jesus Christ	Ииисус Христос	[i:sus hristɔs]
the Holy Spirit	Деза Са	[deza sa]
the Savior	КӀелхьардаьккхинарг	[k:elhardæk:inarg]
the Virgin Mary	Ӏийса-пайхамаран нана	[əi:sa pajhamaran nana]
the Devil	ШайтӀа	[ʃajtha]
devil's	шайтӀан	[ʃajthan]
Satan	Йилбаз	[jɪlbaz]
Satan's	йилбазан	[jɪlbazan]
angel	малик	[malik]
guardian angel	малик-лардархо	[malik lardarhɔ]
angelic	маликан	[malikan]
apostle	апостол	[apɔstɔl]
archangel	архангел	[arhaŋel]
the Antichrist	дажал	[daʒal]
the Church	Килс	[kils]
Bible	Библи	[bibli]
biblical	библин	[biblin]
Old Testament	Къена Весет	[qhena weset]
New Testament	Керла Весет	[kerla weset]
Gospel	Инжил	[inʒil]
Holy Scripture	Жайна	[ʒajna]
Heaven	Стигал, Стигалан Паччахьалла	[stigal], [stigalan patʃahal:a]
Commandment	весет	[weset]
prophet	пайхмар	[pajhmar]
prophecy	пайхмаралла	[pajhmaral:a]
Allah	АллахӀ	[al:ah]
Mohammed	МухьаммадӀ	[muham:ad]
the Koran	КъоӀлан	[qhɔrəan]
mosque	маьждиг	[mæʒdig]
mullah	молла	[mɔl:a]
prayer	ламаз	[lamaz]
to pray (vi, vt)	ламаз дан	[lamaz dan]
pilgrimage	ХьаьжцӀа вахар	[hæʒtsha vahar]
pilgrim	хьаьжа	[hæʒa]
Mecca	Макка	[mak:a]
church	килс	[kils]
temple	зиярат	[zijarat]
cathedral	килс	[kils]
Gothic	готически	[gɔtitʃeski]
synagogue	синагога	[sinagɔga]
mosque	маьждиг	[mæʒdig]

chapel	килс	[kils]
abbey	аббатство	[abːatstvɔ]
convent	монастырь	[mɔnastɪrʲ]
monastery	монастырь	[mɔnastɪrʲ]
bell (in church)	горгал	[gɔrgal]
bell tower	мамсар	[mamsar]
to ring (about bells)	детта	[detːa]
cross	жІара	[ʒeara]
cupola (roof)	бохь	[bɔh]
icon	икона	[ikɔna]
soul	са	[sa]
fate (destiny)	кхел	[qel]
evil (noun)	вон	[vɔn]
good (noun)	диканиг	[dikanig]
vampire	убар	[ubar]
witch (sorceress)	гІам	[ɣam]
demon	йилбаз	[jɪlbaz]
devil	шайтІа	[ʃajtha]
spirit	са	[sa]
redemption	къинойх цІандалар	[qhinɔjh tshandalar]
to redeem (vt)	цІандала	[tshandala]
church service, mass	гІуллакх	[ɣulːaq]
to say mass	гІуллакх дан	[ɣulːaq dan]
confession	дохковалар	[dɔhkɔvalar]
to confess (vi)	дохкодала	[dɔhkɔdala]
saint (noun)	эвлаяъ	[ɛvlaja]
sacred (holy)	деза	[deza]
holy water	деза хи	[deza hi]
ritual (noun)	Іадат	[eadat]
ritual (adj)	Іадатан	[eadatan]
sacrifice (offering)	саІа даккхар	[saɣa dakːar]
superstition	доьгІначух тешар	[døɣnatʃuh teʃar]
superstitious	доьгІначух теша	[døɣnatʃuh teʃa]
afterlife	эхартара дахар	[ɛhartara dahar]
eternal life	даим дахар	[daim dahar]

MISCELLANEOUS

249. Various useful words

background (green ~)	фон	[fɔn]
balance (of situation)	баланс	[balans]
barrier (obstacle)	дуьхьало	[dyhalɔ]
base (basis)	лард	[lard]
beginning	юьхь	[juh]
category	категори	[kategɔri]
cause (reason)	бахьана	[bahana]
choice	харжар	[harʒar]
coincidence	нисдалар	[nisdalar]
comfortable (~ chair)	бегӀийла	[beɣi:la]
comparison	дустар	[dustar]
compensation	меттахӀоттор	[met:ahɔt:ɔr]
degree (extent, amount)	дарж	[darʒ]
development	кхиам	[qiam]
difference	башхалла	[baʃhal:a]
effect (e.g., of drug)	эффект	[ɛf:ekt]
effort (exertion)	гӀора	[ɣɔra]
element	элемент	[ɛlement]
end (finish)	чаккхе	[ʧ̇ak:e]
example (illustration)	масал	[masal]
fact	хилларг	[hil:arg]
frequent	кест-кеста	[kest kesta]
growth (development)	дегӀ даккхар	[deɣ dak:ar]
help	гӀо	[ɣɔ]
ideal	идеал	[ideal]
kind (sort, type)	тайпа	[tajpa]
labyrinth	лабиринт	[labirint]
mistake	гӀалат	[ɣalat]
moment	юкъ	[juqh]
object (thing)	хӀума	[huma]
obstacle	новкъарло	[nɔvqharlɔ]
original (original copy)	оригинал	[ɔriginal]
part (~ of sth)	дакъа	[daqha]
particle, small part	дакъалг	[daqhalg]
pause (break)	сацангӀа	[saʦanɣa]

position	хьал	[hal]
principle	принцип	[printsip]
problem (is there any ~?)	проблема	[problema]
process	процесс	[protses:]
progress	прогресс	[progres:]
property (quality)	башхало	[baʃhalɔ]
reaction	реакци	[reaktsi]
risk	кхерам	[qeram]
secret	къайле	[qhajle]
section (sector)	дакъа	[daqha]
series	сери	[seri]
shape (outer form)	форма	[forma]
situation	хьал	[hal]
solution	дар	[dar]
standard (adj)	стандартан	[standartan]
standard (level of quality)	стандарт	[standart]
stop (pause)	садаlар	[sadaəar]
style	стиль	[stiʎ]
system	къепе	[qhepe]
table (chart)	таблица	[tablitsa]
tempo, rate	болар	[bolar]
term (word, expression)	термин	[termin]
thing (object)	хlума	[huma]
thing (object, item)	хlума	[huma]
truth	бакъдерг	[baqhderg]
turn (please, wait your ~)	парl	[raɣ]
type (sort, kind)	тайпа	[tajpa]
urgent	сиха	[siha]
urgently	чехка	[tʃehka]
use (usefulness)	пайда	[pajda]
variant	вариант	[variant]
way (means, method)	кеп	[kep]
zone	зона	[zona]

250. Modifiers. Adjectives. Part 1

additional	кхин тle	[qin the]
ancient (civilization etc.)	мацахлера	[matsahlera]
artificial	искусственни	[iskus:tweŋi]
back, rear	тlехьара	[thehara]
bad	вон	[vɔn]
beautiful	хаза	[haza]
beautiful (e.g., ~ palace)	тlеххаза	[thehaza]

big (in size)	доккха	[dɔk:ɑ]
bitter (taste)	къаьхьа	[qhæhɑ]
blind (sightless)	бIаьрзе	[bəærze]
calm	тийна	[ti:nɑ]
calm, quiet	тийна	[ti:nɑ]
careless (negligent)	ледара	[ledɑrɑ]
caring (kindly)	гIайгIа йолу	[ɣɑjɣɑ jolu]
central (in location)	юккъера	[jukqherɑ]
cheap (inexpensive)	дораха	[dɔrɑhɑ]
children's	берийн	[beri:n]
civil (of community)	граждански	[graʒdɑnski]
clandestine (secret)	къайлаха	[qhɑjlɑhɑ]
clean (free from dirt)	цIена	[ʦhenɑ]
clear (thinking, argument)	кхетаме	[qetɑme]
clever (smart)	хьекъале	[heqhɑle]
close (near in space)	гергара	[gergɑrɑ]
closed	къевлина	[qhevlinɑ]
cloudless (sky)	екхна	[eqnɑ]
cold (drink, weather)	шийла	[ʃi:lɑ]
compatible	цхьаьна дорIу	[ʦhæːnɑ dɔɣu]
contented	реза долу	[rezɑ dɔlu]
continuous	дехха	[dehɑ]
continuous (uninterrupted)	хаддаза долу	[had:ɑzɑ dɔlu]
cool (weather)	шийла	[ʃi:lɑ]
dangerous	кхераме	[qerɑme]
dark (room)	бодане	[bɔdɑne]
dead (not alive)	делла	[del:ɑ]
dense (fog, smoke)	чорда	[ʧɔrdɑ]
difficult (decision)	хала	[hɑlɑ]
difficult (problem, task)	хала	[hɑlɑ]
dim, faint (light)	беда	[bedɑ]
dirty (not clean)	боьха	[bøhɑ]
distant (faraway)	генара	[genɑrɑ]
dry (climate, clothing)	декъа	[deqhɑ]
easy (not difficult)	атта	[at:ɑ]
empty (glass, room)	даьсса	[dæs:ɑ]
exact (amount)	нийса	[ni:sɑ]
excellent	тIехдика	[thehdikɑ]
excessive (demand)	барамал тIех	[bɑrɑmɑl theh]
expensive	деза	[dezɑ]
exterior	арахьара	[arɑhɑrɑ]
far (distant in space)	генаха	[genɑhɑ]
fast (quick)	маса	[mɑsɑ]

fatty (food)	дерстина	[derstina]
fertile (land, soil)	ялта хьекъа	[jalta heqha]
flat (e.g., ~ panel display)	тӏапа	[thapa]
flat (e.g., ~ surface)	нийса	[ni:sa]
foreign (country, language)	кхечу мехкан	[qetʃu mehkan]
fragile (china, glass)	экам	[ɛkam]
free (at no cost)	маьхза	[mæhza]
free (unrestricted)	парӏат	[parɣat]
fresh (~ water)	теза	[teza]
fresh (e.g., ~ bred)	керла	[kerla]
frozen (food)	гӏорийна	[ɣori:na]
full (completely filled)	дуьззина	[dyz:ina]
good (book etc.)	дика	[dika]
good, kind	дика	[dika]
grateful	баркалле	[barkal:e]
happy	ирсе	[irse]
hard (not soft)	чӏорла	[tʃhoɣa]
heavy (in weight)	деза	[deza]
hostile	мостагӏаллин	[mostaɣal:in]
hot (high in temperature)	довха	[dovha]
huge	тӏехдоккха	[thehdɔk:a]
humid	тӏуьна	[thyna]
hungry	меца	[metsa]
ill (sick, unwell)	цомгуш	[tsɔmguʃ]
illegible	кхеташ доцу	[qetaʃ dɔtsu]
immobile	лелаш доцу	[lelaʃ dɔtsu]
important	ладаме	[ladame]
impossible (not possible)	таро доцу	[tarɔ dɔtsu]
indispensable	оьшу	[øʃu]
inexperienced	доьлла доцу	[døl:a dɔtsu]
insignificant (unimportant)	пайда боцу	[pajda bɔtsu]
interior	чоьхьара	[tʃøhara]
joint (~ decision)	цхьаьна ден	[tshæna den]
last (e.g., ~ week)	дӏадахнар	[dɑadahnar]
last (final)	тӏаьххьара	[thæhara]
left (e.g., ~ side)	аьрру	[ær:u]
legal (legitimate)	законехь	[zakɔneh]
light (in weight)	дайн	[dajn]
light (pale color)	сирла	[sirla]
limited (restricted)	кӏезиг	[k:ezig]
liquid (fluid)	коча	[kɔtʃa]
long (e.g., ~ way)	деха	[deha]
loud (voice etc.)	чӏорла	[tʃhoɣa]
low (voice)	меллаша	[mel:aʃa]

251. Modifiers. Adjectives. Part 2

main (principal)	коьрта	[kørta]
matt	кхоьлина	[qølina]
merry, cheerful	самукъане	[samuqhane]
meticulous (job)	дурсе	[durse]
mysterious	кхета хала	[qeta hala]

narrow (street, passage)	готта	[got:a]
native (of country)	дина	[dina]
near (in space)	гергара	[gergara]
near-sighted	бlорзагал	[bəorzagal]
necessary (indispensable)	хьашт долу	[haʃt dolu]

negative	дацаре	[datsare]
neighboring	лулара	[lulara]
nervous	нервийн	[nervi:n]
new	цlина	[tʃhina]
next (e.g., ~ week)	роrlepa	[rɔɣera]
nice (kind)	хьоме	[hɔme]
nice (voice)	тамехьа	[tameha]

normal (common, typical)	лартlахь долу	[larthah dolu]
not big	доккха доцу	[dɔk:a dɔtsu]
not clear	къаьсташ доцу	[qhæstaʃ dɔtsu]
not difficult	хала доцу	[hala dɔtsu]

obligatory	декхарийлахь долу	[deqari:lah dolu]
old (house)	къена	[qhena]
open	диллина	[dil:ina]
opposite	дуьхьалдоrlу	[dyhaldɔɣu]
ordinary (usual, normal)	гуттар а хьуьлу	[gut:ar a hylu]
original (unusual)	оригинал йолу	[original jolu]

past (recent)	дlадахна	[dəadahna]
permanent	хаддаза	[had:aza]
personal (message, letter)	леррина	[ler:ina]
polite	гlиллакхе	[ɣil:aqe]
poor (not rich)	къен	[qhen]
possible	тарлун	[tarlun]
poverty-stricken	къен	[qhen]

present (in time)	хlинцалера	[hintsalera]
previous	хьалхара	[halhara]
principal (main)	коьрта	[kørta]
private (not for the public)	долара	[dɔlara]
private (personal)	юьхьах хьокху	[juhah hɔqu]
probable (likely)	хила тарлу	[hila tarlu]

public (open to all)	юкъараллин	[juqharal:in]
punctual (person)	дурсе	[durse]

rare (uncommon)	нилха	[nilha]
raw (uncooked)	тӀуьна	[thyna]
right	аьтту	[æt:u]
right, correct	нийса	[ni:sa]
ripe (fruit)	кхиъна	[qina]
risky	кхераме	[qerame]
sad (depressing)	гӀайгӀане	[ɣajɣane]
sad (unhappy)	гӀайгӀане	[ɣajɣane]
safe (not dangerous)	кхерамза	[qeramza]
salty (food)	дуьра	[dyra]
satisfied (customer)	кхачаме	[qatʃame]
second hand	пайда оьцуш хилла	[pajda øtsuʃ hil:a]
shallow (water)	гомха	[gomha]
sharp (blade, scissors)	ира	[ira]
short (in length)	доца	[dotsa]
short, short-lived	йоццача хенан	[jotsatʃa henan]
significant (notable)	доккха	[dok:a]
similar	тера	[tera]
simple (easy)	цхьалха	[tshalha]
skinny (too thin)	оза	[ɔza]
slim (person)	оза	[ɔza]
small (in size)	жима, кегий	[ʒima], [kegi:]
smooth (surface)	шера	[ʃera]
soft (to touch)	кӀеда	[k:eda]
somber, gloomy	бодане	[bodane]
sour (flavor, taste)	муьста	[mysta]
spacious (house, room)	паргӀат	[parɣat]
special	леррина	[ler:ina]
straight (line, road)	нийса	[ni:sa]
strong (construction)	чӀогӀа	[tʃhoɣa]
strong (person)	нуьцкъала	[nytsqhala]
stupid (foolish)	Ӏовдал	[əovdal]
suitable	мегаш долу	[megaʃ dɔlu]
sunny (day)	маьлхан	[mælhan]
superb, perfect	тӀехдика	[thehdika]
swarthy	Ӏаьржачу аматехь	[əærʒatʃu amateh]
sweet (in taste)	мерза	[merza]
tan	маьлхо дагийна	[mælho dagi:na]
tasty	чоме	[tʃɔme]
tender (affectionate)	кӀеда-мерза	[k:eda merza]
the highest	лакхара	[laqara]
the most important	уггар лараме	[ug:ar larame]
the nearest	герггара	[gerg:ara]

the same, equal	цхьатерра	[tshater:a]
thick (e.g., ~ fog)	дуькъа	[dyqha]
thick (wall, slice)	стомма	[stɔm:a]
tired (exhausted)	гӀелделла	[ɣeldel:a]
tiring	кӀаддеш долу	[k:ad:eʃ dɔlu]
transparent	чекх са гун	[tʃeq sa gun]
unique (exceptional)	башха	[baʃha]
warm (moderately hot)	мела	[mela]
wet (e.g., ~ clothes)	тӀеда	[theda]
whole (entire, complete)	дийна	[di:na]
wide (e.g., ~ road)	шуьйра	[ʃyjra]
young	къона	[qhɔna]

MAIN 500 VERBS

252. Verbs A-C

to accompany (vt)	цхьаьнадаьлла даха	[ts̄hænadæl:a daha]
to accuse (vt)	бехкедан	[behkedan]
to act (take action)	дан	[dan]
to add (put together)	тӀетоха	[thetɔha]
to address (speak to)	ала	[ala]
to admire (vi)	гӀаддаха	[ɣad:aha]
to advertise (vt)	реклама ян	[reklama jan]
to advise (give advice to)	хьехам бан	[heham ban]
to affirm (vt)	тӀечӀагӀдан	[thetʃhaɣdan]
to agree (say yes)	реза хила	[reza hila]
to allow (sb to do sth)	маго	[magɔ]
to amputate (vt)	дӀадаккха	[deadak:a]
to anger (vt)	оьгӀаздахийта	[øɣazdahi:ta]
to answer (vi, vt)	жоп дала	[ʒɔp dala]
to apologize (vi)	бехк цабиллар деха	[behk tsabil:ar deha]
to appear (come into view)	гучудала	[gutʃudala]
to applaud (vi, vt)	тӀараш детта	[tharaʃ det:a]
to appoint (assign)	хӀотто	[hɔt:ɔ]
to approach (come nearer)	тӀедан	[thedan]
to arrive (about train)	схьакхача	[shaqatʃa]
to ask (~ sb to do sth)	деха	[deha]
to aspire (vi)	гӀерта	[ɣerta]
to assist (help)	ассистент хила	[as:istent hila]
to attack (military)	атак ян	[atak jan]
to attain (objectives)	даккха	[dak:a]
to avenge (vt)	чӀир леха	[tʃhir leha]
to avoid (danger, task)	уьдуш лела	[yduʃ lela]
to award (give medal to)	совгӀат дала	[sɔvɣat dala]
to bathe (~ one's baby)	лийчо	[li:tʃɔ]
to battle (vi)	лета	[leta]
to be (on the table etc.)	Ӏилла	[əil:a]
to be able to …	мага	[maga]
to be afraid (of …)	кхера	[qera]
to be angry (with …)	оьгӀазъэха	[øɣazʰɛha]

to be at war	тӀом бан	[thom ban]
to be based (on …)	ларда тӀе догӀадала	[larda the doɣadala]
to be bored	сагатдала	[sagatdala]
to be convinced	тешна хила	[teʃna hila]
to be enough	тоа	[tɔa]
to be envious	хьега	[hega]
to be in a hurry	сихдала	[sihdala]
to be indignant	эргӀаддала	[ɛrɣad:ala]
to be interested in …	безам хила	[bezam hila]
to be needed	оьшуш хила	[øʃuʃ hila]
to be perplexed	цецдала	[ʦeʦdala]
to be preserved	диса	[disa]
to be required	оьшуш хила	[øʃuʃ hila]
to be surprised	цецдала	[ʦeʦdala]
to be worried	сагатдан	[sagatdan]
to beat (dog, person)	етта	[et:a]
to become (e.g., ~ old)	хила	[hila]
to become pensive	ойлане дожа	[ɔjlane dɔʒa]
to behave (vi)	лела	[lela]
to believe (think)	теша	[teʃa]
to belong to …	хила	[hila]
to berth (moor)	йистедало	[jistedalɔ]
to blind (of flash of light)	блаьрса дайа	[beærsa daja]
to blow (wind)	хьекха	[heqa]
to blush (vi)	эхь хетта цӀийвала	[ɛh het:a ʦhi:vala]
to boast (vi)	куралла ян	[kural:a jan]
to borrow (money)	юхалург эца	[juhalurg ɛʦa]
to break (branch, toy etc.)	кегдан	[kegdan]
to breathe (vi)	садеӀа	[sadeea]
to bring sth	схьадало	[shadalɔ]
to burn (paper, logs)	даго	[dagɔ]
to burst (vi)	хада	[hada]
to buy (purchase)	эца	[ɛʦa]
to call (for help)	кхайкха	[qajqa]
to call (with one's voice)	кхайкха	[qajqa]
to calm down (vt)	дӀатедан	[deatedan]
to cancel (call off)	дӀадаккха	[dɛadak:a]
to cast off	дӀадаха	[dɛadaha]
to catch (e.g., ~ a ball)	леца	[leʦa]
to catch sight (of …)	ган	[gan]
to cause …	бахьана хила	[bahana hila]
to change (~ one's opinion)	хийца	[hi:ʦa]
to change (exchange)	хийца	[hi:ʦa]

to charm (please, delight)	дагадоха	[dagadɔha]
to choose (select)	харжар	[harʒar]
to chop off (vt)	дӏахадо	[dɛahadɔ]
to clean (from dirt)	цӏандан	[tshandan]
to clean (shoes etc.)	цӏандан	[tshandan]
to clean (tidy)	дӏадаха	[dɛadaha]
to close (window, shop)	дӏакъовла	[dɛaqhɔvla]
to comb hair	ехк хьакха	[ehk haqa]
to come down (the stairs)	охьадан	[ɔhadan]
to come in (enter)	чудаха	[tʃudaha]
to come out (book)	арадала	[aradala]
to compare (vt)	дуста	[dusta]
to compensate (vt)	меттахӏотто	[met:ahɔt:ɔ]
to compete (vi)	къийса	[qhi:sa]
to compile, to make (a list)	хӏотто	[hɔt:ɔ]
to complain (vi, vt)	латкъа	[latqha]
to complicate (vt)	чолхе дан	[tʃɔlhe dan]
to compose (music etc.)	даккха	[dak:a]
to compromise (vt)	сий дайа	[si: daja]
to concentrate (vi)	тӏегулдала	[theguldala]
to confess (criminal)	къардала	[qhardala]
to congratulate (vt)	декъалдан	[deqhaldan]
to consult (doctor, expert)	консультаци эца	[kɔnsuʌtatsi ɛtsa]
to continue (~ to do sth)	дахдан	[dahdan]
to control (verify)	тӏехьажа	[thehaʒa]
to convince (vt)	дӏадада	[dɛadada]
to cooperate (with)	дакъа лаца	[daqha latsa]
to coordinate (vt)	уьйр ян	[yjr jan]
to cost (vt)	деха	[deha]
to count (add up)	лара	[lara]
to count on …	дагахь хила	[dagah hila]
to crack (ab. ceiling, wall)	этӏа	[ɛtha]
to create (vt)	кхолла	[qɔl:a]
to cry (weep)	делха	[delha]
to cut off (vt)	дӏахадо	[dɛahadɔ]

253. Verbs D-G

to dare (e.g., ~ to do sth)	хӏотта	[hɔt:a]
to date from	терахь яздан	[terah jazdan]
to deceive (vi, vt)	Iexo	[ɛeho]
to decide (e.g., ~ to do sth)	сацо	[satsɔ]
to decorate (tree, street)	хаздан	[hazdan]

to dedicate (book etc.)	хьажо	[haʒɔ]
to defend (a country etc.)	лардан	[lardan]
to defend oneself	лардала	[lardala]
to demand (request firmly)	тӀедожо	[thedɔʒɔ]
to denounce (vt)	мотт бетта	[mɔt: bet:a]
to deny (declare untrue)	керстдан	[kerstdan]
to depend on …	даза	[daza]
to deprive (vt)	даккха	[dak:a]
to deserve (vt)	даккха	[dak:a]
to design (machine etc.)	проект хӀотто	[prɔekt hɔt:ɔ]
to desire (want, wish)	лаа	[la:]
to despise (vt)	ца даша	[tsa daʃa]
to destroy (documents etc)	хӀаллакдан	[hal:akdan]
to differ (from sth)	къаьсташ хила	[qhæstaʃ hila]
to dig (tunnel etc.)	ахка	[ahka]
to direct (point the way)	тӀедахийта	[thedahi:ta]
to disappear (vi)	къайладала	[qhajladala]
to discover (new land etc.)	гучудаккха	[gutʃudak:a]
to discuss (talk about)	дийцаре дилла	[di:tsare dil:a]
to dismiss (from job)	мукъадаккха	[muqhadak:a]
to distribute (leaflets etc.)	даржо	[darʒɔ]
to disturb (vt)	новкъарло ян	[nɔvqharlɔ jan]
to dive (vi)	чулелха	[tʃulelha]
to divide (math)	декъа	[deqha]
to do (vt)	дан	[dan]
to do the laundry	дитта	[dit:a]
to double (increase)	шозза алсамдаккха	[ʃɔz:a alsamdak:a]
to doubt (have doubts)	шекьхила	[ʃekʲhila]
to draw a conclusion	сацам бан	[satsam ban]
to dream (daydream)	дагалеца	[dagaletsa]
to dream (in sleep)	гӀенаш ган	[ɣenaʃ gan]
to drink (vi, vt)	мала	[mala]
to drive (a car)	машина лело	[maʃina lelɔ]
to drive sb away	эккхо	[ɛk:ɔ]
to drop (let fall)	охьаэго	[ɔhaeɣɔ]
to drown (ab. person)	бухадаха	[buhadaha]
to dry (clothes, hair)	дакъо	[daqhɔ]
to eat (vi, vt)	даа, яаа	[da:], [ja::]
to eavesdrop (vi)	ладогӀа	[ladɔɣa]
to emit (smell)	даржо	[darʒɔ]
to enter (on list)	юкъаяздан	[juqhajazdan]
to entertain (amuse)	самукъадаккха	[samuqhadak:a]
to equip (fit out)	гӀирс хӀотто	[ɣirs hɔt:ɔ]
to examine (proposal)	къасто	[qhastɔ]

to exchange sth	хийцадала	[hi:tsadala]
to exclude, to expel	дӏадаккха	[dəadak:a]
to excuse (forgive)	бехк ца билла	[behk tsa bil:a]
to exist (vi)	хила	[hila]
to expect (anticipate)	дагахь хила	[dagah hila]
to expect (foresee)	синхаам хила	[sinha:m hila]
to explain (vi, vt)	кхето	[qeto]
to express (vt)	схьаала	[sha:la]
to extinguish (a fire)	дӏаяйа	[dəajaja]
to fall in love (with ...)	дезадала	[dezadala]
to feed (provide food)	хӏума яла	[huma jala]
to feel (fear, regret)	хаадала	[ha:dala]
to fight (against the enemy)	къийсам атто	[qhi:sam at:ɔ]
to fight (vi)	лета	[leta]
to fill (glass, bottle)	дуза	[duza]
to find (~ lost items)	каро	[karɔ]
to find out (make enquiries)	хаа	[ha:]
to finish (vt)	чекхдаккха	[tʃeqdak:a]
to fish (with a line)	чӏерий леца	[tʃheri: letsa]
to fit (about dress etc.)	гӏехьа хила	[ɣeha hila]
to flatter (vi, vt)	хесто	[hestɔ]
to fly (bird, plane)	лела	[lela]
to follow ... (come after)	тӏаьхьадаха	[thæhadaha]
to forbid (not allow)	дехка	[dehka]
to force (compel)	дайта	[dajta]
to forget (vi, vt)	дицдала	[ditsdala]
to forgive (pardon)	геч дан	[getʃ dan]
to form (constitute)	кхолла	[qɔl:a]
to get dirty (vi)	бехдала	[behdala]
to get infected (with ...)	кхета	[qeta]
to get irritated	карзахдала	[karzahdala]
to get married	зуда яло	[zuda jalɔ]
to get rid of ...	хьалхадала	[halhadala]
to get tired	гӏелдала	[ɣeldala]
to get up (arise from bed)	хьалагӏатта	[halaɣat:a]
to give a hug, to hug (vt)	марадолла	[maradɔl:a]
to give in (yield to)	дита	[dita]
to go (by car, train etc.)	даха	[daha]
to go (to walk)	даха	[daha]
to go for a swim	лийча	[li:tʃa]
to go out (for dinner etc.)	арадала	[aradala]
to go to bed	охьадижа	[ɔhadiʒa]
to greet (vt)	маршалла хатта	[marʃal:a hat:a]

to grow (plants)	кхио	[qiɔ]
to guarantee (assure)	юкъара хила	[juqhara hila]
to guess right	хаа	[ha:]

254. Verbs H-M

to hand out (distribute)	дӀасадекъа	[dəasadeqha]
to hang (curtains etc.)	хьалаолла	[halaɔl:a]
to have (vt)	хила	[hila]

to have a try	гӀорта	[ɣɔrta]
to have breakfast	марта даа	[marta da:]
to have dinner	пхьор дан	[phɔr dan]
to have fun	сакъера	[saqhera]
to have lunch	делкъана хӀума яа	[delqhana huma ja:]

to head (group etc.)	куьйгалла дан	[kyjgal:a dan]
to hear (vi, vt)	хаза	[haza]
to heat (vt)	дохдала	[dɔhdala]
to help (assist, aid)	гӀо дан	[ɣɔ dan]
to hide (e.g., ~ something)	дӀадилла	[dəadil:a]

to hint (vi)	къедо	[qhedɔ]
to hire (e.g., ~ a boat)	лаца	[latsa]
to hire (staff)	лаца	[latsa]
to hope (vi, vt)	догдаха	[dɔgdaha]
to hunt (for food, sport)	талла эха	[tal:a ɛha]
to hurry sb	сихдан	[sihdan]

to imagine (to picture)	сурт хӀотто	[surt hɔt:ɔ]
to imitate (vt)	тардан	[tardan]
to implore (vt)	деха	[deha]
to import (vt)	импорт ян	[impɔrt jan]
to increase (vi)	доккха хилар	[dɔk:a hilar]
to increase (vt)	доккха дан	[dɔk:a dan]

to infect (vt)	далийта	[dali:ta]
to influence (vt)	Ӏаткъам бан	[əatqham ban]
to inform (~ sb about ...)	хаам бан	[ha:m ban]
to inform (vi, vt)	информаци ян, хаам бан	[infɔrmatsi jan, ha:m ban]
to inherit (property, right)	верасалла кхача	[werasal:a qatʃa]

to insist (vi, vt)	тӀера ца вала	[thera tsa vala]
to inspire (vt)	иракарахӀоттор	[irakarahɔt:ɔr]
to instruct (teach)	инструкцеш яла	[instruktseʃ jala]
to insult (offend)	сий дайа	[si: daja]

| to interest (vt) | безам хила | [bezam hila] |
| to intervene (vi) | юкъаэккха | [juqhaɛk:a] |

to introduce (present)	довзо	[dɔvzɔ]
to invent (machine etc.)	кхолла	[qɔl:a]
to invite (ask to come)	схьакхайкха	[shaqajqa]
to iron (laundry)	тоха	[tɔha]
to irritate (annoy)	карзахдаккха	[karzahdak:a]
to isolate (vt)	дӏакъасто	[dəaqhastɔ]
to join (political party etc.)	дӏакхета	[dəaqeta]
to joke (be kidding)	забарш ян	[zabarʃ jan]
to keep (old letters etc.)	Ӏалашдан	[əalaʃdan]
to keep silent	диет ца хила	[diet tsa hila]
to kill (vt)	ден	[den]
to knock (at the door)	детта	[det:a]
to know (sb)	довза	[dɔvza]
to know (sth)	хаа	[ha:]
to laugh (at the joke)	дела	[dela]
to launch (start up)	кхосса	[qɔs:a]
to leave (abandon)	дита	[dita]
to leave (e.g., ~ for Mexico)	дӏадаха	[dəadaha]
to leave (forget)	дита	[dita]
to liberate (vt)	мукъадаккха	[muqhadak:a]
to lie (be in lying position)	вижина Ӏилла	[wiʒina əil:a]
to lie (tell untruth)	аьшпаш ботта	[æʃpaʃ bɔt:a]
to light (e.g., a campfire)	лато	[latɔ]
to light up (illuminate)	серладаккха	[serladak:a]
to like (e.g., I like …)	хазахета	[hazaheta]
to like (enjoy)	тӏера хила	[thera hila]
to limit (vt)	доза тоха	[dɔza tɔha]
to listen (vi)	ладоӏа	[ladɔɣa]
to live (e.g., ~ in France)	даха	[daha]
to live (exist)	хила	[hila]
to load (gun)	дуза	[duza]
to load (vehicle etc.)	тӏедотта	[thedɔt:a]
to look (out of the window)	хьежа	[heʒa]
to look for … (search)	леха	[leha]
to look like (resemble)	тера хила	[tera hila]
to lose (umbrella etc.)	дайа	[daja]
to love (sb)	деза	[deza]
to lower (blind, head)	охьадахийта	[ɔhadahi:ta]
to make (e.g., ~ dinner)	кечдан	[ketʃdan]
to make a mistake	гӏалатдала	[ɣalatdala]
to make copies	даржо	[darʒɔ]
to make easier	дайдан	[dajdan]
to make use (of …)	пайда эца	[pajda ɛtsa]

to manage (business)	куьйгаллз дан	[kyjgal:z dan]
to mark (make a mark)	билгало ян	[bilgalɔ jan]
to mean (signify)	хила	[hila]
to meet (get acquainted)	довза	[dɔvza]
to memorize (vt)	дагахь латто	[dagah lat:ɔ]
to mention (talk about)	хьахо	[haho]
to miss (school etc.)	дита	[dita]
to mix (combine, blend)	вовшахъэдан	[vɔvʃahʰɛdan]
to mix up (confuse)	тило	[tilɔ]
to mock (deride)	дела	[dela]
to move (wardrobe etc.)	дӏататта	[dəatat:a]
to multiply (math)	эца	[ɛtsa]
must	хьакъ долуш хила	[haqh dɔluʃ hila]

255. Verbs N-S

to name, to call (vt)	цӏерш яха	[tsherʃ jaha]
to negotiate (vi)	дагабовла	[dagabɔvla]
to note (write down)	билгалдан	[bilgaldan]
to notice (see)	ган	[gan]
to obey (vi, vt)	муьтӏахь хила	[mythah hila]
to object (vi, vt)	дуьхьал хила	[dyhal hila]
to observe (see)	тергам бан	[tergam ban]
to offend (person)	халахетар дан	[halahetar dan]
to omit (word, phrase)	юкъахдита	[juqhahdita]
to open (vt)	схьаделла	[shadel:a]
to order (in restaurant)	заказ ян	[zakaz jan]
to order (military)	омра дан	[ɔmra dan]
to organize (concert, party)	дӏахӏотто	[dəahɔt:ɔ]
to overestimate (vt)	мах юхахӏотто	[mah juhahɔt:ɔ]
to own (possess)	хила	[hila]
to participate (vi)	дакъа лаца	[daqha latsa]
to pass (go beyond)	тӏехдала	[thehdala]
to pay (vi, vt)	ахча дала	[ahtʃa dala]
to peep, spy on	хьежа	[heʒa]
to penetrate (vi)	чудала	[tʃudala]
to permit (allow)	магийта	[magi:ta]
to pick (flowers)	даккха	[dak:a]
to place (put, set)	хила	[hila]
to plan (~ to do sth)	план хӏотто	[plan hɔt:ɔ]
to play (actor)	ловза	[lɔvza]
to play (children)	ловза	[lɔvza]

to point (e.g., ~ the way)	гайта	[gɑjtɑ]
to pour (liquid)	дотта	[dɔt:ɑ]
to pray (vi, vt)	ламаз дан	[lɑmɑz dɑn]
to predominate (vi)	тоьлушха хила	[tøluʃhɑ hilɑ]
to prefer (like better)	гӏоли хета	[ɣɔli hetɑ]
to prepare (~ a plan)	кечдан	[ketʃdɑn]
to present (sb to sb)	довзийта	[dɔvzi:tɑ]
to preserve (peace, life)	лардан	[lɑrdɑn]
to progress (move forward)	хьаладала	[hɑlɑdɑlɑ]
to promise (vt)	валда дан	[vɑədɑ dɑn]
to pronounce (say)	ала	[ɑlɑ]
to propose (vt)	хьахо	[hɑhɔ]
to protect (e.g., ~ nature)	лардан	[lɑrdɑn]
to protest (vi)	дуьхьал хила	[dyhɑl hilɑ]
to prove (vt)	тешо	[teʃɔ]
to provoke (vt)	питана таса	[pitɑnɑ tɑsɑ]
to pull (e.g., ~ the rope)	озо	[ɔzɔ]
to punish (vt)	тӏазар дан	[tɑəzɑr dɑn]
to push (e.g., ~ the door)	дӏататта	[dɑtɑt:ɑ]
to put away (vt)	дӏадаха	[dɑədɑhɑ]
to put in (insert, include)	тийса	[ti:sɑ]
to put in order	къепе дало	[qhepe dɑlɔ]
to put, to place	дилла, охьадилла	[dil:ɑ], [ɔhɑdil:ɑ]
to quote (cite)	дешнаш дало	[deʃnɑʃ dɑlɔ]
to reach (arrive at)	дӏакхача	[dɑəqɑtʃɑ]
to read (vi, vt)	еша	[eʃɑ]
to realize (achieve)	кхочушдан	[qɔtʃuʃdɑn]
to recall (~ one's name)	дагадаийта	[dɑgɑdɑi:tɑ]
to recognize (admit)	кхета	[qetɑ]
to recognize (identify sb)	вовза	[vɔvzɑ]
to recommend (vt)	мага дан	[mɑgɑ dɑn]
to recover (~ from flu)	тодала	[tɔdɑlɑ]
to redo (vt)	юхадан	[juhɑdɑn]
to reduce (speed etc.)	жимдан	[ʒimdɑn]
to refuse (~ sb)	ца дала	[tsɑ dɑlɑ]
to regret (be sorry)	дагахьбаллам хила	[dɑgɑhbɑl:ɑm hilɑ]
to reinforce (position)	чӏагӏдан	[tʃhɑɣdɑn]
to remember (not forget)	дагадан	[dɑgɑdɑn]
to remind (vt)	дагадаийта	[dɑgɑdɑi:tɑ]
to remove (~ an obstacle)	дӏадаккха	[dɑədɑk:ɑ]
to remove (e.g., ~ a stain)	дӏадаккха	[dɑədɑk:ɑ]
to rent (of a tenant)	лаца	[lɑtsɑ]
to repair (mend)	тодан	[tɔdɑn]
to repeat (say again)	юхаала	[juhɑ:lɑ]

to report (make a report)	доклад ян	[dɔklad jan]
to reproach (vt)	бехкаш даха	[behkaʃ daha]
to reserve, to book	бронь ян	[brɔɲ jan]
to restrain (hold back)	сацо	[satsɔ]
to return (come back)	юхада	[juhada]
to risk, to take a risk	кхерам баккха	[qeram bak:a]
to rub off (erase)	дӀадайа	[dəadaja]
to run (move fast)	дада	[dada]
to satisfy (please)	реза дан	[reza dan]
to save (rescue)	кӀелхьардаккха	[k:elhardak:a]
to say (e.g., ~ thank you)	ала	[ala]
to scold (vt)	дов дан	[dɔv dan]
to scratch (with claws)	сизаш дан	[sizaʃ dan]
to select (to pick)	схьахаржа	[shaharʒa]
to sell (goods)	дохка	[dɔhka]
to send (a letter)	дӀадахьийта	[dəadahi:ta]
to send back (vt)	юхадахьийта	[juhadahi:ta]
to sentence (vt)	кхел ян	[qel jan]
to serve (in restaurant)	хьашт кхочушдан	[haʃt qɔtʃuʃdan]
to settle (a conflict)	дӀадерзо	[dəaderzɔ]
to shake (vt)	дегадан	[degadan]
to shave (vi)	даша	[daʃa]
to shine (vi)	къега	[qhega]
to shoot (vi)	кхийса	[qi:sa]
to shout (vi)	мохь бетта	[mɔh bet:a]
to show (to display)	гайта	[gajta]
to shudder (vi)	тохадала	[tɔhadala]
to sigh (vi)	са даккха	[sa dak:a]
to sign (document)	куьг тӀало	[kyg taəɔ]
to signify (mean)	маьӀна хила	[mæəna hila]
to simplify (vt)	чолхаза дан	[tʃɔlhaza dan]
to sin (vi)	къинош лето	[qhinɔʃ letɔ]
to sit (be seated)	Ӏан	[əan]
to smash (~ a bug)	вичӀадаккха	[witʃadak:a]
to smell (have odor)	хьожаэха	[hɔʒaɛha]
to smell (sniff at)	хьожа яха	[hɔʒa jaha]
to smile (vi)	дела къежа	[dela qheʒa]
to solve (problem)	дан	[dan]
to sow (seed, crop)	ден	[den]
to spill (liquid)	Ӏано	[əanɔ]
to spit (vi)	туйнаш кхийса	[tujnaʃ qi:sa]
to stand (toothache, cold)	сатоха	[satɔha]

to start (begin)	доло	[dɔlɔ]
to steal (money, property)	лечкъо	[letʃqhɔ]
to stop (cease)	дӀасацо	[dəasatsɔ]
to stop (for pause etc.)	саца	[satsa]
to stop talking	вист ца хила	[wist tsa hila]

to stroke (caress)	хьеста	[hesta]
to study (vt)	Ӏамо	[əamɔ]
to suffer (feel pain)	бала хьега	[bala hega]

to support (cause, idea)	тӀетан	[thetan]
to suppose (assume)	мотта	[mɔt:a]
to surface (ab. submarine)	тӀедала	[thedala]
to surprise (amaze)	цецдаккха	[tsetsdak:a]
to suspect (of wrongdoing)	шекьхила	[ʃəkʲhila]
to swim (vi)	нека дан	[neka dan]
to switch on (vt)	йолаялийта	[jɔlajali:ta]

256. Verbs T-W

to take (get hold of)	схьаэца	[shaətsa]
to take a bath	дила	[dila]
to take a rest	садала	[sadaəa]
to take a seat	охьахаа	[ɔhaha:]
to take aim (at the target)	хьежо	[heʒɔ]

to take away	дӀадахьа	[dəadaha]
to take off (airplane)	хьалагӀатта	[halaɣat:a]
to take off (remove)	схьадаккха	[shadak:a]
to take pictures	сурт даккха	[surt dak:a]

to talk to …	къамел дан	[qhamel dan]
to teach (give lessons)	Ӏамо	[əamɔ]
to tear off (vt)	схьадаккха	[shadak:a]
to tell (story, joke)	дийца	[di:tsa]

to thank (vt)	баркалла баха	[barkal:a baha]
to think (believe)	лара	[lara]
to think (vi, vt)	ойла ян	[ɔjla jan]
to threaten (vt)	кхерам тийса	[qeram ti:sa]
to throw (stone)	кхийса	[qi:sa]

to tie (~ sb to a tree)	дӀадехка	[dəadehka]
to tie up (prisoner)	дӀадехка	[dəadehka]
to tire (exhaust)	кӀаддан	[k:ad:an]
to touch (one's arm etc.)	хьекхадала	[heqadala]
to tower (over …)	ирахдахна хила	[irahdahna hila]

to train (animals)	караламо	[karaəamɔ]
to train (vi)	Ӏама	[əama]

to train sb	**Iамо**	[əamɔ]
to transform (vt)	**хийца**	[hi:tsa]
to translate (word, text)	**талмажалла дан**	[talmaʒal:a dan]
to treat (patient, illness)	**дарба лело**	[darba lelɔ]
to tremble (with cold)	**дего**	[degɔ]
to trust (vt)	**теша**	[teʃa]
to try (attempt)	**гIорта**	[ɣɔrta]
to turn (change direction)	**дIадерза**	[dəaderza]
to turn away (vi)	**агIордерза**	[aɣɔrderza]
to turn off (the light)	**дIадайа**	[dəadaja]
to turn over (stone etc.)	**ха харца**	[ha hartsa]
to underestimate (vt)	**кхоччуш ца лара**	[qɔtʃuʃ tsa lara]
to underline (vt)	**билгалдаккха**	[bilgaldak:a]
to understand (vi, vt)	**кхета**	[qeta]
to undertake (vt)	**юьхьарлаца**	[juharlatsa]
to unite (join)	**цхаьнатоха**	[tshænatoha]
to untie (vt)	**схьадаста**	[shadasta]
to use (phrase, word)	**пайда эца**	[pajda ɛtsa]
to vaccinate (vt)	**маха тоха**	[maha tɔha]
to vote (vi)	**кхаж таса**	[qaʒ tasa]
to wait (vi, vt)	**хьежа**	[heʒa]
to wake sb (vt)	**самадаккха**	[samadak:a]
to want (wish, desire)	**лаа**	[la:]
to warn (of the danger)	**дIахьедан**	[dəahedan]
to wash (clean)	**дила**	[dila]
to water (plants)	**хи тоха**	[hi tɔha]
to wave (the hand)	**лесто**	[lestɔ]
to weigh (have weight)	**оза**	[ɔza]
to work (vi)	**болх бан**	[bɔlh ban]
to worry (make anxious)	**сагатдан**	[sagatdan]
to worry (vi)	**сахьийзо**	[sahi:zɔ]
to wrap (goods, parcel)	**юкъахьарчо**	[juqahartʃɔ]
to wrestle (sport)	**лата**	[lata]
to write (letter etc.)	**яздан**	[jazdan]
to write down	**дIаяздан**	[dəajazdan]

Printed in Great Britain
by Amazon.co.uk, Ltd.,
Marston Gate.